Succeeding at Assessment Centres For Dummies®

Cheat Sheet

Knowing What to Expect

Not sure what to expect at an Assessment Centre? Here are a few points to shed some light for you:

- Your performance is measured in terms of job-related skills.
- You're asked to participate in job-related business simulations that assess your skills and potential.
- Your performance is assessed by several Assessors.
- You're assessed along with a number of other candidates.
- Each assessor provides an independent and objective input on your performance.
- Your overall performance is judged against a set standard, rather than against the other candidates.
- The process is fair and equal to all candidates.
- You can gain a realistic preview of the job.

The chapters in Part I give you loads more information about the nature of Assessment Centres.

Ten Tips for Success

Here are our best tips for maximising your chances of success:

- Arrive in good time, ready for action.
- Be positive – expect to succeed and you probably will.
- Pay close attention to all instructions.
- Focus on the objectives of each activity.
- Take a moment to think before you act.
- Make a positive impact – stand out from the crowd.
- Monitor and manage your time (make sure you wear a watch!).
- Don't dwell on any disappointments; stay calm.
- Be yourself and don't act out of character.
- Enjoy the experience – it's fun and you can learn a lot!

The chapters in Part IV have heaps more tips to help you to shine at an Assessment Centre.

For Dummies: Bestselling Book Series for Beginners

Succeeding at Assessment Centres For Dummies®

Variations in Assessment Centres

Assessment Centres can have different purposes, so be clear about the purpose of your Centre:

- ✔ Assessment Centres are usually used for selection or promotion decisions.

- ✔ Development Centres tend to be used to identify future potential or areas for development.

Assessment Centres can include any combination of the following items:

- ✔ **Group Exercises:** Team tasks with fellow candidates.

- ✔ **One-to-One Exercises:** Interacting with another person.

- ✔ **Work Alone Exercises:** Written analytical output.

- ✔ **Interviews:** The Assessors can determine your previous experiences.

- ✔ **Psychometric Tests:** These can reveal ability or personality.

- ✔ **Other Activities:** These can include icebreakers, presentations about the organisation or job-role and so on.

The chapters in Part II go into a lot more detail about each type of exercise.

Preparing for an Assessment Centre

Don't underestimate the power of presentation. Follow these tips to help you remain calm and in control before you even arrive at an Assessment Centre:

- ✔ Research the organisation and the job role.

- ✔ Ensure you know what the Assessors are looking for – speak to the organisers if you need to.

- ✔ Complete allocated pre-centre tasks in good time.

- ✔ Think about how you can display your strengths.

- ✔ Ask other people about your strengths and weaknesses.

- ✔ Learn from others' Assessment Centre experiences.

- ✔ Practice the tasks you expect to face.

- ✔ Plan what to wear and how to get there.

- ✔ Get all the things you need ready the night before.

- ✔ Make sure you're well rested; get an early night before your big day.

For Dummies: Bestselling Book Series for Beginners

Succeeding at Assessment Centres

FOR

DUMMIES®

Succeeding at Assessment Centres FOR DUMMIES®

by Nigel Povah and Lucy Povah

A John Wiley and Sons, Ltd, Publication

Succeeding at Assessment Centres For Dummies®

Published by
John Wiley & Sons, Ltd
The Atrium
Southern Gate
Chichester
West Sussex
PO19 8SQ
England

E-mail (for orders and customer service enquires): cs-books@wiley.co.uk

Visit our Home Page on www.wiley.com

Copyright © 2009 John Wiley & Sons, Ltd, Chichester, West Sussex, England

Published by John Wiley & Sons, Ltd, Chichester, West Sussex

For general information on our other products and services, please contact our Customer Care Department within the U.S. at 800-762-2974, outside the U.S. at 317-572-3993, or fax 317-572-4002.

For technical support, please visit www.wiley.com/techsupport.

Wiley also publishes its books in a variety of electronic formats. Some content that appears in print may not be available in electronic books.

British Library Cataloguing in Publication Data: A catalogue record for this book is available from the British Library

ISBN: 978-0-470-72101-8

Printed and bound in Great Britain by TJ International, Padstow, Cornwall

10 9 8 7 6 5 4 3 2 1

WILEY

About the Authors

Nigel Povah is a Chartered Occupational Psychologist and is the Managing Director and founder of A&DC, which is one of the UK's leading HR consultancies in the Talent Management field (www.ADC.uk.com).

Upon graduating from Leeds University in Psychology and obtaining a Masters at London University's Birkbeck College in Occupational Psychology, he decided to pursue a career as a professional chess player. During a five-year spell he represented England on a number of occasions, wrote four books on chess, became an International Master and taught and coached numerous players, including some of England's current crop of Grandmasters.

In the early 1980s Nigel decided to return to his interest in psychology and embarked upon a career in Human Resource consultancy which included stints in recruitment and training, before he founded Assessment & Development Consultants (A&DC) in 1988.

Nigel is widely regarded as one of the UK's leading experts in the Assessment Centre field, having co-authored *Assessment and Development Centres* (Gower). He was also one of the members of the British Psychological Society's Steering Committee who produced the 'Best Practice Guidelines on the Design, Implementation and Evaluation of Assessment and Development Centres'.

As well as his executive role at A&DC, Nigel continues to write articles on Assessment and Development Centres and delivers papers at various conferences.

Nigel lives in Guildford with his wife Gill and their children and he still tries to find time to pursue his interest in chess as a keen amateur.

Lucy Povah is a Senior Consultant at A&DC where she has worked with her father for the last five years since graduating from Warwick University in Psychology and obtaining her Masters in Occupational Psychology from Surrey University.

During those five years she's designed and run many Assessment Centres, both in the UK and internationally, for a wide range of public and private sector organisations such as Acas, BAA, Boots, HMRC, Syngenta, and the UK Fire and Rescue Service.

These Assessment Centres have been targeted at staff at all levels from graduates through to senior management and executives, where she has enabled organisations to adopt best practice selection processes.

Lucy has a particular interest in Positive Psychology, which focuses on enabling people to take full advantage of their strengths, especially within Assessment Centres.

Lucy currently lives in London, where she splits her time between visiting her family and friends in Surrey and enjoying the attractions of London.

Dedication

To our family and loved ones for putting up with numerous weekends and evenings of neglect; we hope you'll forgive us. We would also like to thank you for your encouragement and support throughout this project and beyond.

Authors' Acknowledgements

We would like to thank the people at Wiley, including Wejdan Ismail for recognising the value of a book such as this, tracking us down and offering us this opportunity, and Rachael Chilvers for being highly supportive and encouraging us during the writing.

We would also like to thank all the clients we've worked with over the years for providing the rich tapestry of experiences that have given rise to the numerous anecdotes and useful lessons that we've been able to share with you in this book.

Finally, we'd like to thank numerous fellow practitioners, including past and present colleagues at A&DC (too many to mention by name but you know who you are), with whom we have exchanged stories over many years, because many of the observations and recommendations within this book are based on their experiences as much as our own.

Thank you to you all!

Publisher's Acknowledgements

We're proud of this book; please send us your comments through our Dummies online registration form located at www.dummies.com/register/.

Some of the people who helped bring this book to market include the following:

Acquisitions, Editorial, and Media Development

Project Editor: Rachael Chilvers

Development Editor: Tracy Barr

Content Editor: Jo Theedom

Copy Editor: Christine Lea

Proofreader: David Price

Technical Editor: Angela Baron, CIPD

Commissioning Editor: Wejdan Ismail

Executive Project Editor: Daniel Mersey

Cover Photos: Front cover © Tay Junior/GettyImages; back cover © John Rowley/GettyImages

Cartoons: Ed McLachlan

Composition Services

Project Coordinator: Lynsey Stanford

Layout and Graphics: Reuben W. Davis, Andrea Hornberger, Melissa K. Jester, Ronald Terry

Proofreader: David Faust

Indexer: Cheryl Duksta

Special Help

Brand Reviewer: Carrie Burchfield

Contents at a Glance

Introduction:..*1*

Part I: Introducing Assessment Centres..............*5*
Chapter 1: Demystifying Assessment Centres.......................................7
Chapter 2: How an Assessment Centre Works.....................................27
Chapter 3: Maximising Your Chances of Success...............................47

*Part II: Mastering Assessment
Centre Exercises*..*61*
Chapter 4: Standing Out in Group Exercises.......................................63
Chapter 5: Impressing in Oral Presentations.......................................81
Chapter 6: Starring in Role-Plays...99
Chapter 7: Shining in Fact-Finding Exercises....................................119
Chapter 8: Achieving in Analysis Exercises.......................................131
Chapter 9: Performing in Planning and Scheduling Exercises..........145
Chapter 10: Managing In-Basket or Inbox Exercises.........................157

*Part III: Excelling at Non-Exercise Assessment
Centre Activities*...*175*
Chapter 11: Responding Effectively in Interviews.............................177
Chapter 12: Perfecting Your Approach to Psychometric Tests........199
Chapter 13: Tackling Other Activities...217
Chapter 14: Learning from Attending an Assessment Centre...........233

Part IV: The Part of Tens....................................*255*
Chapter 15: Ten Ways to Impress the Assessors...............................257
Chapter 16: Ten Ways of Behaving Effectively..................................265
Chapter 17: Ten Tips for Achieving Peak Performance....................273

Index...*279*

Table of Contents

Introduction *1*

About This Book 1
Conventions Used in This Book 2
Foolish Assumptions 2
How This Book Is Organised.....................................3
Part I: Introducing Assessment Centres 3
Part II: Mastering Assessment Centre Exercises 3
Part III: Excelling at Non-Exercise Assessment
Centre Activities...3
Part IV: The Part of Tens 4
Icons Used in This Book..4
Where to Go from Here 4

Part I: Introducing Assessment Centres *5*

Chapter 1: Demystifying Assessment Centres.........7

What Assessment Centres Are (and Aren't)............................7
Defining Assessment Centres...8
What an Assessment Centre isn't...................................10
Answering common questions about Assessment
Centres 12
Key Features of Assessment Centres 13
Measuring job-related competencies............................14
Using job-related simulations 14
Involving more than one assessor...................................14
Gathering independent data for making decisions 15
Assessing multiple participants 15
Advantages of Using Assessment Centres............................16
Predicting future potential with greater accuracy 16
Providing a fair and equal opportunity to all candidates....17
Providing a realistic job preview 19
Common Uses of Assessment Centres....................................19
External recruitment 20
Internal promotion 22
Development 22

Chapter 2: How an Assessment Centre Works 27

Knowing about Measuring Performance.............................27
    Job-related skills, or competencies............................28
    Levels of performance 31
Attending the Assessment Centre 31
    Timetabling...32
    Tackling the exercises 34
Ways of Working...35
    Working in groups...36
    Working one-to-one..36
    Working on your own 38
'Independent' Exercises versus 'Themed' Exercises............39
Additional Activities...40
    Competency Based Interview 40
    Psychometric tests...41
    Other activities 41
Discovering Who's Who 42
    Other candidates 42
    Centre manager and centre administrators 42
    Role-players...43
    The assessors...43
Decision-Making Time 44
    During the activities 44
    Coming to a decision...45

Chapter 3: Maximising Your Chances of Success 47

Researching the Organisation 47
Finding Out about the Job 49
    Reviewing the job description 49
    Reading the job advert.......................................50
    Identifying your questions...................................51
Soaking Up Your Briefing Material 51
    Scrutinising the tasks 52
    Doing practice tests...53
Preparing for the Assessment Centre 54
    Linking the job accountabilities with skills being
        assessed 54
    Displaying the necessary skills and competencies....55
    Matching competencies to your skills
        and strengths.......................................56
    Planning how to compensate for weaknesses 57
Clearing Your Path to the Assessment Centre 57
    Notifying the centre of a disability 58
    Taking account of previous Assessment
        Centre feedback 59

Part II: Mastering Assessment Centre Exercises 61

Chapter 4: Standing Out in Group Exercises 63

Looking into Group Exercises 63
    Group size and timing 64
    Activity-based group exercises.....................................65
    Discussion-based group exercises 66
    Assigned role group discussions....................................68
Common Competencies Being Assessed 70
Behaving Effectively 72
    Helping the group to get organised...............................72
    Speaking now or forever holding your peace! 73
    Staying in the game 74
    Managing the opposition 74
    Giving the quieter group members a chance...............75
    Being prepared to compromise 75
    In the firing line: Dealing with challenges...................76
    Trying to ignore the assessors.......................................77
Gearing Up for the Group Exercise.......................................77
    Before the assessment centre...78
    During the assessment centre...78

Chapter 5: Impressing in Oral Presentations......... 81

Figuring Out the Format..81
    As a stand-alone exercise 82
    Linked to other exercises 83
Prep, Delivery and Q&A: The Three Stages 84
    The preparation stage..84
    The delivery stage 86
    The question and answer (Q&A) stage......................87
Different Types of Presentation 88
    Presenting on your own to a few 88
    Presenting on your own to a group................................89
    Presenting as part of a team..89
Common Competencies Being Assessed 90
Behaving Effectively 92
    Building in appropriate content 92
    Using visual aids 92
    Starting with a bang!..93
    Controlling your nerves...94
    Projecting positive body language 95

Tuning into your audience 95
Using humour appropriately 96
Finishing with a flourish 97
Avoiding the Seven Deadly Sins of Presenting 97

Chapter 6: Starring in Role-Plays. 99

Recognising Role-Play Exercises 99
One-to-one role-play exercises 100
Multiple role-play exercises 102
Popular Scenarios 105
Internal role-plays 105
External role-plays 106
Role of the Role-Player 108
Common Competencies Being Assessed 108
Behaving Effectively 110
Having a well-prepared plan 110
Building the relationship 110
Making your point 113
Handling resistance 113
Expecting the unexpected 114
Balancing individual and organisational needs 114
Summarising the outcome 115
Avoiding Ineffective Behaviours 115
Becoming angry or aggressive 115
Getting frustrated 116
Starting to panic 117
Gearing Up for the Role-Play Exercise..............................117
Before the Assessment Centre 117
During the Assessment Centre 118

Chapter 7: Shining in Fact-Finding Exercises 119

Fathoming Fact-Finding Exercises 119
Phase 1: Planning and preparing 120
Phase 2: Questioning and interpreting 121
Phase 3: Evaluating and deciding 122
Phase 4: Reviewing and justifying 122
Common Competencies Being Assessed 123
Behaving Effectively 125
Thinking on your feet 125
Taking brief notes 125
Weighing up the information 126
Coping with the pressure 126

Avoiding Ineffective Behaviours 127
    Jumping to conclusions 127
    Freezing in the headlights 127
    Being prejudiced and having preconceived ideas....127
    Asking ineffective questions 128
Gearing Up for the Fact-Finding Exercise............................129
    Before the Assessment Centre................................129
    During the Assessment Centre................................130

Chapter 8: Achieving in Analysis Exercises 131

Analysing Analysis Exercises 131
Outlining Analysis Exercise Formats....................................132
    Analysis exercise written reports.............................133
    Analysis exercise presentations 135
    Analysis exercise group discussions 136
Common Competencies Being Assessed 137
Behaving Effectively 139
    Managing your time well..139
    Deciding what information is missing.......................140
    Analysing the pros and cons.....................................140
    Giving reasons for decisions 141
    Remembering other effective behaviours 142
Gearing Yourself Up for the Analysis Exercise....................142
    Before the Assessment Centre.................................142
    During the Assessment Centre................................143

Chapter 9: Performing in Planning and Scheduling Exercises 145

Introducing Planning and Scheduling Exercises.................146
Six Steps for Project Planning and Implementation 149
Common Competencies Being Assessed 150
Behaving Effectively 151
    Following the rules 151
    Recording your thoughts...151
    Reviewing your final solution....................................152
Avoiding Ineffective Behaviours 152
    Creating confusion...152
    Overlooking dependencies..152
Preparing for Action 153
    Before the Assessment Centre.................................153
    Reading up on project planning................................154
    Practising producing a project plan.........................154
    During the Assessment Centre................................155

Chapter 10: Managing In-Basket or Inbox Exercises 157

In-Basket or Inbox? 158
Tackling the Task Before You 160
    Setting priorities with a matrix 161
    Tackling paper-based in-basket exercises 162
    Dealing with electronic inbox exercises 163
Common Competencies Being Assessed 165
Behaving Effectively 166
    Looking before you leap 166
    Making things stand out 167
    Checking priorities 167
    Looking for links 168
    Tuning into your audience 168
    Using all available resources......................................169
    Watching the clock 170
Avoiding Ineffective Behaviours 171
    Being superficial 171
    Being overly detailed 171
    Never-ending paper shuffling.....................................173
Gearing Yourself Up for the Exercise.................................173
    Before the Assessment Centre...................................173
    During the Assessment Centre....................................174

Part III: Excelling at Non-Exercise Assessment Centre Activities 175

Chapter 11: Responding Effectively in Interviews ... 177

Staffing the Interview 178
    One-to-one interviews 178
    Two-to-one interviews..179
    Panel interviews 180
Taking the Structured Approach...181
    Situational interviews 182
    Behavioural description interviews............................183
Highlighting Competency Based Interviews 183
    Step 1: Describing the context/scenario....................185
    Step 2: Describing what you did 185
    Step 3: Describing what happened 186
Common Competencies Being Assessed 188

Behaving Effectively 190
   Making a good first impression......................190
   Listening attentively..............................191
   Getting on the right track 192
   Putting your failings positively 192
Avoiding Ineffective Behaviours 193
   Sitting in painful silence..........................193
   Appearing too laid-back.............................194
   Talking hypothetically..............................194
   Telling blatant lies 194
Preparing for Action 195
   Before the Assessment Centre........................195
   During the Assessment Centre........................197

Chapter 12: Perfecting Your Approach
to Psychometric Tests 199

Studying Common Psychometric Tests 200
   Administration 200
   Interpretation and scoring 201
Performing at Ability Tests 202
   Verbal ability tests................................203
   Numerical ability tests.............................205
   Abstract ability tests..............................205
   Mechanical and spatial ability tests................207
Answering Personality Questionnaires.......................210
Handling Situational Judgement Tests 212
Completing 360° Feedback Questionnaires.....................214
Psyching Yourself Up for the Test...........................216
   Before the day......................................216
   On the day 216

Chapter 13: Tackling Other Activities 217

Getting Off to a Quick Start.................................218
   Controlling your nerves upon arrival 218
   Making an impactful introduction 219
   Tackling icebreakers................................221
Making Your Mark on the Assessment Activities 222
   Participating in business games 222
   Undertaking outdoor activities......................224
   Reviewing personal performance......................225

Taking Part in Information Sessions 227
 Responding to company presentations 228
 Tackling Q&A sessions with recent recruits 229
Providing Feedback on the Assessment Centre..................230

**Chapter 14: Learning from Attending
an Assessment Centre........................ 233**

Reviewing Your Own Performance 234
 Reviewing each activity 234
 Reviewing your performance as a whole..................235
 Discovering what you've learned 239
Getting Feedback on Your Performance 240
 Asking for feedback..241
 Getting your feedback...242
 Receiving feedback in style 244
 Optimising different forms of feedback 245
Bringing Together What You've Learned 247
 Peeking through the Johari Window 248
 Putting all the information together.........................250
Preparing for the Next Time 251
 Your path to improvement: Using the Ability-
 Awareness model...251
 Applying your learning 253

Part IV: The Part of Tens *255*

Chapter 15: Ten Ways to Impress the Assessors 257

Dress to Impress 257
Align Yourself with the Organisation's Values....................258
Play to Your Strengths...259
Be Prepared 259
Exhibit Your Enthusiasm and Commitment 260
Signal a Willingness to Learn..260
Retain Your Composure 261
Show Respect Towards Others 261
Convince the Organisation of Your Worth..........................262
Get It Right for the Assessors...262

Chapter 16: Ten Ways of Behaving Effectively 265

Behave Assertively 265
Show Confidence...266
Earn the Respect of Others...267
Gain the Support of Others..267
Be Genuine and Sincere 268

Be Friendly and Approachable...268
Act with Assurance...269
Stay Focused..270
Use Appropriate Body Language 270
Make Sure You Get Noticed 271

**Chapter 17: Ten Tips for Achieving
   Peak Performance 273**

Arrive in Good Time, Relaxed and Ready to Perform 273
Pay Careful Attention to All Instructions
   (Oral or Written) 274
Focus Clearly on the Aim of the Task...................................275
Use Preparation Time Effectively..275
Manage Your Time 276
Focus on One Task at a Time...276
Don't Dwell on Disappointments 277
Relax During Breaks..277
Be Yourself 278
Enjoy the Experience!...278

Index *279*

Introduction

*W*elcome to *Succeeding at Assessment Centres For Dummies!* Did you pick up this book because you're due to attend an Assessment Centre and, like most people, you're not really sure what to expect? Well, rest assured, this book will remove the veil of mystique and provide you with a clear appreciation of what Assessment Centres are all about.

Assessment Centres have been around for over half a century during which time they've grown steadily in popularity, mainly because organisations trust them to help them make effective selection decisions. One of the main attractions of an Assessment Centre is that they're one of the most comprehensive and accurate ways of identifying the skills and abilities required for success in a given job. An Assessment Centre enables you to display all your qualities, so you have a great opportunity to show what you're capable of and realise your full potential.

About This Book

Assessment Centres can appear complicated, so we've set about providing you with a clear explanation of how they work and what you need to know, to give you the best possible chance of success.

Having designed and run literally hundreds of Assessment Centres of varying duration and content, we have channelled our knowledge of what exercises aim to assess and what assessors generally look for from your performance, to provide you with some focused advice.

You can dip in and out of this book as you like; don't feel compelled to read it from cover to cover. However, if you've received an invitation to an Assessment Centre, the following approach is useful:

- If you know very little about the Centre and have never attended an Assessment Centre before, the first three chapters in Part I provide a useful background.

- If you know what exercises you're likely to face, refer to the relevant chapters in Part II.

- If you believe that you'll sit a psychometric test and/or perhaps have an interview, head to the chapters in Part III.

- Finally, as part of your general preparation, follow the advice in Chapters 3 and 13 and read the tips in Chapters 15 to 17 in Part IV.

Conventions Used in This Book

To help you as you go through this book we use the following conventions:

- *Italics* have been used to highlight quotations and definitions.

- Monofont is used for occasional web addresses which we suggest you might wish to use to access useful information.

- We use male pronouns in odd chapters and female pronouns in even chapters to be fair to both genders!

Foolish Assumptions

While writing this book we made some assumptions about your knowledge of Assessment Centres, why you might be interested in this book, and what you want to get out of it. We assume that your reason for picking up this book might be one or more of the following:

- You don't know anything at all about Assessment Centres and you want to gain some understanding, which could range from knowing the basics through to having a fairly thorough grasp of what they're all about.

- You've been invited to attend an Assessment Centre for the first time and want to know what to expect.

- You have a pretty good idea of the activities you'll face on an Assessment Centre but you want to be as thoroughly prepared for it as you can, because you're keen to do well.

How This Book is Organised

This book is divided into four major parts. The chapters within each part go into greater detail of specific aspects or elements of an Assessment Centre. Each chapter provides self-contained coverage of that particular aspect, so you don't need to read all of the chapters or read them in sequence. The Table of Contents provides a comprehensive list of everything we cover, enabling you to jump around the book as you like.

Part I: Introducing Assessment Centres

This part provides you with an introductory overview to Assessment Centres. Starting with an introduction to the basic principles and a description of what an Assessment Centre looks like, we then go into greater detail about how they actually work. These first two chapters provide you with a foundation upon which to build your understanding. We also focus on some of the general preparation you can do before your Assessment Centre to ensure you maximise your chances of success.

Part II: Mastering Assessment Centre Exercises

This part explains each of the different types of exercises that are used most frequently on Assessment Centres. Knowing what to expect and how to handle these types of exercise will boost your confidence no end, enabling you to feel you can tackle whatever's thrown at you.

Part III: Excelling at Non-Exercise Assessment Centre Activities

This part covers interviews, psychometric tests and various briefing sessions. Attending an Assessment Centre is likely to be one of the most insightful events of your career, so we also cover how to ensure you make the most of the opportunity to learn from this enriching experience.

Part IV: The Part of Tens

This part provides a series of general tips that apply to the Assessment Centre as a whole, rather than being aligned with any specific aspect of a Centre. We start by covering some practical tips about how to impress the Assessors, because your success at a Centre is very much in their hands. We then provide some suggestions about how best to behave, with appropriate warnings about behaviours to avoid! Finally, we offer some classic tips about how to ensure you're at the top of your game, so you can leave the Assessment Centre feeling positive and knowing you gave it your best.

Icons Used in This Book

We use a number of different icons throughout this book to draw your attention to particular pieces of information.

The knotted string highlights particularly important information to remember.

This icon relates to technical stuff that you don't necessarily need to know and can skip over if you want to. However, we include it in case you want to understand the underlying theory behind some of the points covered.

This icon refers to useful ideas and suggestions.

The bomb signals something to be careful about and highlights behaviours to avoid.

Where to Go from Here

What to read next? The choice is yours. You can just dip in and out of the different chapters, depending on which bits appear most relevant and useful to you. Or you can go down the traditional route and read this book from cover to cover.

We hope that this book helps you to perform more effectively in an Assessment Centre, so you can achieve your ambition of getting that job or promotion you want. Give the best performance you can, and remember to always be yourself. Good luck!

Part I
Introducing Assessment Centres

'He's certainly keen and in very good time —
his assessment is not until next week.'

In this part . . .

For many people the term Assessment Centre conjures up an image of somewhere that you go to be prodded and probed until your innermost secrets are exposed. Little wonder that being asked to attend an Assessment Centre can be an intimidating prospect for the uninitiated!

This part aims to remove the mystique of Assessment Centres, so you can attend armed with the confidence to succeed.

Chapter 1

Demystifying Assessment Centres

● ●

In This Chapter

▶ Understanding what an Assessment Centre is and what it isn't

▶ Knowing why and when Assessment Centres are used

▶ Appreciating why you're being invited to an Assessment Centre

● ●

*F*or many people an Assessment Centre and what goes on there is a complete mystery. In this chapter we explain just what an Assessment Centre is and what it isn't. We're also going to attempt to dispel many of the myths accompanying Assessment Centres, so that if you're invited to attend a centre you can happily go armed with knowledge and confidence.

We also tell you about the different purposes for which Assessment Centres are used and how they're run so that you know what to expect when attending an Assessment Centre.

What Assessment Centres Are (and Aren't)

Hearing the term Assessment Centre for the first time, you may naturally assume that an Assessment Centre is a place where assessments are carried out. This popular misconception is based on the fact that the earliest such assessment events were run at a place called the Assessment Centre, so the name stuck. Nowadays, an Assessment Centre is a particular *type* of assessment process used for selecting the right person for the right job, and which has been steadily growing in popularity since the Second World War. In short, it is a process not a place.

Defining Assessment Centres

No single, universally accepted definition exists for an Assessment Centre, but there are many versions all tending to say much the same thing. Here's a typical example:

> *An integrated system of tests and other measures, including simulation exercises designed to generate behaviour similar to that required for success in a target job or job level.*

So what does this tell you? Read on to find out.

Activities are relevant to the actual job you're seeking

First, you can expect the Assessment Centre to include activities relating to the sorts of things you expect to do in the job you're being assessed for. For example, if you're applying for a job as a customer service agent in a call centre, then you may well find that you're asked to handle one or more customer queries over the phone. This type of activity simulates the real job and is an essential principle of an Assessment Centre.

Assessment Centres set out to use realistic tasks serving to give you a useful insight into the nature of the job that you're applying for, helping both you and the organisation to decide whether there is a good fit.

The process lets you display behaviours you're actually going to need

Second, an Assessment Centre is designed to let you display the behaviour that's considered relevant to the job in question. So, unlike an interview, where you have the opportunity to talk about yourself and what you *would* do or *did* do in a given situation, at an Assessment Centre you need to show what you *can* do, the exercise simulations being both practical and realistic.

If you've applied for a particular job and you've been invited to attend an Assessment Centre as part of the selection process, try to identify what successful performance in that job would look like. What are the sorts of things a successful job performer would do? These behaviours are what the Assessors will be looking for and this can guide you as to how to behave on the Centre.

An integrated system is designed to give a full picture of your abilities

Third, the reference to an 'integrated system' highlights the fact that the various parts of the Assessment Centre process all contribute to the assessment of the behaviours needed in the job you're being assessed for. This shows that Assessment Centres are carefully constructed events and not simply a set of unrelated tasks that have been thrown together.

History of Assessment Centres

The Assessment Centre method was developed during the Second World War when there was an urgent need to find people with the capability to lead under very difficult circumstances. The milestones for Assessment Centres (ACs) are:

1942: German, UK and US Armed Forces use ACs for the selection of officers

1945: UK Civil Service Selection Board (CSSB) – first non-military use of ACs

1956: Telecoms provider AT&T first use ACs for management development purposes

1960s: Interest grows in the US: IBM, Standard Oil, General Electric

1970s: Interest grows in the UK: ICL (now part of Fujitsu), Post Office, consumer brand giant Grand Metropolitan

1980s: Increasing use of Assessment Centres for development (DCs)

1990s: Growth in use of AC/DCs in US and UK in public and private sectors

2000s: Growing global interest in use of ACs

Your overall performance is determined by how well you did on the assessment as a whole; a less effective performance on one activity can be compensated for by a more than effective performance on another. So give each activity your 'best shot' and don't be discouraged if you feel you've slipped up on one, because you may still have the opportunity to recover.

Well-designed Assessment Centres share certain key features, which we describe in 'Key Features of Assessment Centres' later in this chapter.

What an Assessment Centre isn't

An Assessment Centre is a structured process for assessing the capabilities you're going to need to be successful in a particular job. This description can lend itself to all sorts of misunderstandings about what an Assessment Centre actually is, as the following sections explain.

A real-life version of The Apprentice

In the popular TV series *The Apprentice*, a group of contestants carry out a series of tasks and are gradually whittled down to a winner, who gets the much sought-after job. The TV show is very different from the structure and purpose of an Assessment Centre because:

✔ Assessment Centres make sure that the requirements of the job are clearly defined before the assessment takes place.

✔ A group of observers, known as assessors, are fully trained in what to look for in the various tasks that the participants are asked to do.

✔ The tasks are chosen to simulate different aspects of the job in question. Although this may be true for some of the tasks in *The Apprentice*, it certainly isn't true for them all, because the contestants are frequently asked to carry out bizarre tasks totally unrelated to the job.

✔ Participants at an Assessment Centre aren't competing with one another because they're all being measured against a common standard, allowing each participant to pass or fail. For the success of the show, Sir Alan Sugar has to hire *someone*, even if none of the candidates come up to scratch!

A series of interviews or a battery of psychometric tests

You may find that you're invited to an assessment event which is referred to as an Assessment Centre, but which is made up of the following:

- ✔ A series of interviews (See Chapter 11)
- ✔ A battery of psychometric tests (See Chapter 12)
- ✔ An interview and some psychometric tests
- ✔ Exercise simulations or activities – but not measuring specific job-related behaviours

Any assessment event that doesn't include at least one exercise simulation requiring you to actually demonstrate job-related behaviour doesn't qualify as an Assessment Centre.

For example, an organisation runs an event that they call an Assessment Centre, made up of an interview, psychometric tests, and an activity such as a team task – constructing the tallest tower possible out of Lego bricks. The organisations' justification for including this type of task is that you're going to need to display various qualities required in the job, such as teamwork, communication skills, planning, leadership, and so on. However, the potential flaw in this form of assessment is that unless the job needs you to build Lego towers from time to time, this particular task bears no resemblance to the demands of the job. Although the skills being observed may be relevant, the task itself may impact on how those skills are displayed and you may not display those behaviours in the way you would with a more realistic task, thus undermining the validity of the task within the assessment process.

You aren't in a position to question the choice of tasks, so try focusing on doing your best at whatever tasks are set before you, regardless of their suitability. Avoid being distracted by any irritation or the nagging question: 'What does this have to do with the job?' Try figuring out what behaviours the organisation is looking for and do your best to show that you have those qualities. Hopefully, you're going to have the opportunity to vent your frustration at the end of the event when you're asked for feedback. However, be very careful not to be too critical, as you may come across as a 'moaner' or the organisation may think you're making excuses for a less than effective performance. Make sure that your feedback is couched constructively, like: 'I would have preferred it if the task had been closer to the XYZ role, as I believe that communication skills are very important in this role and I don't feel that I had sufficient opportunity to demonstrate my abilities in this area.'

Answering common questions about Assessment Centres

In this section we describe some of the typical questions which highlight candidates' concerns when they're invited to attend an Assessment Centre.

What's more important: Past experience and achievement or performance at an Assessment Centre?

You may be tempted to think that your experience and achievements to date are more important than how you perform on an Assessment Centre. Not so! Assessment Centres focus on identifying your future potential. What you've done up to this point in your life may not show what you're truly capable of achieving. Indeed, Assessment Centres are most usefully employed in those situations where you're about to make a step-change, such as graduating from university and taking up your first full-time job, or being promoted to a first-line manager. In both cases, the change is quite significant and you're going to need to display skills in a totally new setting.

Do people who have previously attended an Assessment Centre have an advantage?

No, not really. Each Assessment Centre is different in terms of the behaviours being assessed, the exercises or activities being used, the make-up of the group of candidates, and the team of assessors doing the assessing. Even if a candidate has previously attended a similar centre, it's unlikely that this is going to be of any great benefit. It's very difficult to put on a performance and to keep it up when it's 'the real you' who's on display and being tested.

Am I competing against other candidates?

Strictly speaking, no. Assessment Centres aim to assess people against a predetermined standard, which is defined in relation to the requirements of the job for which you're being assessed (the target job). In theory, everyone can meet or exceed the standard required, or fail to meet the standard. However, in reality there are usually only so many vacancies available, and if everyone exceeds the required standard, then the organisation usually picks the best performers.

Aim to do your best, but don't be obsessed with 'beating' the other candidates, because overly competitive behaviour may not go down well in that particular organisation. Avoid being seen as a poor team player who's too self-centred. On the other hand, don't be a 'shrinking violet' who's dominated by the other participants. The key is striking a sensible balance by displaying and earning respect for others through an appropriate amount of give and take.

How do assessors avoid bias based on prior knowledge about me?

Bias can be a concern when the Assessment Centre is for internal promotion, and you perhaps feel that some of the assessors have preconceived views about you, influencing how they'll judge your performance. However, if the Assessment Centre is well designed and properly managed, then this concern shouldn't arise, as only relevant, observed behaviour will be evaluated. Any attempts to include irrelevant information are likely to be challenged and almost certainly ignored when considering your performance.

Key Features of Assessment Centres

You've got to grips with what an Assessment Centre is and what it isn't (see the preceding sections); now we describe some of the key features in further detail, so as to make you more familiar with the process and increase your chances of success.

Measuring job-related competencies

If you're invited to attend an Assessment Centre you can safely assume that the event is designed to assess a set of job-related competencies, which have been identified through some form of job analysis. You're usually told in advance of the competencies that the centre is going to be assessing. You need to give some thought to what the Assessment Centre is trying to measure and how you can show that you possess those qualities.

For a more detailed explanation of Competencies and the role they play in an Assessment Centre, check out Chapter 2.

Using job-related simulations

Your next step is to think about which exercise simulations are likely to be used on the Assessment Centre to measure those competencies. It's important that the exercises reflect the types of activities that you're going to meet in the job you're being assessed for. You can expect to be presented with more than one exercise simulation, as it's generally considered desirable to have several sources of evidence for each of the competencies being assessed. A typical Assessment Centre may have between three and five exercises, possibly along with an interview, and one or more psychometric tests.

Chapter 2 gives you an overview of the types of exercise simulations you're likely to meet and Chapters 4 to 10 go into a detailed description of each of these different types.

Involving more than one assessor

One of the most important features of an Assessment Centre is that more than one assessor evaluates your performance. By involving multiple assessors, the risk of individual bias influencing the final outcome is much reduced. Best practice recommends that there's one assessor for every two partici-pants (candidates), so if you're one of eight participants then it's likely that there are also four assessors. If the Assessment Centre is made up of four different exercise simulations, then each assessor is tasked with observing and evaluating your performance in a different exercise.

It's almost certain that you're going to need to impress more than one assessor if you wish to succeed at your Assessment Centre. So don't fall into the trap of trying to impress just one particular assessor, even if that assessor seems to be giving you more attention by sending out positive signals such as a lot of eye contact and smiling.

The assessor's role is described in more detail in Chapter 2.

Gathering independent data for making decisions

Each assessor is expected to work independently to come to an objective evaluation of your performance on a particular exercise. Any discussion between the assessors about your performance is discouraged to prevent the assessors from unduly influencing one another before the marking is completed.

After the assessors finish their marking, they then come together for a final evaluation meeting to share their findings. This is a critical and important feature of the Assessment Centre. If four different assessors independently conclude that your performance is deficient on a particular competency you can be sure that you're being judged fairly and accurately.

See Chapter 2 for a more detailed explanation of how the assessors make their collective decision about your overall performance.

Assessing multiple participants

The Assessment Centre is often referred to as a Multiple Assessment Process, because it measures multiple competencies, using multiple exercise simulations, evaluated by multiple assessors, all of which involve multiple participants (candidates). Most Assessment Centres invite 6 to 12 participants, although in theory it's possible to run an Assessment Centre with any number of participants, or even just one!

It can happen that you're the one and only participant at the Assessment Centre. If you find yourself in this position, respond in exactly the same way as you would for a centre with more participants, as the assessment is likely to be made up of much the same activities. For example, you may be given a written task, followed by a presentation, a one-to-one role-play, as well as being interviewed. The one obvious difference is that you're unlikely to be asked to take part in a group discussion exercise, unless the assessors use stand-ins to make up the group numbers.

Take heart! Attending an Assessment Centre as a solitary participant probably means that you're on the shortlist of candidates being considered for that position.

Advantages of Using Assessment Centres

Assessment Centres have grown steadily in popularity ever since they first came on the scene during the Second World War. But what is it that has made them popular and what does this mean for you?

Predicting future potential with greater accuracy

Every organisation wants to find the best people for the job so that it can maximise its productivity and become the best in the field. Key to achieving this goal is being able to predict who among a multitude of applicants for a particular job is going to be the most successful in that post. This requirement is a perpetual challenge for organisations, which have been experimenting with many different assessment methods over the years. The Assessment Centre consistently shows itself to be one of the most effective ways of predicting future job success.

Providing a fair and equal opportunity to all candidates

Assessment Centres are recognised for giving candidates a fairer and more equal opportunity in the job selection process. This is because Assessment Centres are designed to assess your ability to tackle job-related activities, rather than relying on someone making a superficial judgement about your capabilities, based on some abstract and seemingly irrelevant measures.

Researching Assessment Centres

Psychologists have carried out many research studies over the decades, comparing different job selection methods. The following figure is based on a combination of such studies and shows how well each method is at predicting job success.

Unsurprisingly, no absolutely certain way exists of predicting future job success.

Work Samples are the most reliable because getting you to actually do part of the job provides the clearest indication of your capability. This is fine with certain practical jobs but for any office-based job, where you need to know a lot about procedures and the organisational structure, it's unrealistic to expect you to step into that role for a limited period of time, so work samples only have limited scope. They also lack the ability to assess your future potential as they are rooted in the 'here and now'.

Ability/Aptitude Tests are a highly effective way of measuring your intellectual capability in a general context, but they don't show how you can apply your intellect to tackle the practical challenges within that job.

Biodata involves answering a series of focused biographical questions, which provide data that specifically relate to the job for which you're applying. Such questionnaires can be useful for screening large numbers of applicants, but they're costly and time-consuming to produce, and are only economical for large-scale recruitment.

Other selection processes include: the Interview, References, Personality Tests, and the Assessment Centre, which is by far the most effective method for predicting future job success.

So, if you're invited to attend an Assessment Centre, you can be reassured that the organisation is using what is generally regarded as one of the most valid selection methods, hopefully reinforcing your opinion that this is a professional organisation that you'd want to work for.

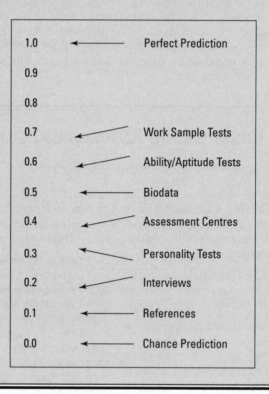

1.0	⟵ Perfect Prediction
0.9	
0.8	
0.7	⟵ Work Sample Tests
0.6	⟵ Ability/Aptitude Tests
0.5	⟵ Biodata
0.4	⟵ Assessment Centres
0.3	⟵ Personality Tests
0.2	⟵ Interviews
0.1	⟵ References
0.0	⟵ Chance Prediction

When you attend an Assessment Centre you do so in the knowledge that you and the other candidates are going to be assessed against an objectively defined standard, rather than being compared with one another. That standard applies equally to everyone, regardless of background or at what stage in your career you're attending the centre. The standard acts as a yardstick and is updated regularly to reflect changing demands of the job whenever they occur.

Providing a realistic job preview

Another advantage of the Assessment Centre over other selection methods is that an Assessment Centre gives you a useful insight into what that particular job is going to involve if you are appointed. This is a real benefit because it allows you to decide if this particular job in this organisation is the one for you.

It's in everyone's interest to give you the opportunity of considering carefully if the job is right for you; if you're going to be able to cope and find the job fulfilling. The advantage of the Assessment Centre is that it acts as a shop window, where 'what you see is what you get'!

Common Uses of Assessment Centres

Assessment Centres are highly sophisticated events which are costly and time-consuming to design and carry out, but despite this they've been used for a number of different purposes over the years, as Table 1-1 shows.

Table 1-1	Uses for Assessment Centres
Uses for Assessment Centres	*Percentage Use*
Other external recruitment	57%
Diagnose development needs	56%
Identify high potential	50%
Graduate recruitment	49%
Inform internal promotion	45%
Succession planning	38%

Reproduced with the kind permission of The A&DC Group.

The results in Table 1-1 are from an international survey carried out in 2007, of 437 respondents from 43 countries on five continents, showing that the top six uses for Assessment Centres fall into three broad categories, as we describe in the following sections.

External recruitment

External recruitment has always been the most popular use for Assessment Centres and still is today. Typically Assessment Centres are used for two types of external recruitment: large-scale recruitment such as graduate recruitment and senior or key appointments.

Graduate recruitment

Assessment Centres are often used in situations where there are large numbers of vacancies and even larger numbers of candidates, such as in graduate recruitment.

You may be about to graduate or have recently graduated, and you're applying for a graduate trainee position with a number of big employers. Most of these organisations are planning to take on a large pool of graduates, perhaps in excess of 100, and they often get upwards of 5,000 applicants. This means a large-scale employer needs to screen out those applicants whom they judge as being unsuitable for their organisation. Many organisations do this by using a series of screening activities, each more refined than the last, and culminating in the Assessment Centre.

Often the initial screening criteria are by necessity very crude, which could include only considering candidates with a 2.1 degree, even though many with a 2.2 or even lower are viable candidates. Generally the intention at this stage of screening is to significantly reduce applicant numbers, so your first challenge is to get past this initial hurdle.

You need to stand out from the crowd, by showing the organisation you have the skills they're looking for. Most organisations' application forms are now online. Form filling is time-consuming, particularly because you need to repeat the process for each organisation you're applying to. Try building up a set of standard examples in a Microsoft Word document of how you demonstrate behaviours such as Teamwork,

Planning, Influencing, and so on. After making sure that your examples are clear and well thought through you can then cut and paste them into different application forms.

If you get through the initial screening you may be invited to complete an online psychometric test, which is used to reduce applicant numbers even further. Go to Chapter 12 for advice on how to tackle psychometric tests.

After getting through this stage you're then likely to be invited to attend an Assessment Centre, which is usually the last stage of the selection process.

Getting to the Assessment Centre stage is a good reason for giving yourself a big pat on the back because you've managed to get through to the last few hundred. At this stage your chances of success are likely to be approximately one in three, so you have every reason to be proud of your achievement. However, the job isn't done yet and you need to go to the appropriate chapters within this book to help you make the most of your chance when it comes up. It's very important to re-read your application form, so as to make sure you give consistent answers in an interview, not forgetting that the answers you gave on your application form helped you to get to this stage of the selection process.

Senior or key appointments

Assessment Centres are also used to recruit people into senior positions where the consequences of getting it wrong are highly significant. If you've been invited to attend an Assessment Centre for a senior post such as an executive or a general manager, then the likelihood is that you're on a short-list of around three to six candidates. In this situation it's usual for the candidates to be seen on an individual basis, to avoid any embarrassment, particularly if the applicants are likely to know one another because of coming from the same industry or line of business.

Whatever the outcome, make a point of asking for feedback. You can discover a lot about yourself and you also gain useful insights as to how the Assessment Centre process works, which is likely to be beneficial if you get to attend another centre in the future.

Internal promotion

Assessment Centres are sometimes used for important internal promotions, such as appointments to a first-line managerial position or other key roles within the organisation. The centre can also be used for succession planning, helping to identify people with the potential to move into senior roles in the future.

Unfortunately a few organisations using Assessment Centres fail to make their purpose clear. Sometimes this is simply an oversight but occasionally it's because the organisation has a hidden agenda. For example, they may claim that they wish to assess their employees in readiness for a switch over to a new working environment, but they fail to disclose that those employees not showing the appropriate skills may end up being made redundant. We're certainly not implying that all Assessment Centres carry such threats, but it's always advisable to ask what the centre is aiming to achieve.

Hopefully, the organisation that you're aiming to join is going to be one following best practice and providing a clearly written brief, accompanied by a Question and Answer session explaining exactly what they are trying to do and why.

Development

Since the 1980s Assessment Centres have been used more and more for development purposes. The detailed nature of the data produced from an Assessment Centre provides a rich source of information, which can be used to pinpoint areas for development and provide powerful feedback. Such Assessment Centres are often referred to as 'Assessment Centres for development' or perhaps more fittingly 'Development Centres'. The relationship between Assessment Centres and Development Centres is illustrated in Table 1-2.

Table 1-2 The Asset-Development Centre Relationship

Features	Assessment Centre	Development Centre		
Purpose	Recruitment or internal promotion	Identifying future potential	Diagnosing development needs	Developing areas that need addressing
Use	Selection event	Succession planning	Skills audit	Changing behaviour
Role of assessor	Assess	Assess	Observing and giving feedback	Coaching and developing
Duration	About 1 day	1–2 days	2–3 days	2+ days
Feedback	After the event	After the event	During the event	During the event
Outcome	Select for immediate appointment	Define gaps against future job	Define gaps against current job	Close gaps within current job

Development Centres can have a number of different purposes and sometimes they even have joint purposes, as outlined below.

Fully understanding the purpose of a Development Centre and how the event is going to be run is vital to the outcome of your attendance. Many organisations provide a clear brief covering questions such as:

 ✔ What is the purpose of the Development Centre?

 ✔ Who is the Development Centre targeted at?

 ✔ How are participants nominated?

 ✔ Who are going to act as assessors? What training do the assessors have?

✔ How are the results from the Development Centre going to be used?

✔ Who is going to have access to the data/results from the Development Centre?

✔ What is the policy/procedure on feedback?

✔ Where are the results from the Development Centre going to be stored?

✔ Are there opportunities for reassessment?

It's important to ask the organisation for a clear brief if they don't produce one for participants.

For further guidance on this or any other matters about Assessment Centre standards visit the British Psychological Society's website and check out its Guidelines on Assessment Centre Best Practice, which you can find at www.psych testing.org.uk.

Identifying future potential

Although Development Centres have many of the characteristics of the traditional Assessment Centre, the principal difference is that Development Centres are looking to spot candidates for future senior appointments or for a fast- track development programme to help someone acquire the skills and qualities needed for a senior role.

Being invited to attend a Development Centre of this type (sometimes they're still called Assessment Centres) should be regarded as a positive step, as you're either going to be assessed to see if you should join a fast-track programme or you've already been earmarked for progression. Either way, make sure you rise to the challenge by showing your commitment to working on your development needs, because most organisations respond favourably to employees showing willingness to invest time and effort into fulfilling their potential.

Diagnosing strengths and development needs

Another aspect of Development Centres is focusing on diagnosing individual strengths and development needs. This may be carried out as part of a general skills audit, for example, to support an organisational need such as the adoption of a new set of corporate values and behaviours. In the late 1990s and early 2000s many organisations were trying to implement a 'Change Programme' and needed their staff to 'get on board' with the message. Development Centres are seen as an effective way of reinforcing changes in behaviour that are needed on an individual and corporate level.

Providing coaching on identified development needs

Coaching for developmental purposes, such as tackling areas needing particular attention, is another feature of Development Centres. Providing coaching represents a much more radical departure from the traditional Assessment Centre approach and is often built into training and development events.

Chapter 2

How an Assessment Centre Works

In This Chapter

▶ Looking at what is being measured and how

▶ Finding out who does what

▶ Understanding how decisions are reached

*F*earing the unknown is perfectly normal. Perhaps you're feeling just a bit apprehensive about your trip of a lifetime trekking in the Amazon rainforest. You don't know what to expect or whether the experience is going to be positive or negative. Luckily, an expedition to an Assessment Centre isn't nearly as awesome as trekking in the Amazon; nevertheless having a few qualms is quite natural. But as a participant, the more you know about the workings of an Assessment Centre, the better you're going to perform.

To help you get the most out of your Assessment Centre experience, we're going to try to allay any concerns you may have by explaining exactly how an Assessment Centre works.

Knowing about Measuring Performance

Assessment Centres are designed to enable you to prove your suitability and capability for a particular job, by asking you to carry out exercises planned to simulate the job on offer. At the Assessment Centre a candidate's knowledge, skills, abilities and attitudes required to do the target job are measured in a fair and objective manner. However, these can only be observed through your behaviour and this is why your behaviour is assessed during an Assessment Centre.

Your performance on the exercises gives the assessors a good idea of how you're likely to behave in the real job on a day-to-day basis, where your strengths or development needs lie, and how your performance compares with what is needed for carrying out that job successfully.

 Every job is different, requiring different skills. Employers carry out job analysis to identify those behaviours that are required to be effective in a particular job. For example, to be a successful, a judge has to demonstrate knowledge of the law, display honesty and integrity, have good listening skills, show the ability to analyse a lot of information quickly and accurately, and be able to come speedily to valid and just decisions.

Job-related skills, or competencies

Standards for testing a person's suitability for a particular job are called *competencies*: they can also be called 'criteria', 'dimensions', 'attributes' and 'characteristics'. Assessment Centres use competencies for measuring whether you're likely to be successful in the role that you're applying for.

A competency is an underlying characteristic of a person; it may be a motive, trait, skill, aspect of one's self-image, or social role or body of knowledge.

What's behaviour and why focus on it?

One of the simplest ways of defining human behaviour is: *What an individual 'says' or 'does' or 'does not say' or 'does not do', when something is expected of him or her.*

Your behaviour is a physical expression of what you're thinking and how you're putting your thoughts into action. The way you're behaving is the basis for allowing someone else to make value judgements about you.

Job analysis – why bother?

Job analysis is a formal procedure for looking at a job in detail, both in terms of the content of a job and what makes someone successful within that role. The information collected from a job analysis is used as a yardstick for testing suitability and successful job performance.

One way of getting this information is to interview people who have first-hand experience of the job and who can provide information about the job content and the essential skills and expertise needed to do the job

successfully. Job analysis interviews are often carried out by psychologists with the job holders, and their managers or senior management.

Interviewing people at both levels is important so as to get a detailed picture of the job in question. Job holders are able to describe the specific tasks that make up the job, while the managers explain what 'good performance' looks like in that job and how the job may change in line with the organisation's future needs.

You need to be absolutely clear about the difference between the terms 'competencies' and 'competences', which are both used in the job selection process. Competencies relate to the person and how he or she *behaves* in order to achieve a task required by the job. Competences are about having the *ability* to complete a certain task required by the job. Table 2-1 lists the key differences between 'competencies' and 'competences'.

Table 2-1	Competencies Versus Competences	
Key Differences	*Competencies*	*Competences*
Focus	The Person	The Job/Role
Nature	People characteristics *Example:* Interpersonal skills	Job tasks *Example:* Dealing with payroll
Performance indicators	Behaviours *Examples:* Shares information Gains support	Task outputs *Examples:* Replies within a day Inputting data accurately

Table 2-1 *(continued)*

Key Differences	Competencies	Competences
Levels of complexity	Context for the behaviour	Complexity of output
	Examples: Develops relationships with colleagues (level 1)	Examples: Processes information on new staff (level 1)
	Develops relationships with key clients (level 2)	Manages complexity of tax records (level 2)
	Delivers excellence	Develops standards

Competencies are made up of three parts: title, definition, and a set of positive and negative behavioural indicators. Some organisations tell you before the assessment starts what competency titles and definitions are going to be used in the recruitment process. A 'title' is the label given to the competency being assessed and the 'definition' outlines the key behaviours that are going to be observed within that competency, for example:

Title: Teamwork (TWK)

Definition: Willingness to participate as a full member of a team of which he/she is not necessarily leader. Effectively contributes and/or shares information even though it's of no direct personal interest.

Behavioural indicators:

+ Acknowledges and expands on others' ideas

+ Contributes throughout to the discussion

– Causes arguments with other team members

– Withdraws from the group when his or her suggestions are rejected

If you're not told what competencies are going to be assessed at your Assessment Centre – it doesn't hurt to ask! Most organisations have a clear policy on disclosing such information. Being given this information in advance allows you to compare your skill set with the competencies being assessed, helping you to decide your overall level of 'fit'.

Levels of performance

As well as the type of behaviour you display in your assessment your *level* of behaviour is also assessed to check if you've displayed an acceptable standard of performance. This measurement of behaviour is known as a 'benchmark' and means the required standard of behaviour needed in the target job. For example, the level of communication skills needed by a scientist are very different from that of a politician. While a scientist needs the skill of communicating scientific information clearly and precisely to a peer group, a politician needs to be able to communicate effectively with a much wider range of people: the general public, parliament, the media. The 'benchmark' or level of behaviour required for each job is different.

When an assessor awards a rating of, say, 3 (on a scale of 1 to 5) on a competency such as Persuasive Oral Communication in a group discussion exercise, the assessors are saying:

> *You displayed an acceptable level of Persuasive Oral Communication in this group discussion exercise, compared with the likely demands of the target job.*

This statement about the demands of the target job is absolutely fundamental to the success of the Assessment Centre's ability to predict your capacity to carry out the target job successfully.

Knowing in advance what competencies you're going to be assessed on means you can start thinking about how each competency relates to the day-to-day activities within the target job. This gives you an idea of what behaviours you need to demonstrate in those tasks and the level of behaviour that's expected on the job by the assessors.

Attending the Assessment Centre

Your attendance at an Assessment Centre is likely to last for between one and two days. Assessment Centres for development (Development Centres – refer to Chapter 1) can last for as long as three to five days due to the developmental purpose. A one-day Assessment Centre is the most popular, because it strikes the right balance between the input needed by all involved in the event, and the need to gather enough data upon which to base a decision about your suitability for the job.

Although the structure and content of the Assessment Centre varies according to the requirements of the job on offer, we're going to try to outline what a typical Assessment Centre looks like.

Timetabling

Before attending the Assessment Centre, you're sent information about: how to get to the Assessment Centre, the timetable, the dress code (note these exercises don't require shorts and trainers!), any recreational facilities, who to speak to if you have any queries, and details of any preparatory work you need to do.

As well as the information you receive before attending the Assessment Centre, most likely you'll have another briefing on the morning of the centre, including information about the exercises, the role of the assessors, and what is expected of you.

You may be given specific details about the types of exercises that you're going to do. For example: you're going to be working in groups to discuss various issues, you'll be having an interview, and you're going to be doing written work.

Given the likely time constraints of the exercises, you must listen carefully to any briefings throughout the day, and respond immediately if you have any doubts or if the instructions aren't clear.

You can see an example of an Assessment Centre timetable in Figure 2-1.

After being briefed you spend most of the day doing exercises, interviews and tests. Usually at the end of the day comes a closing session. Organisers thank you for your time and explain when and how you're likely to hear about the outcome. You may also be asked to give feedback as to how the event went for you. Find out more about feedback in Chapters 13 and 14.

TIME	SCHEDULE
08:00	Registration & Coffee
08:20	Welcome & Introductions
08:50	Group Discussion
09:50	Break
10:10	Preparing for a One-to-One Meeting
10:45	One-to-One Meeting
11:40	Preparing for a One-to-One Meeting
12:15	One-to-One Meeting
12:55	Lunch
13:55	Analysis Exercise Report Writing
16:00	Break
16:15	Analysis Exercise Presentation Preparation
16:40	Analysis Exercise Presentation
17:00	Close and Depart

Figure 2-1: An example of an Assessment Centre timetable.

Understanding how the Assessment Centre is structured helps you prepare yourself for the day ahead. For example, if you're given a timetable like the one shown in Figure 2-1, then you must focus on your first exercise, the group discussion, and try not to think about the one-to-one role-plays or analysis exercises that you're going to be doing later on. Keeping yourself focused is very important for a successful performance at the centre.

Tackling the exercises

Your day at the Assessment Centre is made up of carrying out a set of simulation exercises. These exercises give you the opportunity to display behaviour relevant to the target job and provide a realistic and honest picture of what the job involves.

The choice of exercises on an Assessment Centre will be influenced by the competencies that need to be assessed. Employers look to measure a competency at least twice during an Assessment Centre to make sure that they're making an accurate judgement of your behaviour for that competency. An example showing which competencies can be measured in different exercise types is given in the Competency Exercise Matrix in Table 2-2.

Table 2-2	Competency Exercise Matrix				
Competency	*Exercises*				
	Non-Assigned Analysis Role Group Discussion	Assigned Role Group Discussion	Role-play	In-Basket	Analysis Exercise
Planning and Organising (P&O)		✓	✓	✓	✓
Problem Analysis (PA)	✓	✓		✓	✓
Commercial Awareness (CA)			✓	✓	✓
Customer Service (CS)	✓		✓	✓	✓

Competency	Exercises			
Persuasive Oral Communication (POC)	♪	♪	♪	♪
Initiative (I)	♪	♪	♪	♪
Teamwork (TWK)	♪	♪		

When you're preparing for attendance at an Assessment Centre, think about what competencies are likely to be measured in the different types of exercises for the target job. For example, if you know that Customer Service is going to be measured and you have a good idea which exercises you're going to be asked to complete, think about the behaviours you should display to ensure an effective performance. For example, in a group discussion exercise you may be asked to discuss the impact your decisions have on customers. In a role-play exercise you meet the customer and have to resolve the customer's specific issues. And in an analysis exercise you have to make recommendations about how to attract new customers to your company. The different types of exercises and ways of working are explained in more detail in the next section.

Ways of Working

In your normal job you're expected to respond to a range of different situations and the Assessment Centre exercises are designed to simulate what happens in the real world.

Usually you find yourself regularly working in one of three contexts:

- ✔ In groups
- ✔ One-to-one
- ✔ On your own

We describe below the different types of exercises associated with each of the three ways of working.

Working in groups

Most jobs require you to spend some time working with other people in groups and the nature and purpose of these group activities can take various forms.

Group discussion exercises are a popular way of simulating the way you work in a group. There are two main features that determine the nature of group discussions:

 ✔ **Co-operative or Competitive:** This will strongly deter-mine the format and content of the group discussion and how it will operate.

 A *co-operative group* discussion requires you to analyse a number of ideas or facts and come up with recommenda-tions within an allotted timeframe. This type of exercise is often called a 'Non-Assigned Role Group Discussion', because all the participants are given the same informa-tion and no one is assigned any particular role.

 A *competitive group* discussion requires you to persuade and negotiate, to get the best deal you can. In this type of exercise, the group usually receives some common infor-mation, as well as information that is exclusive to you. This type of exercise is often called an 'Assigned Role Group Discussion', because each of the participants is given a different brief.

 ✔ **Leadership allocation:** Another key feature of group dis-cussions is whether or not to allocate the leadership role. Participants are sometimes asked to take it in turns to lead the discussion. The allocation of leadership of the group depends on the extent to which leadership is an important competency in the target job.

To find out more about group discussions go to Chapter 4.

Working one-to-one

Jobs often require you to spend some time working with one other person and these interactions can take various forms.

Assessment Centres often use the following three exercises to assess candidates in one-to-one situations.

| ✔ **Oral presentation:** For example, you're asked to present facts or sell an idea to colleagues.

| ✔ **Role-play:** For example, you have to counsel someone or negotiate with a buyer.

| ✔ **Fact-finding:** For example, you're asked to investigate a problem and decide on a course of action.

Oral presentations

In an oral presentation exercise you're asked to prepare and make a presentation. Although an oral presentation is often delivered to an audience of two or more people, it may also to be run as a one-to-one session. If so, this is likely to be less formal and may not include the use of visual aids. The level of formality and the nature of the presentation are usually determined by the demands of the target job.

For more information on oral presentations, please see Chapter 5.

Role-play

Role-play exercises simulate one-to-one interactions between the role-player in the guise of a customer, colleague, boss or subordinate and you in the target job role. However, although you're asked to behave as if you're in the target job, you're *not* asked to role-play a character. The usual format for this type of exercise is to give the candidate a detailed brief with general background information, a description of a particular situation, and some notes about the person you're about to meet with.

You can find out more about role-play exercises in Chapter 6.

Fact-finding

A fact-finding exercise is about testing your analytical skills. You're given a brief outline description about an incident or problem and are asked to prepare questions to put to someone who possesses a large amount of relevant information, in order to solve the problem. You're then allowed to question her for a fixed period, at the end of which you need to come to a decision and make an appropriate recommendation. After presenting your decision, you're questioned to test the soundness of your arguments.

Turn to Chapter 7 for more information on fact-finding exercises.

Working on your own

The majority of jobs require you to spend some time working by yourself, to analyse information, plan activities or produce some form of written output.

The most commonly used exercises assessing your ability to work on your own are the written in-basket and analysis exercises. You may also come across the less common planning and scheduling exercise.

In-basket exercise

The in-basket exercise is about managing the paperwork: handling letters, internal memos, reports, junk mail, and so on, simulating the target job. Your task is to sort through the items, prioritising, delegating and taking action. This includes writing letters, planning meetings, making phone calls. The in-basket exercise is now also available in an email format, called the inbox exercise.

For more information on in-basket or inbox exercises, see Chapter 10.

Analysis exercise

The analysis exercise requires you to look at some prepared data, which is presented in writing or numerically, analyse the data and present a logical interpretation. The content and time taken to do the exercise are designed to simulate the target job. Typically you're given four to five pages of text, possibly accompanied by tables and/or graphs (depending on the type of job) and allowed 1 to 2 hours to take in the information and write a report with recommendations.

You can find out more about analysis exercises in Chapter 8.

Planning and scheduling exercise

Planning and scheduling exercises are used by Assessment Centres for assessing project management skills and they simulate the skills required in the target job. You're given background information and a description of the project, and asked to prepare a plan, showing how you're going to use the resources to achieve a specific objective.

For more information on planning and scheduling exercises, see Chapter 9.

'Independent' Exercises versus 'Themed' Exercises

You may find that the exercises used on an Assessment Centre are independent of each other or linked together by a theme. Both approaches have advantages and disadvantages. The approach taken depends on the preference of the organisation.

If the exercises you're asked to undertake are independent of each other, you assume a new role within a different organisation, and sometimes a different industry in each exercise. Generally you're fully briefed at the start of each exercise. Each new exercise means adjusting to a new role, in a new organisation, with a new line manager. Having to change direction gives you the benefit of making a 'fresh start'. So, if you feel you've performed poorly in one exercise, having finished it you can move on to the next exercise and start anew.

Some employers choose to design an Assessment Centre simulating a 'typical working day', planning the exercises around one theme or topic. This approach is sometimes called 'A day in the life. . .', giving you continuity, because you take on just one role in the organisation for the whole day. Most likely, you'll be briefed at the beginning of the day detailing your role and where you fit into the organisation that you're working for.

You can also be asked to do the 'A year in the life. . .' exercise, which is based on the same principles, as the 'A day in the life. . .' but with a longer timeframe. Again you're faced with a series of interlinked exercises, but time at the Assessment Centre doesn't represent real time. Instead, one day represents several months or even years, and therefore the exercises are designed around how the organisation changes during this period. This is done by having two or three hours of exercises set in one period of time, two or three hours set six months later, and a final couple of hours set the following year. This type of event allows the assessor to test how you change and adapt your behaviour to the various developments within the organisation.

If you find yourself facing the 'A day in the life . . .' approach, try using the interlinked exercises to your advantage. Bringing what you've learned from an earlier exercise into a later exercise helps you come to a more informed decision. This is a useful feature of the interlinked approach, which doesn't happen with independent exercises.

Additional Activities

As well as doing simulation exercises, the Assessment Centre may involve you completing some other form of assessment activities. The purpose of the additional activities is to get a complete picture of your performance relating to the competencies being assessed and to help assessors come to fully informed decisions. The more information the assessors have about you means more comprehensive feedback. This can be invaluable for taking action and planning your future career.

Knowing what the additional activities are and how to tackle them is important. The most popular types of additional activities that you may be asked to do are described in the following sections.

Competency Based Interview

Having at least one interview is a common feature of an Assessment Centre. The most used interview is the Competency Based Interview (CBI). In this type of interview you're asked questions focusing on gathering evidence about the competencies being assessed on the Assessment Centre. The evidence from the CBI is then considered alongside the evidence collected from the simulation exercises.

For certain competencies the interview is the best source of evidence for the assessors. For example, competencies such as Integrity or People Development are more easily explored within an interview than through simulation exercises.

For more information on the Competency Based Interview, turn to Chapter 11.

Psychometric tests

Tests of verbal and numerical reasoning, known as psychometric tests are popular for measuring your intellectual capabilities and how you'll perform in the target job. The job analysis process can help to pinpoint where links exist between the psychometric test results and the competencies being assessed.

Personality questionnaires such as Hogan, 16PF or OPQ show your preferred ways of working. For example, being open-minded or focusing on detail, or your level of commitment. Such information can be used to complement your behaviour in the competencies that you've been tested on, and can help show how well you're likely to fit in with the team and culture of the organisation to which you're applying.

Chapter 12 has much more to say about psychometric testing.

Other activities

There are a variety of instruments, forms and questionnaires, such as 360° questionnaires used to find out more about you and the way you behave. You may be asked to fill in a 360° questionnaire during your assessment or even before the event. Your boss and/or colleagues may also be asked for input. However, the data about you may be viewed as subjective, and because of this the information is less commonly used for assessment purposes.

For more information on 360° questionnaires or other activities, head to Chapters 12 and 13.

Discovering Who's Who

So that you give your best at an Assessment Centre, make sure you recognise the different roles and responsibilities people have there and who you're going to be meeting and when.

Other candidates

For a start you're going to be meeting your fellow candidates, who are likely to be feeling as nervous as you! Like you they're going to be doing the same exercises, trying to find out as much about the organisation as they can, focusing on the target job, and checking out the job's suitability for them.

Importantly, don't view your fellow participants as 'competition'. Instead, chat to the other candidates, find out more about them, their backgrounds, why they're interested in this job, and what other jobs they've applied for. You may well find that the information you glean is going to be useful for planning your future career.

Centre manager and centre administrators

Most Assessment Centres have a centre manager and centre administrators. The centre manager and administrators are responsible for making sure the event runs smoothly and that you're in the right place at the right time. They're going to be your main point of contact for the day and are there to answer any questions or queries that you may have during the event.

Make contact with the centre manager and administrators as early on in the assessment process as possible. This early contact means that you can feel more comfortable about approaching them during the course of the day, should you have any queries or problems. For example, you may begin to feel unwell and need to speak to them about your options of continuing with the assessment or going home.

Role-players

If you're taking part in a role-play exercise you meet a role-player. Role-players are trained and given specific guidance about how to play their role and interact with you, the candidate. Most likely, the organisation doing the assessing will try to limit the contact you have with the role-player outside of the exercise in order to maintain the realism of the situation. So, don't feel offended if the role-player walks straight past you and doesn't stop to chat!

The assessors

Assessors play a key role at an Assessment Centre. The assessors are responsible for observing your behaviour during the exercises and afterwards making decisions about your performance. To make sure that the process is fair and objective for each candidate, assessors have formal training to make sure they're competent. To prevent there being any bias in assessors' judgements, interaction with the candidates is kept to a minimum. The use assessors who don't have any prior knowledge of the candidates attending the Assessment Centre is considered best practice.

During an exercise the assessor's role is simply to collect data. Assessors write down everything you say relating to the exercise. Make sure you speak clearly and can be heard, otherwise you won't get credit for your contributions!

Assessors also need to have a thorough and detailed understanding of the following:

- ✔ The organisation and job being assessed.
- ✔ The competencies being assessed and how they relate to job performance.
- ✔ How to evaluate a candidate's behaviour based on performance within the exercises.
- ✔ How to make decisions based on behavioural evidence.
- ✔ How to present accurate oral and written feedback about the candidate's behaviour and performance.

You must therefore strive to impress the assessors with your knowledge of what the job involves and your ability to operate and behave at a level that is required.

Assessors aim to be fair and unbiased. They try to give you the opportunity to show what you're capable of, so that they can gather as much evidence as possible to decide how you fit the target job. Assessors aren't there to block your success; they really do want to see you do well!

Decision-Making Time

You may wonder how decisions about you are made on Assessment Centres. In the following sections we explain the most common approach.

During the activities

The assessors are trained to carry out a behavioural assessment process in which they Observe, Record, Classify and Evaluate (ORCE). Assessors *observe* and *record* your behaviour while you're performing the exercises, in much the same way as a video camera, by simply looking at and recording what is actually happening and only making judgements when they have a complete picture of your behaviour.

Only after you've finished the exercise session and you've moved on to another task do the assessors start to *classify* your observed behaviour against the competencies being measured in that exercise. Afterwards the assessors *evaluate* the behavioural evidence that has been gathered for each competency on a given exercise. This involves looking at all the evidence, both positive and negative, in terms of both quantity and quality for that competency and then awarding a rating that summarises your ability on that competency within that exercise. The process is then repeated for each competency in turn. A rating or evaluation is then given corresponding to the benchmark.

Coming to a decision

The decision-making meeting (or 'wash-up') is the most critical stage of your assessment. The performance of each candidate is discussed in turn, partly to make a decision about whether you've been successful, but also to collect evidence so that the assessors can provide you with feedback.

Assessors discuss the evidence they've collected about you competency by competency. Assessors read out the evidence they have for each competency in each exercise and then discuss this as a group to decide on an overall competency score. Sometimes an Overall Assessment Rating (OAR) is also given. This is usually the sum total of all the group consensus competency scores. Candidates are then ranked in terms of 'job fit' according to the OAR. All the evidence is then used to allow the assessors to make a Yes/No decision.

A document, called 'A participant wash-up matrix', is used to help structure the discussion around the behavioural evidence that's been collected, so that the assessors can reach consensus scores. The wash-up matrix is shown in Figure 2-2.

Certain factors play an important part in the decision-making process. For example, some competencies are thought to be essential, based on the job analysis research, while other competencies are labelled desirable. In this case candidates may have to score a higher mark in the essential competencies than the desirable competencies. For example, it would be a critical requirement of a teacher or lecturer to have good oral communication skills.

Another important consideration is whether or not a competency is readily trainable. For example, if a candidate scores poorly on a competency that's very difficult to improve through training, such as analytical skills, then this is a serious problem. On the other hand, if a candidate scores poorly on a trainable competency, such as interpersonal skills, then this candidate may still be worthy of consideration.

Name: Jane Bennett	Exercises					Overall Evaluation
Competency	CBI	Assigned Role GD	Non-Assigned Role GD	Role-play 1	Role-play 2	
Customer Service	2		2		4	2
Teamwork		2	3			2
Initiative	3			3	3	3
Leadership		2	4	4		4
Planning & Organising	2	3		3		3
Influencing	4	3			2	3
Developing Others	2		1	2		2
				Overall Assessment Rating		19

Figure 2-2: A participant wash-up matrix.

Once the decision is made, candidates will need to be informed of the decision and specific feedback will need to be provided. The only exception to giving feedback may be on external selection events. For more information on Assessment Centre feedback, please see Chapter 14.

Chapter 3

Maximising Your Chances of Success

In This Chapter
▶ Investigating the organisation and the job
▶ Matching your skills to the job
▶ Getting ready for the assessment

*Y*ou've been invited to attend an Assessment Centre – congratulations! Now's the time to start preparing for the great day. Doing your homework means getting yourself in the right frame of mind for the event and increasing your chances of a successful outcome.

In this chapter we focus on helping you to find out about the organisation you're hoping to work for, making sure you have a high level of 'fit' to the target job, and show you how to get the most out of your time at the Assessment Centre.

Researching the Organisation

Finding out as much as you can about the ethos, culture and long-term goals of the organisation you're hoping to work for is going to help you greatly on the Assessment Centre. Having the full picture of the organisation gives you a better chance of getting to grips with the thinking behind the exercises you're going to be asked to perform and the way you carry them out. You're also likely to have a more positive attitude towards the organisation: whether it's a multinational, a government agency, public service, small business or in the City.

Log on to the Internet and take a look at the organisation's Home page, the About Us page, and the Careers page if they have one. You can get a good feel about an organisation's culture from its website. Read the language on the website and what the organisation values most. An organisation's values give you an insight into how customer-centric they are, how important ethics and diversity are to them and also how they build successful internal working environments.

Organisations are often looking to grow and expand and need dedicated and committed people working for them. An employer is going to be impressed if you can show that you understand their business and the marketplace in general. Arm yourself with the answers to the following questions:

- ✔ What does the organisation do?
- ✔ Where is the organisation based?
- ✔ Who are the organisation's competitors?
- ✔ What are their corporate values?
- ✔ What are the organisation's strategic aims over the next two to three years?
- ✔ What kind of people is the organisation looking for?
- ✔ What career opportunities is the organisation offering and what career development do they provide?

Try speaking directly to the organisation you're hoping to join. Phone the Head Office and ask to speak to someone in the Human Resources department. The staff in Human Resources can fill you in about the job and their recruitment process. Perhaps if you ask you may be able to talk to a current job holder. This is the best person to give you an up-to-date and honest perspective about what it's like working for the organisation. If you're given the opportunity of speaking to someone in the organisation make sure you're well prepared by having a list of questions ready, because you don't want to end up wasting anyone's time.

Make your research work for you during the Assessment Centre by impressing the assessors with what you've found out about the organisation and the target job. This also includes asking any specific questions you may have outstanding from your research. During the day there'll be set time for asking such questions – astute questions can impress assessors.

Finding Out about the Job

Having a thorough understanding of what the target job involves is critical to your success on the Assessment Centre. Going back to the original job advert and job description is a useful way of double-checking your facts.

 If you can't find the original job description or the advert doesn't have enough information to remind you why the job especially appealed to you in the first place, contact the organisation and ask for a copy or try searching for the advert on the Internet.

Reviewing the job description

Your job description sets out the main role and responsibilities of the job holder. Here's an extract from a job description for an Office Manager, which you can compare with the target job description.

JOB TITLE: *Office Manager*

JOB LOCATION: *London*

REPORT TO: *Administration Manager*

DIRECT REPORTS: *2 Office Assistants, 1 Receptionist*

MAIN JOB PURPOSE: *To manage the Admin Production Team and ensure an effective, high standard of support service to internal staff and external clients. To manage and maintain general office facilities and procedures.*

PRINCIPAL ACCOUNTABILITIES:

1. To manage and co-ordinate the work of the Admin Team, incorporating external resources where necessary, to maintain effective and productive administration support.

2. To oversee production and distribution of all products and materials, ensuring accuracy, timeliness, compliance with organisation quality standards, and minimal errors and wastage.

3. To assist with recruitment, development and appraisal of Admin team staff, and continually seek ways of improving and maintaining staff motivation, communication and development.

4. To ensure the effectiveness of the administrative function and all office procedures, devising and implementing new procedures as appropriate.

5. To manage relationships with external suppliers such as printers, couriers, stationery providers and temp agencies, and negotiate best possible rates.

All the skills needed to do the job are listed in the Accountabilities section. To be a successful Office Manager you need to have:

✔ Effective management skills (points 1 and 3).

✔ Ability to find ways of improving and updating processes and systems and putting them into action (points 3 and 4).

✔ Ability to place staff in the right job, supervise performance and make sure the job is done to a high standard (points 1and 2).

✔ Effective communication and people skills (points 3 and 5).

If you haven't yet got some of the skills featured in the job description, you may want to think about building them into a development plan.

From your own job description pick out the essential requirements of the job and map them to your current skills, experience and achievements. This can form the basis for thinking about how you're going to tackle the target job.

Reading the job advert

A job advert acts as the shop window to the organisation. Advertisements are designed to be eye-catching and inspiring, encouraging the best people to come and work for the organisation. Go back to your job advert as it most likely summarises the requirements of the job and is a useful checklist for sorting out what skills and experience you can transfer from your current job to the target job. A typical job advert includes:

✔ Title of the job: for example, 'Marketing Manager'

✔ Salary

- ✔ Location of the job
- ✔ Description of the job
- ✔ Skills required
- ✔ Experience
- ✔ Educational requirements
- ✔ Benefits
- ✔ Contact name, address and website
- ✔ Closing date for applications

Identifying your questions

You may find that there are gaps in the description of the target job and that you have questions that still need to be answered. For example, you may want more detail about specific job responsibilities, whether the job is for a fixed period, if you need a driving licence, or if you're likely to be moved to a new location and for how long. Make sure you note down questions as you think of them, and that you have your list to hand when you get a chance to ask questions at the Assessment Centre.

Think over what you value in your current job, and if there are any aspects of the target job that you're unsure about, add those questions to your list. If you're not currently in a job or this is your first job application and assessment, get friends or family to help you pinpoint questions you may want to ask.

Soaking Up Your Briefing Material

When you're invited to an Assessment Centre you receive a briefing pack, containing basic information about the date, time, location, dress code and who you have to reply to confirming your attendance.

Your briefing pack may also give you more detail about the target job and include a list of the skills and competencies against which you're going to be assessed. This information gives you a clear understanding of the target job.

Also included in the briefing pack may be some specific preparation for the assessment, which you need to do in advance and send in to the target organisation, or bring with you on the day.

Whatever level of information the organisation gives you, it's very important that you read all the briefing material, making sure you understand what you're being asked to do, so that you can focus your preparation as needed. (See the later section 'Preparing for the Assessment Centre' for suggestions on how to use the briefing material to your advantage.)

Read through your briefing pack twice, making sure you take action where asked. Then read through the brief again on the night before attending the Assessment Centre, and on the morning of the centre. In this way you have all the information firmly fixed in your mind, giving yourself a good start to your day.

Scrutinising the tasks

Organisations often prepare you by giving you information about the types of activities you can expect at the Assessment Centre. For example, an organisation may say:

> *During the course of the Assessment Centre, you will be asked to participate in a number of exercises simulating major parts of the job you are applying for. You will also have an interview and be asked to complete psychometric tests. You will be told on the day exactly which exercises to do and in which sequence.*

Sometimes the information you're given about the Assessment Centre exercises is limited, although the target job should indicate what exercises are likely to come up. Chapters 4 to 13 go into detail about many of the Assessment Centre exercises you're likely to be doing.

Some organisations go into more detail, for example, they tell you exactly what types of exercises you're going to take part in; such as a Group Discussion, a Role-Play, an In-basket exercise, a Competency Based Interview (CBI) and an ability test. Obviously having more detail allows you to prepare more thoroughly for the day.

If you think the briefing on the specific exercises or activities doesn't give enough detail, then get in touch with the organisation and ask for more information. The organisation may not always respond, but it's in your interests to ask.

Look at similar tasks or activities you've done in the past and compare them with the exercises and activities you're likely to be doing on the Assessment Centre. Think about how you tackled those activities, what behaviours you displayed, what worked, and where different behaviours may have worked better. Going over these points can help you see where you may need to alter your behaviour in the Assessment Centre exercises.

Doing practice tests

Some organisations may ask you to do a practice psychometric test before the Assessment Centre. The practice test will be an ability test (a type of psychometric test; see Chapter 12 for much more on psychometric testing) which you work at on your own and has right or wrong answers. You won't be asked to complete practice tests for personality tests, as these are about your working preferences and don't have a right or wrong response. Organisations want you to do your best on an ability test and so they allow you the chance to practise to understand the format of the test, so that when you do it for real on the day, you know what to expect and your performance reflects your ability to answer the questions.

You do the psychometric test on paper or online and your briefing pack explains what you need to do. You can also do your own practice tests by going online and downloading practice tests for free.

Try the following website to practise ability tests for free: `www.shl.com/SHL/en-int/CandidateHelpline/`.

Get going with a few practice tests well in advance of the Assessment Centre to give yourself a good idea of what the tests are about and how you perform in them. Practising such tests doesn't necessarily help you improve your score, but they help you understand what's expected of you when doing a test for real.

Preparing for the Assessment Centre

By now you have all the details at your fingertips of the key skills being assessed in the target job, the accountabilities (key info you dug out of the job description), and the exercises that you're going to be doing. You're now ready to start putting a plan together showing how suitable you are for the job.

Linking the job accountabilities with skills being assessed

Imagine that you've applied for the job of Office Manager outlined in the earlier section 'Finding Out About the Job'. From the job description (see the earlier section 'Reviewing the job description'), you can check what the five accountabilities are.

The job description also gives briefing information on:

- ✔ Key Skills: Attention to Detail, Planning and Organising, Leadership, Judgement, Interpersonal Sensitivity, Initiative and Customer Service.

- ✔ Assessment Centre exercises: In-Basket, Internal Role-Play and a Competency Based Interview (CBI).

Having this information, start linking the accountabilities with the key skills. Think about what behaviours you're going to demonstrate in which exercises in relation to the target job.

Here are examples of how the accountabilities and your skills can be linked:

✔ Effective management skills link well to the Leadership competency. This can be tested in the Internal Role-Play as it's likely that this role-play will be with a direct report (that is, someone you supposedly line manage).

✔ The ability to find ways of improving processes and systems and putting them into action links to the Initiative, Planning and Organising and Attention to Detail competencies. These three competencies can be tested in the In-Basket, as some of the items are about improvement to processes.

You can then do the same for the other accountabilities, linking skills to the competency.

You're never going to know for sure which competencies are going to be assessed in which exercises. It's important that you use this tool of linking accountabilities to skills broadly. You need to think of all possible scenarios you may meet in the Assessment Centre and how you're going to respond. Don't focus on one situation and then expect this to occur in the Assessment Centre. The chances are that it won't! Avoid displaying predetermined behaviours that may not be right for the exercise.

Displaying the necessary skills and competencies

After linking the accountabilities to your skills, you can start thinking about how you're going to respond to a particular situation.

Give some thought to how you've behaved in situations in the past: at work, university or in your social life, or when attending a previous selection process.

Also look at what sorts of behaviour other people displayed in the same situations. Think about what behaviours worked well and what behaviours didn't work so well. Make a list of suitable and unsuitable behaviours against each competency in different situations.

 Ask colleagues, friends or family to check over your list. They may come up with alternative behaviours. Look over your new list and think about whether you agree or disagree with their points.

 Simply being yourself gives you the best chance of doing well on an Assessment Centre. Don't do anything you wouldn't normally do, because you may look and feel uncomfortable in a situation that isn't natural for you.

Matching competencies to your skills and strengths

Everyone has his own particular skills and strengths, which are recognised and applauded. Give some thought to what you're good at, or ask friends and family for a few ideas.

After listing your skills and strengths consider how they relate to the competencies that are going to be assessed. For example, if you're an organised person, then it's likely that you have strengths in the competency Planning and Organising. You can then think about the exercises and activities where you can best show these skills.

 Spend five minutes at the beginning of each exercise planning your approach to the task and telling yourself exactly how much time you're going to spend on each part to make sure you finish the task.

Knowing how to use your strengths to your advantage helps to reassure you that you're going to be able to do at least some of the exercises on the Assessment Centre and probably do them well.

Planning how to compensate for weaknesses

Everyone has a few weaknesses – areas that need developing or improving. It's worthwhile spending some time identifying what your weaknesses are so that you can take action.

After you've identified where your weaknesses lie, think how best you can minimise their impact during the course of the Assessment Centre.

What are the ways you can compensate? Well, for example, you recognise that you're not especially good at picking up on detail. You often miss typos and make careless mistakes when you're under a time pressure. You know that it's likely that the competency Attention to Detail is going to be assessed.

You need to turn the situation around. Use your strength in Planning and Organising to help minimise any adverse affect of Attention to Detail, which you're not so good at. You can do this by making sure you build into your initial plan enough time check or double-check your work before the end of the exercise.

You're likely to find that you're using more than one competency to respond to the same situation, giving you the chance of finding more than one way of minimising your weaker areas. Spending time thinking about real-life scenarios and how you compensate for your weaknesses can help guide your behaviour in the Assessment Centre.

Clearing Your Path to the Assessment Centre

Before attending the Assessment Centre, you may need to sort out extra things, which depend upon your particular circumstances. Here are two important things for your attention.

Notifying the centre of a disability

In 1995 the *Disability Discrimination Act* (DDA) was passed to prevent unlawful discrimination against any person(s) with a disability. The DDA makes it illegal for employers to discriminate against existing or prospective staff if they have a disability. The Act also applies to recruitment, selection opportunities for training, promotion and redundancies.

Also, employers have a duty to make 'reasonable adjustments' where necessary to both selection procedures and the way the work is done, to make sure people with disabilities fit in.

The Act defines a disability as '. . .a physical or mental impairment, which has a substantial and long-term adverse effect on one's ability to carry out normal day-to-day activities such as those involved in mobility, manual dexterity, physical co-ordination, speech, hearing, eyesight or communication, or permanent condition, which is controlled by medication'.

If you have a disability, such as visual impairment or dyslexia, then it's essential that you let the Assessment Centre know in advance. This gives the organisers time to make the necessary changes to ensure that there aren't any obstacles standing in the way of your performance.

For example, if you're dyslexic, tell the organisers and give them all information they need to give you the support or help you require. Your needs can be based how your disability was taken care of in the past, such as at school or university, or ask your GP to write to the Assessment Centre.

A person with dyslexia may need changes in the timings of activities, a computer for carrying out certain activities, and possibly someone to do reading for the whole event.

Changes that need to be made are going to vary from person to person and from disability to disability, so it's essential that you speak to the organisers personally to make sure everything is done in the best possible way to help you.

Taking account of previous Assessment Centre feedback

Preparing for attending an Assessment Centre is like being at a dress rehearsal: it gives you a good idea how things are going to go on the opening night (or day)!

You may have attended an Assessment Centre before, so it's likely you were given detailed feedback on how you performed and where your strengths or weaknesses lie, and suggestions for development.

If you're being assessed for a similar job, go back to that feedback and think about how your strengths and areas for development relate to the competencies being assessed this time round. The more similar the two jobs are, the more useful this information is going to be in helping in your performance in the coming assessment. Reassessing your pattern of behaviours and looking at where you may need to make changes, as well as drawing on your earlier assessment experience is going to help greatly in bringing about a successful outcome.

Part II
Mastering Assessment Centre Exercises

'That's not very encouraging, Mr Wislethorpe.'

In this part . . .

*T*his part covers the seven different types of exercise that you're most likely to encounter in an Assessment Centre, and in each case we describe the nature of that exercise and provide an example of what a typical brief looks like. We also describe some of the variations in the formats of the different exercise types, and we highlight the most common competencies that each exercise is generally used to assess. For each of the different exercise types, we provide you with a guide to what are generally regarded as the most effective behaviours – and those to avoid! Finally, we provide some advice on how to prepare yourself, so you really can master each exercise.

Chapter 4

Standing Out in Group Exercises

In This Chapter

▶ Identifying different types of group exercises

▶ Spotting good behaviour

▶ Practising for assessment day

*P*hrases such as 'playing the game' and 'it's not the winning; it's the taking part that counts' are buried deep in the British consciousness. As it's highly likely that you're going to find yourself taking part in at least one group activity during your assessment, knowing how to come across as a team player but at the same time standing out from the crowd is the name of the game!

In this chapter we explain the different types of group exercises on an Assessment Centre and how to balance achieving the group task with meeting your own individual goals.

Looking into Group Exercises

Group exercises are an obvious way of seeing how a team works together and are a much used assessment tool. Group exercises are popular with candidates because working in a team and problem solving is a familiar and comfortable task. For this reason, group exercises often occur early in the Assessment Centre and are even used as an 'icebreaker', allowing the candidates to settle into the day's activities and to get to know one another.

An important feature of Assessment Centre exercises is that they simulate as far as possible the target job. There are a number of different ingredients that go into the various group exercises and knowing the make-up and how the exercise is being run is going to help you to adjust your performance as necessary.

Group size and timing

Usually a group exercise lasts for between 30 and 60 minutes, with three or more people working together to achieve a set task. Groups of 4 to 6 are the most popular because they're a practical size for carrying out an activity, and re-create normal working practice. (Two people aren't officially considered to be a 'group', as this represents a one-to-one scenario; see Chapters 5 to 7 for details.)

Typical topics

Topics can range from the very business-focused to the bizarre. You might be part of a committee discussing which projects to implement to help improve business performance. Alternatively, you might find yourself discussing which products to take with you when abandoned on a desert island.

Getting your airtime

How much and how often you contribute to the group exercise depends on your levels of comfort within the group and with the activity you're asked to do. However, think about your input as a way of using your share of *airtime*. Airtime simply means the amount of time you, as an individual, give to the exercise. The amount of airtime you're likely to have depends on the size of the group and how much time is given for doing the exercise. If you're in a group of three people and the exercise is set to last 45 minutes, you can expect to each have about 10 to 12 minutes of airtime, if everyone takes an equal share.

Your airtime is also affected by the group dynamic. This is the way each person in the group interacts with the other members. You can do little about the group dynamic, so you have to change your behaviour when needed to help keep the group working together. For example, if you have three quiet individuals in the group, then you may need to take more airtime than you'd intended to get the group going. Or, one member of the group is inclined to take over and you're struggling to get your share of airtime.

Although it's important that you make the most of your allotted airtime, allowing you to contribute to the task and share your ideas, you need to be aware that taking another candidate's airtime can work against you, especially if it's done in a hostile way (see Chapters 15 and 16 for more details).

Working out your airtime (the time allowed for the task divided by size of group) means you can then spend the right amount of time contributing and making sure your contributions are worth hearing. Always try to use your airtime wisely: helping the group to get the task finished while making your presence felt, without being overbearing or hogging centre stage.

Activity-based group exercises

An activity-based group exercise aims at developing team-working skills. For example, you're asked to build a tower made out of Lego, or as many paper boats as you can within a set time.

It is unlikely that you'll ever get asked to undertake a 'real group activity' as this would require technical knowledge that might advantage some candidates over others. However, the activity will vary in how closely it simulates the target job. Either way the activity is designed to create a situation allowing you show suitable job-related behaviours. These behaviours can include the following:

✔ Planning and organising the task to be done within a fixed time. This activity may require the group to assign its members specific jobs or roles to make sure the task gets done; such as three people being responsible for making the boats and the fourth member of the group being responsible for checking the quality of the boats.

✔ Getting the team working together successfully by making sure the whole team is involved and communicating effectively to achieve the group's goal.

Unless you're applying for a job in a manufacturing environment where practical tasks might be more applicable, you're more likely to come across the more popular discussion-based group exercise that we talk about in the following section.

Discussion-based group exercises

A discussion-based group exercise is a round-table discussion. The discussion can be about a single weighty subject or a number of lighter topics. Generally, the topics are chosen in advance by the Assessment Centre but sometimes the candidates are asked to come up with their own topics for discussion. If you're asked to start a discussion, make sure you've a suitable topic already prepared, such as a high-profile legal case currently in the news that the group can't fail to have heard about. Avoid topics like your favourite hobby, as it's likely to be of little interest to the group or stimulate interesting debate, as well as failing to impress the assessors.

 If you're about to attend an Assessment Centre, get yourself up to date with what's going on in the world. Read as many different newspapers as you can and watch the TV news for at least one to two weeks before your assessment. Try choosing a topic of your own and discussing it with family or friends. This can help you see the other person's point of view and the other side of the argument, as well as giving you the chance to practise your debating skills.

You're very likely to be given an exercise based around issues that you're going to be facing in the target job. You need to show the assessors how you respond to such issues as if they were for real so that they can see what you're able to bring to the organisation and the target job.

Being a leader in a group discussion

Being appointed as 'leader' can make people do funny things, as they try to adopt what they think is an appropriate leadership style. Some people take on the dictatorial 'command and control' approach with gusto, while others adopt an equally ineffectual style of an indecisive people pleaser.

 If you find yourself designated as the leader, focus on these four areas of responsibility:

✔ **Establish the task objectives and key issues.** Summarise the aim of the task described in the brief and what issues needed to be considered to achieve the aim.

✔ **Utilise each individual's strengths.** Find out what individuals know about the task, and whether they have any previous experiences in a particular area. Do they have relevant information to share with the group?

✔ **Delegate appropriately.** Ask others to take on roles such as timekeeper, scribe, and so on.

✔ **Take decisions.** Know when to move the discussion on to ensure the task is achieved in the allotted time.

What to do when the discussion is leaderless

Unless leadership is a key requirement for the job, you're more likely to find yourself in a leaderless group discussion, where the focus is on effective teamwork. This removes the power dynamic and forces the group to come to a compromise solution.

You're usually given your own brief containing all the information necessary to complete the task. Sometimes your brief has the same information as those of the other members of the group and sometimes you have more information, known only to you. The kind of information you get depends on whether you're taking part in a non-assigned role or an assigned role group exercise (we explain non-assigned role and assigned role group discussions in the next sections).

Non-assigned role group discussions

A non-assigned role group discussion is a co-operative problem-solving exercise, in which each group member is given an identical brief and therefore no roles are 'assigned'. Your collective task is to analyse this information and to make suitable recommendations about how to tackle the problem(s) or issue(s) before you.

Non-assigned role group discussions typically last for between 30 and 60 minutes and you're not given time to prepare your response. This means you have to read, discuss and make your recommendations about the issues within the 30 to 60 minute timeframe.

Here's an extract from a non-assigned role group discussion brief:

The Situation

You have recently joined a large department store chain and have been asked to meet with a group of your colleagues as a member of a Quality Circle Team, to consider a number of issues and come up with recommendations aimed at improving customer service.

The exercise is scheduled to last for 45 minutes.

Issue 1

The department store has just launched a new quality customer service drive. The drive is designed to enhance service levels in an increasingly competitive marketplace. Your Manager feels the store needs to improve its image and recently introduced a new staff dress code. Half of the staff do not wear the regulation dress code as they do not see any added value in it. At the same time, research shows that older customers only approach staff wearing regulation dress.

The Department Store Manager, would like your input on how to sell the dress code regulations to your colleagues and improve professionalism?

First of all the group has to decide how much time is needed to successfully finish the task. For example, if there are four issues to be discussed during the 45 minutes, you need to give a certain amount of time to each issue (probably 10 minutes in this case), with the remaining 5 minutes used to organise the group. You also have to decide if there are any specific roles to be given to individual members of the group. You may want someone to act as timekeeper, or someone to keep a written record of your recommendations.

After agreeing how the group is going to work, the group can then start carrying out the task.

Assigned role group discussions

An assigned role group discussion is a competitive exercise. Each person in the group is assigned a specific role. For example, each candidate represents a different department of an organisation such as Finance, HR, Marketing or IT. You each have your own brief containing information that is relevant to your department outlining the goals that you need to achieve. What you're aiming to achieve is likely to conflict with the views and opinions of other team members in the other departments. You have to 'sell' your ideas to the other members of your group, so that your department gets the best deal, as well as meeting the company's goals.

Assigned role group discussions typically last between 60 and 90 minutes. You're given a short time to prepare (15 to 30 minutes) before the discussion begins, to plan how best to present your case to the other group members.

Here's an extract from an assigned role group discussion brief:

Introduction

This exercise involves each participant assuming one of six managerial roles. These are: Personnel Manager, Research and Development Manager, Production Manager, Sales and Marketing Manager, Information and Systems Manager, and Finance Manager.

Exercise Duration

Upon receiving your brief you will have 15 minutes to read through and prepare any relevant notes concerning the brief and the company profile. The group discussion will then commence and should continue for no more than 60 minutes.

Brief for the Personnel Manager

You are the Personnel Manager within Technex Limited, a small but highly innovative and successful Electronics Company. In fact, the Company has recently won an 'Innovation in Technology' award worth £75,000. This followed the news that Cybertel, a major US multinational, had acquired Technex.

Cybertel has decided to match this figure with a further £75,000. This money is to be used at the discretion of Technex's management, the only stipulation being that the combined sum is spent on special projects and/or capital improvements.

A meeting has been arranged to consider how the combined figure of £150,000 is to be used. Each manager has his or her own uses for the money, but if a mutually agreed allocation cannot be reached by the end of the meeting, the money will be distributed at the discretion of the US organisation. If this were to occur, Technex's allocation could be minimal.

You have had discussions with various members of your Department, and have compiled a number of issues that you may wish to raise during the meeting. These are detailed below for you to consider. You do not have to raise all the issues outlined.

Your Brief

There is a general feeling within the Personnel Department that demographic changes will mean it is increasingly important to retain and develop existing staff. The issues you can raise reflect concerns about turnover and utilisation of the present Human Resources.

You are particularly concerned about the rise in staff turnover. Although it is true to say that job mobility within the electronics industry generally has increased, this is of little comfort when faced with ever higher recruitment costs (these are currently around £5,000 for each position). In an attempt to identify where problems may exist, a Job Satisfaction survey has been proposed. The intention is to be in a position to take action and improve the situation before it adversely affects turnover. Use of a consultancy to carry out such a survey for the whole organisation would cost approximately £35,000.

Common Competencies Being Assessed

Your performance is assessed against a set of competencies linked to the activity. (For more about competencies take a look at Chapter 2.) The most common competencies you're likely to meet in a group exercise are the following, together with a definition of each competency:

- ✔ **Flexibility:** The ability to modify own behaviour, that is, adopt a different style or approach, to reach a goal.

- ✔ **Planning and Organising:** Able to establish efficiently an appropriate course of action for self and/or others to accomplish a goal.

- ✔ **Leadership:** Able to motivate, enable and inspire others to succeed, utilising appropriate styles. Has a clear vision of what is required and acts as a positive role model.

- ✔ **Problem Analysis:** Effectiveness in identifying problems, seeking pertinent data, recognising important information and identifying possible causes of problems.

- ✔ **Judgement:** The ability to evaluate data and courses of action and to reach logical decisions. An unbiased, rational approach.

- ✔ **Persuasive Oral Communication:** Able to express ideas or facts in a clear and persuasive manner. Convince others to own expressed point of view.

- ✔ **Teamwork:** Willingness to participate as a full member of a team of which she is not necessarily leader; effective contributor even when team is working on something of no direct personal interest.

- ✔ **Initiative:** The ability to actively influence events rather than passively accepting; sees opportunities and acts on them. Originates action.

Not all of the eight competencies in the list are necessarily going to appear during your assessment. However, if you're taking part in a group exercise, the Assessment Centre is likely to be assessing at least some of the competencies.

Keeping track of what competencies are being assessed at each stage of the group exercise is important for finishing the exercise successfully. Table 4-1 shows the various stages of a group exercise and competencies being assessed.

Table 4-1	Typical Competencies Assessed at Each Stage of a Group Exercise
Stage	*Competencies*
1. Drawing up an action plan	Planning and Organising Leadership
2. Discussion and coming up with ideas.	Problem Analysis Flexibility Teamwork Initiative
3. Weighing up ideas and voting on solutions and/or recommendations.	Judgement Persuasive Oral Communication

Behaving Effectively

Knowing how to behave in a group setting isn't always easy. Should you be trying to be the centre of attention or should you focus on listening to others? In these sections we describe some top tips for behaving effectively during a Group Exercise.

Helping the group to get organised

Showing your commitment to the group exercise is going to impress the assessors. Helping to get the group organised for the exercise is your first opportunity, so use it to your advantage. Even if you haven't been appointed as leader, try helping to direct the group by asking the following questions:

- ✔ How are we going to organise ourselves?
- ✔ How are we going to split up the time?
- ✔ Does anyone want to act as timekeeper?
- ✔ Are we going to make notes on the flip chart?
- ✔ Who wants to keep a record of what we're doing?

Beware! You need to be careful not to come across as a know-all and be seen by the rest of the team and the assessors as someone who's manipulating the group. Make sure the other group members get a chance of doing their share of contributing. Volunteering to take on one of the suggested roles, especially if no one else seems inclined, shows your commitment to helping the team succeed.

After the group agrees who's doing what and when, the group can turn its attention to discussing the brief, identifying problems and coming up with solutions.

Speaking now or forever holding your peace!

Candidates sometimes have difficulty in knowing when to speak and when to stay quiet. To get this right it's important that you think about the following three aspects of how the group works:

- ✔ **Process:** The group needs to quickly get organised in order to get going on the task. Ongoing discussion helps makes sure the group is on track for achieving the goal. For example, highlight how much time is left for finishing the task or summarise what's been achieved so far.

- ✔ **Content:** Before contributing to the content of the discussion, you need to think about the relevance of the point you're making. For example, if you're making a new point, is it meaningful to the discussion, does your point add anything to what's already been discussed, or does your point offer an entirely new way of looking at what is being discussed?

- ✔ **Volume:** Remember that you won't get marks for what you don't say. Avoid mumbling! Speak up and speak clearly so that everyone in the group and the assessors can hear you. Also beware of speaking too loudly as you get too excited or determined to get your point across. Remember to speak clearly enough to be heard, but don't shout over others!

Staying in the game

Your aim is to shine and impress the assessors that you're the one for the job. But while you're looking to be the winner you have to balance this against making sure the group reaches its set goal. Although making your mark is part of your game plan, if the group fails to achieve the task this reflects negatively on each group member as well as yourself. So put all your energy into working with the other members of the group to achieve the task.

Managing the opposition

Do remember other candidates are going to be as keen as you to get involved in the discussion. It's important that you let others have their say. But chances are you're going to have someone in the group who's eager to take centre stage and do all the talking! Here are a couple of strategies for dealing with such a person without coming across as overbearing yourself:

- ✓ **The group member is making good points but is talking too much:** Think of ways of involving other members of the group in a constructive way. For example, 'That's a really interesting point Mike, what do you think Amal?' Or, 'Yes Linda, that's exactly what I thought too and I was also thinking that . . .'

- ✓ **The group member has a lot to say but what's being said isn't well thought through:** Think of ways of challenging the suggestions without coming across as rude or impatient. For example, 'I hadn't considered it from that angle, how did you come to that conclusion . . .?' Or, 'I actually had a different point of view . . . what does everyone else think?'

Although it can be frustrating when other group members appear to be speaking without having anything constructive to say, it's essential that you're not seen as demolishing the contributions other members of the group are making towards the task.

Giving the quieter group members a chance

Keep reminding yourself that the group exercise is all about teamwork. In practice this means giving every team member the chance to contribute. Some team members may be hesitant about speaking up. The assessors are going to give you credit if they see you actively seeking to get quieter group members joining in the discussion. Here are a few phrases you can use to encourage the quieter group members:

- ✔ 'What do you think, John?'

- ✔ 'Maybe we can go round the table and each say what we think is the best way forward here . . .'

- ✔ 'I think that's a really good point, Emily.'

Encourage group members *to listen* to what the rest of the group has to say. To make sure the quieter group member is listened to, you can say, for example, 'I think it's important that we understand what everyone thinks about this . . .'

Being prepared to compromise

Repeatedly making a point that the group doesn't agree with isn't going to do you any favours! You have to consider whether your contribution is going to be for the greater good of the group. Although in an assigned role exercise you're asked to persuade the other group members to see your point of view, sometimes you have to recognise that the group has agreed to go in another direction. At this point you have to accept the general agreement and refocus on doing all you can to help the group to achieve its goal. Compromising can win you brownie points and shows you as a good team player.

In a group discussion, usually only one winning idea gets the overall agreement of the group. This doesn't mean that the rest of you are losers! It may simply mean that the way the idea was presented made the suggestion look like the best way forward for the group exercise.

In the firing line: Dealing with challenges

During a group discussion it's highly likely that a point you're making is going to be challenged. The challenge can be made constructively, for example, such as you being asked to explain your reasoning or by the other person saying why she holds a different view from yours. Give and take, and the challenging of ideas are the hallmarks of creative discussion in group exercises, which can help the group to reach an informed decision as to the best way forward.

However, if another group member flatly states that you're wrong or that your idea is rubbish, then you may (rightly?) see her as being confrontational. What is seen by you to be a personal attack can make responding difficult. But often the challenge is an expression of the person being desperate to get her idea accepted by the whole group. Even though the person is going the wrong way about getting her point across, it doesn't always mean that the point won't be accepted, if it's felt that the person's idea is going to help the group achieve its task.

In a challenging situation it's important to stay calm because aggravating the situation isn't going to help you or the group. Instead try turning the challenge on its head by saying something like, 'Okay Chris, that's your opinion; do you mind telling me why you think that – maybe you have a different perspective that I haven't considered?' Responding in this way helps to defuse the situation and allows the challenger to explain her thinking. If the situation reaches a stage where you're both still holding fast to different views, you may want to invite other members of the group to comment and offer a solution.

When you're challenged, it's important that you continue to contribute to the discussion and not withdraw. If you withdraw, the assessors may think that you don't respond well to criticism or that you're not able to explain the reasoning behind your decisions. Take hold of the situation by showing the assessors you welcome criticism when it's constructive, and that your principal aim is making sure the group achieves its goal.

Each member of the group is being assessed against her input to the group discussion. When a group member becomes confrontational, that person inevitably damages her chances of succeeding in the group exercise. If other members of the group join in and are equally confrontational then they damage themselves and the rest of the group. By reacting positively and constructively to a challenge you're going to win the approval of the assessors as well as the group by presenting yourself in a positive and team-focused way.

Trying to ignore the assessors

Throughout the group exercise the assessors are busy observing and recording the input being made by each member of the group. They're present during the whole exercise to make sure they have all the evidence needed to make a fair and honest assessment of your performance. In this respect, assessors are a necessary evil!

Assessors recognise that their presence can be off-putting and try to position themselves out of your line of vision by sitting in a corner of the room. In this way, they hope to limit the chances that you're going to spot them or even draw them into the group discussion, both of which the assessors want to avoid.

As a candidate your goal is to complete the group exercise and it's the assessors' task to observe and record the group's performance. These tasks should never become confused. For this reason, you must not involve anyone outside your group in helping you to achieve your goal.

Gearing Up for the Group Exercise

In this section we talk about ways to prepare yourself for a group exercise to ensure you behave at your best.

Before the assessment centre

Getting practice in for a group exercise is an excellent way of preparing for the event. Ask family, friends or colleagues to form a group where you can practise suitable behaviours in an imaginary situation. You can also practise your discussion skills by selecting a simple topic such as, 'Where is the best place you've ever visited and would you go there again?.' To bring the topic to life think of things that actually happened to you while you were on your travels and how you successfully resolved any problems, while selling the idea to your group that your nearby or far-flung holiday destination is a place not to be missed.

Come up with four different ideas. Turn these ideas into problems needing to be solved. Write the four problems on a piece of paper and give each member of your group a copy. Set a limit of 30 to 40 minutes for the group to discuss all four issues. After you've finished the exercise get some feedback by asking the other group members to say what they thought of your performance. To structure this feedback ask each person in the group to tell you one thing that you did well, one thing that didn't go so well, and one thing that you could do differently. Having this feedback is valuable for helping you to make any changes to your behaviour for the real group exercise coming up at the Assessment Centre.

During the assessment centre

You can do several things throughout the course of the Assessment Centre to ensure that you're ready to perform at your best during the Group Exercise.

Mingling with the other group members

Feeling comfortable and relaxed with the members of your group is important for making a success of your time at the Assessment Centre. Because group exercises often come early on in the assessment process, start mixing with the other candidates as soon as you can. Get to know the other candidates by introducing yourself and asking their names – you can bet that your fellow candidates are feeling as apprehensive as you are and welcome the chance to chat and exchange a friendly smile.

Reading your brief

Take time to read your brief carefully. At this stage you may not know whether you have the same brief as the other group members or a completely different brief. Use any time given for preparation to read the information and make notes on the key issues. You may find that your brief suggests you prefer a specific outcome to the issue, and you may want to consider the pros and cons to this outcome. As well, notice any gaps in the information and what other information you may need to ask to help you in your assessment.

Contributing as early as you can

After the group exercise starts, getting your say in as early as you can helps to build your confidence. The longer you stay silent the more difficult it becomes to break into the discussion. But remember, it's important only to join in the discussion when you have something to say that has a bearing on the matter in hand.

Being forthright with information

If, during the course of the discussion, you suspect that your brief has different information to that of someone else, it's important that you share this with the group to reach an informed decision. If you withhold, lie about, or make up information, you're going to be put at a disadvantage, as well as the group. The assessors are likely to penalise you for giving misinformation, especially if this stops the group from reaching a decision or causes the group to reach a wrong decision. Even if the group manages to achieve the task the assessors may call into question your integrity, so always remember – nobody likes a cheat or a liar!

Chapter 5

Impressing in Oral Presentations

In This Chapter

▶ Understanding your challenge

▶ Considering your audience

▶ Delivering the goods

Knowing how to make an oral presentation work for you is vital to your success in the assessment process and a skill that is going to stand you in good stead for the rest of your life. Captivating your audience and bowling over the assessors is going to be a challenge – but you can rise to it – and we're going to tell you how.

In this chapter you find out what goes into a winning oral presentation and how to set about it. Taking time out to prepare for the event and matching your presentation to your audience are essential ingredients for getting your message across, confidently, clearly, and giving you the result that you want.

Figuring Out the Format

Sorting out the type of oral presentation you're going to be making and applying a few basic rules is the first step towards communicating successfully.

At the Assessment Centre you're often given a topic together with relevant data and you're asked to prepare and deliver your presentation to an audience within a specific timeframe. From the information, you need to decide what to include in the content of your presentation so that your presentation matches the expectations of your target audience.

An oral presentation can be run as stand-alone exercise or as part of another exercise, such as a Group Exercise (refer to Chapter 4) or an Analysis Exercise (see Chapter 8).

As a stand-alone exercise

A stand-alone oral presentation is simpler to set up, and gives you the opportunity of displaying your talent on centre stage, allowing the assessor to focus on observing and recording your true capability.

If the presentation is to be run as a stand-alone exercise then you may be asked to prepare a presentation on the set topic in advance of the Assessment Centre. For example, 'Please prepare a 10-minute presentation for the HR team on what you can bring to Hoffman Clothing', or 'Prepare a 20-minute presentation for the Board on what you see as the key challenges in the current economic climate for Wiles Banks'. Alternatively, you may be given your topic during the Assessment Centre, around an important business issue or case-study.

As well as being given a topic for presentation, which can take the form of both written and numerical information, you're also given suitable equipment for preparing your presentation. These are a flip chart, paper and pens, an overhead projector (OHP) and materials, acetates and pens, or a laptop for preparing a PowerPoint presentation. The example below shows a typical brief for an oral presentation.

In this example you have a timeframe in which to prepare, deliver, and take questions from your audience on your presentation. Head to the later section 'Prep, Delivery and Q&A: The Three Stages' for finding out more about preparing and delivering your presentation, and handling questions.

Your Role

In this exercise you are to assume the role of an Area Sales Manager for Delightful Dinners, a major food company. You have recently been given responsibility for launching a new product into a test market.

Background

The information that follows is drawn from two principal sources. The Marketing Department have developed a number of incentives to support the product launch, while your own intimate knowledge of your area suggests a number of suitable target outlets in the South-East of England.

Your Task

Your National Sales Manager, Anna Lacey, is naturally keen to ensure this test market is carried out successfully. As Anna is in your area for a brief visit today, you have been asked to make a 10-minute presentation. The presentation should include the most significant aspects of your launch strategy and should stipulate who you have decided to use for the test market and why.

Due to limited production capacity you have been asked to nominate just two customers in your area who would be suitable to carry out this test market under the criteria set by Marketing, i.e. that the customer(s) should have a good geographical spread throughout the Southern region and that they are capable of, either singularly or jointly, taking up the full production capacity.

You should be prepared to explain your strategy and the reasoning behind your decision, to gain Anna's approval. You should also be prepared to answer questions for a further 5 minutes on various aspects of your presentation.

You have 40 minutes to prepare your presentation.

Linked to other exercises

Your oral presentation can be linked to other exercises, such as a group discussion. For example, your group is given the task of deciding which of a number of projects is to receive funding. After discussing the options as a group for 30 minutes, each of you is then asked to make an oral presentation on your findings to the assessors in front of your group members.

Alternatively, you may be asked to take part in an Analysis Exercise. For example, you're asked to write a report for your business associates suggesting possible mergers with other organisations. After writing your report you're asked to present your recommendations orally to a Board member.

Prep, Delivery and Q&A: The Three Stages

Getting ready to make an oral presentation follows three stages: preparation, delivery and question and answer (Q&A). (The Q&A stage is actually part of the delivery stage, but because it has a different purpose – rather than presenting, you're responding to your audience's questions – we're treating Q&A as a separate stage.)

The amount of time allowed for an oral presentation can vary widely, for example, from 5 to 30 minutes. The more time given for the presentation, the more time you're given to prepare, deliver and fit in the question and answer session.

The preparation stage

You need to make the most of your preparation time. Start by reading your brief, analysing the information, planning what you're going to say, and deciding how you're going to present your findings.

Being given the opportunity to prepare a presentation in advance of the Assessment Centre has advantages. You can spend as much time as you like researching your topic and an unlimited time preparing. When researching a topic, the Internet is a fantastic place to start. The Internet gives you reams of material for the content of your presentation, and also brings to your attention hot topics so that can show how up to date you are on the subject. Other good sources of information are newspapers, journal articles, books and talking to an expert in the field. Make sure you use a number of sources for your research, so that you know you're including the most relevant and accurate material.

Getting yourself ready

Get going by thinking about the following points and building them into your presentation:

✔ Set out the key issues and goals – how best can the issues and goals be presented?

✔ Analyse and decide what actions you're going to take – how can you justify your strategy?

✔ Think about the topic from your audience's perspective – what does your audience need to know to be persuaded to take on board your recommendations?

✔ How can you best deliver these key messages – what are you going to include?

✔ What issues or concerns is your presentation going to raise – what questions are you likely to be asked?

To help you tackle possible questions from your audience, fix your mind on real issues such as managing human resources, coping with a merger, or a financial crisis, and come up with some answers. For more info on what to expect and how to deal with this part of your presentation, go to the section later in this chapter 'The question and answer (Q&A) stage' for details.

✔ What visual aids are you going to use to help you get your message across?

Visual aids act as a medium for communicating your message to your audience and as a prompt for explaining the points you're making. Never let your visual aids become your full script! Head to the section 'Using visual aids' later in the chapter for more detail.

After putting together your presentation allow time for a rehearsal, checking the following:

✔ **Length:** Am I keeping within the time allowed or am I running over?

✔ **Clarity:** Am I making the key points easily understandable?

✔ **Delivery:** Can I remember my words?

✔ **Impact:** Am I delivering confidently?

When you're satisfied with the content of your presentation and know exactly what you want to say, you're ready to make your presentation.

Getting the room ready

You think you're ready but it's crucial that you don't allow the simple things to trip you up . . . literally! It's hard to make an impact and maintain credibility when you're going head over heels having tripped on a cable that you didn't notice! Make sure you double-check everything. Keep in mind your principal aim is to impress the assessors and you need to show them you've paid attention to detail:

- ✓ **Arranging the room layout (if possible):** Think about where your audience is going to sit and where you are in relation to your audience. Your audience needs to be able see you and your visual aids, as well as hear you.

- ✓ **Making sure your audience is sitting comfortably:** While on an Assessment Centre, you're likely to have limited control over your surroundings. If available, providing your audience with light refreshments makes a good start; making sure the lighting is satisfactory, and if possible keeping the room free from unwanted noise or other distractions all add to a trouble-free presentation.

- ✓ **Using the technology:** If you're planning to do a PowerPoint presentation, check the equipment before you begin to prevent any embarrassing situations, such as your laptop running out of battery halfway through your presentation! Always look to see your laptop is plugged into the power and is connected to the projector. And make sure your mobile phone is switched off!

The delivery stage

You're now ready to stand and deliver! Your audience (this includes the assessors) is sitting comfortably and anticipating your every word.

When thinking about the delivery stage, keep in mind the well-known saying:

Tell your audience what you are going to tell them, then tell them, and then tell them what you told them.

Use this advice well. It can help make sure you keep your presentation on track. The three important stages of your presentation are the:

✔ **Opening:** When you introduce your topic and set expectations. At the opening of your presentation explain your plan of campaign to your audience, so the audience knows what to expect and when, and if there is going to be time for questions.

✔ **Message:** Here you're saying what you've planned to say. During this part of your presentation try drawing the audience in, noting any non-verbal cues showing any reactions to what you're saying. See the section 'Tuning into your audience' later in this chapter for tips on spotting audience reactions.

✔ **Summary:** This is the point where you summarise for the benefit of your audience what you've been talking about. After your summary your audience is likely to want to join in and ask questions.

Although the *format* of your presentation depends on the exercise you're doing, the *approach* is always the same – prepare and deliver, meaning that many of the behaviours that you demonstrate while presenting, whatever the format, are going to stay the same.

The question and answer (Q&A) stage

To prevent any distractions during your presentation and to allow you to manage your time more effectively, structuring your question and answer (Q&A) session at the end is your best policy. Now is the time for gearing yourself up to face some challenging questioning, so you need to be well prepared.

When preparing your presentation try to anticipate likely questions and prepare suitable answers, so you can make sure this final stage of your presentation runs as smoothly as possible. During the Q&A session listen carefully to the questions, and if necessary repeat the question to make sure you've understood what's being asked. This buys you some thinking time. If time allows, give everyone in the room a chance to ask a question by saying something like 'did anyone else have a question?' or 'we just have time for a couple more questions.'

Don't start guessing answers to questions. If you don't know the answer it's better to say so and offer to find out and come back to the person with an answer later, rather than guessing and end up getting it wrong.

Different Types of Presentation

Three key aspects of oral presentations have a bearing on how you approach your task. These are:

- ✓ The size of your audience
- ✓ Presenting on your own
- ✓ Presenting as part of a team

It's one thing to successfully deliver a meaningful presentation but quite another to deliver a truly memorable one. The key to success with an oral presentation is to match your presentation to your audience.

Presenting on your own to a few

Traditionally, an oral presentation on an Assessment Centre is carried out by one person on his own to a small audience. Each candidate on the Assessment Centre is given the same brief and asked to present on the same topic or scenario.

As only two or three of you will be in the room when you're making your presentation, you have to decide the most appropriate way of communicating your message. Think about whether your presentation is best delivered formally or informally. Are you going to stand up, distancing yourself from your audience, or are you going to sit and present across a desk? Are you going to deliver a more formal PowerPoint presentation or can you present from notes and a flip chart?

Typically, most Assessment Centres ask you to make a formal oral presentation, but if you think presenting informally may be more appropriate then ask if this is possible. However, if in doubt, it's probably safer to take the formal approach.

Presenting on your own to a group

Some Assessment Centres prefer you to make your presentation to a group. For example, you may be involved in a linked exercise where a group discussion is taking place. Then each candidate in the group is asked to take it in turns presenting his findings to the assessors and the rest of the group. Although you're mainly directing your presentation to the assessors, there may be up to 12 people in the room, and it may be appropriate to include and engage your fellow candidates as part of your wider audience.

Be careful not to get 'missile locked' on one or two members of your audience. This sometimes happens when an individual in the audience gives you a lot of eye contact or smiles at you, causing you to give that person a greater share of attention, having been drawn in by the person's body language. A similar situation is when a member of your audience asks one or more questions demanding your attention. Or, you may find yourself focusing on the most senior or experienced person in the room, looking for his reaction to your performance. Whatever the reason, you need to be careful that your behaviour doesn't cause the other members of the audience to disengage, which can result in you being penalised for failing to communicate effectively to the whole group. If you find yourself falling into this trap, try disciplining yourself by making eye contact with everyone in the audience, or keep glancing round at your audience. You can also work at keeping your audience engaged by directing questions to different individuals, keeping everyone involved and interested.

Presenting as part of a team

In many jobs it's essential that the team works together effectively and is geared to presenting the group effort to an audience. Likewise, in a simulated exercise on an Assessment Centre you may be asked to act as part of a sales team, working together to prepare and deliver a pitch to clients in order to win new business.

A sales-focused Assessment Centre team exercise might split the candidates into two sales teams. Each team is given a brief explaining that they're bidding against the other team for an assignment. The task for each group is to work together to decide on their bid and at the end of the day deliver a team presentation to the Board, who decide which team wins the bid.

An important aspect of this exercise is co-ordinating the team effort and making effective use of everyone's talents. You have first to decide how you're going to work together in creating your bid, and next decide who's going to deliver which parts of the presentation, making sure that everyone has a share of the input. You have also to decide the approach you're taking so that everyone in the team is working towards the same goal. To achieve the task the team has to take into account each team member's strengths, and which roles are suitable for each person, in order to deliver an effective presentation to the Board and win the bid.

Common Competencies Being Assessed

Your performance is assessed against a set of competencies linked to the activity. (For more about competencies take a look at Chapter 2.) The most common competencies you're likely to meet in an oral presentation are the following, together with a definition of each competency:

- ✔ **Stress tolerance:** Stability of performance under pressure and/or opposition. Makes controlled responses in stressful situations.

- ✔ **Flexibility:** The ability to modify own behaviour to reach a goal, that is, adopting a different style or approach.

- ✔ **Planning and organising:** Able to establish efficiently an appropriate course of action for self and/or others to accomplish a goal.

- ✔ **Judgement:** The ability to evaluate data and courses of action and to reach logical decisions. Shows an unbiased, rational approach.

- ✔ **Listening:** Able to pick out important information in oral communication. Questioning and general reactions indicate 'active' listening.

✔ **Persuasive oral communication:** The ability to express ideas or facts in a clear and persuasive manner, and able to convince others to own expressed point of view.

✔ **Impact:** Makes a good first impression on other people and maintains that impression over time.

✔ **Interpersonal sensitivity:** Awareness of other people and environment and own impact on these. Actions indicate a consideration for the feelings and needs of others (but not to be confused with 'sympathy').

✔ **Initiative:** Actively influences events rather than passively accepting, sees opportunities and acts on them. Originates action.

Not all the nine competencies in the list are necessarily going to appear during your assessment. However, when you're making your oral presentation the Assessment Centre is likely to be assessing at least some of the competencies.

Keeping track of what competencies are being assessed at each stage of your oral presentation is important for finishing the exercise successfully. Table 5-1 shows the three stages of an oral presentation and the competencies being assessed.

Table 5-1   Typical Competencies Assessed at Each Stage of an Oral Presentation

Stage	Competencies
Preparation	Planning and Organising Judgement
Delivery	Impact Persuasive Oral Communication Interpersonal Sensitivity Initiative
Question and answer (Q&A)	Listening Stress Tolerance Flexibility

Behaving Effectively

You can follow a number of behaviours to help you deliver an effective and memorable presentation.

Building in appropriate content

Appropriate content is content that is relevant to your audience, including the right level of technical information and considering the topic from your audience's point of view. If you were talking about recycling to local residents you might focus on what they should be doing, as opposed to the technical effects landfill has on the atmosphere, which they may not understand. Appropriate content will vary according to topic and the backgrounds and expertise of the audience members. By choosing particular issues to put into your oral presentation you're making assumptions about your audience. Once you know who your audience will be, think about the likely make-up of your audience: the age of your audience, and background. Or, think about the occupations of members of your audience and how they're likely to respond to the topic. Are they likely to know a little or a lot, are they beginners or experts? Is using plain English the right medium for getting your ideas across or are you going to need to use technical language, or even jargon (see the section 'Behaviours to avoid' later in this chapter)? Having found out what makes your audience tick, you can put yourself in their shoes and think about what is likely to be of interest to them.

Try bringing the content of your presentation to life by including anecdotes that are within your audience's experience. If you don't know any, ask friends and colleagues to come up with a few you can use. Alternatively, draw on stories you've picked up from newspapers or TV.

Using visual aids

An audience is likely to expect you to use visual aids to support your presentation. The visual aid can be a neat way of getting across to your audience what you're setting out to do: your overall plan, key messages and conclusion. You can also use visual aids such as charts or graphs to illustrate complex ideas or numerical data. Whether you're using PowerPoint, OHPs or slides, think about what type of information is best shown visually.

If the visual aid isn't going to actively *support* your presentation, then the visual aid is unnecessary, and may even get in the way of your message.

You may opt for using OHPs or doing a PowerPoint presentation. The key to success is keeping the text simple, brief, easy to read and consistent. Don't add too much detail, and make sure your handwriting/font is easy to read from a distance and only use colour to highlight the essential points. Remember: The more complicated the info displayed on an OHP or PowerPoint, the easier it is for your message to get lost.

Visual aids are a prompt and *not* a script! Don't put everything you want to say on a slide, OHP or PowerPoint. If you do, you're going to end up reading it out word for word to an audience who are fast asleep!

Starting with a bang!

Grab the attention of your audience. Make your audience sit up, take note and listen. To get your audience listening, you have to build rapport. So start by:

- ✔ **Setting your audience's expectations**. Say who you are, why you're here, and how long you're going to be speaking for.

- ✔ **Telling your audience what you're going to tell them but at the same whetting the audience's appetite for more!** Get going by say something controversial or posing a rhetorical question.

Try thinking of a nugget of information that's going to be interesting to your audience and get it in early – don't leave it until the end, by which time your audience may be starting to tune out!

Go back to the earlier section in this chapter 'The delivery stage' for reminding yourself what goes into the opening of your presentation.

Controlling your nerves

Feeling nervous is perfectly normal – anyone who says he doesn't suffer from nerves is probably putting on a brave front. He might mean he's found a way of controlling his nerves. Presenting in front of group, whatever the size, can be a daunting experience.

How do you overcome your nerves? Try talking yourself out of being nervous by thinking positively, like 'I'm the expert, they're longing to hear what I've got to say' or 'I've rehearsed this presentation eight times so I must be master of the subject'. Also, putting your oral presentation into perspective can help in calming you down and keeping you that way, so ask yourself, 'What's the worst thing that can possibly happen?.'

If you're finding it difficult to be positive and are resigned to feeling nervous, then try working at hiding your nervousness. The audience isn't likely to pick up on your nerves unless you start showing the signs, such as pacing up and down, sweating, fidgeting, hands shaking.

Avoid replacing one nervous mannerism with another, such as putting your hands in your pockets to hide your shaky hands and jingling coins thinking your audience isn't going to notice. Unfortunately, such behaviours are immediately obvious and confirm the audience's suspicions that you're feeling nervous.

Practising your presentation in front of a mirror or even making a video is a great way of spotting give-away signs of nervousness. If you discover that you don't have any, congratulations! But if like most people, you do, try thinking of ways of limiting appearing nervous. Work out your most comfortable method of presenting yourself and stick to it.

Your best way of combating stress and nervousness is by being well prepared for the event. Make sure you know what you're going to say off by heart, and that you've given enough time to rehearsing, especially your introduction, which can often be the most terrifying bit!

Projecting positive body language

Projecting positive body language makes you look and feel confident. Take a look at the following body language:

- **Your face:** Your facial expression shows what you're thinking and feeling: for example, you're happy, serious, enthusiastic, determined. Just because you're on an Assessment Centre doesn't mean that you have to go around looking serious or businesslike all the time, so don't forget to smile now and then.

- **Your posture:** Stand straight with your head held high so that it's easy to take in what's going on around the room (you don't want to give the impression that you're avoiding eye contact). While standing, avoid swaying. You're likely to make your audience feel seasick!

- **Your hand gestures:** It's okay to use your hands as a form of visual aid. For example, use your hands to illustrate, reinforce or emphasise a particular point – just don't do this every sentence! If you feel uncomfortable using gestures, then it's best to let your arms hang by your side in a relaxed manner, or if you're standing at a lectern, resting your hands on both sides of the lectern but without gripping it; however, don't feel confined to standing behind the lectern, walk around as appropriate.

For lots more tips and insight into body language, get hold of a copy of *Body Language For Dummies* by Elizabeth Kuhnke.

Tuning into your audience

When delivering your presentation, you need to be able to 'read your audience' and respond accordingly. It's vital that you know if your audience is engaged or bored by your presentation so that you can take appropriate action. You also need to make sure you're connecting to the whole audience and not just one or two individuals.

Look out for the following worrying signs from your audience:

- Avoiding eye contact
- Fidgeting

✔ Checking mobile phones or PDAs, reading notes, gazing out of the window

✔ Talking or whispering

✔ Arms folded with head resting on chest and looking down

If you spot any signs that your audience isn't engaged, try figuring out why not. It's a good idea in this situation to start asking questions or inviting opinions to get your audience involved. Alternatively, be adventurous by introducing a controversial or provocative idea, or injecting a dose of humour.

Using humour appropriately

Humour can be used as an icebreaker and as a way of establishing rapport with your audience. Humour is also useful for putting everyone at ease and settling any nerves. Although it's good to include humour in a presentation, if it's forced, it can often fail to serve its purpose.

If you're good at telling jokes and are planning to share one with your audience, appreciate what your audience is going to find funny and match your joke accordingly. The last thing you need to do is offend anyone in your audience!

Of course, humour isn't only about telling jokes. If you're not good at telling jokes, steer clear of them. Another way of raising a smile is by telling an amusing story about yourself, for example, an embarrassing or tight spot you once found yourself in. Talking about yourself is an easy way of bringing the story to life. If you can't think of any suitable stories, think about including meaningful quotes, cartoons or droll quips such as: 'I am free of all prejudices. I hate everyone equally' (WC Fields).

Don't feel you *have to* inject humour into your presentation. If you can't find anything that fits or you're unhappy about delivering jokes, then best leave the jokes out and concentrate on your key message. You may just find that something funny to say comes in a moment of genius during your delivery or when you're answering questions.

Finishing with a flourish

This is your last chance of impressing the assessors and your audience while also being your last chance of ruining the positive impression you've made so far!

Keep your conclusion brief and memorable. Sum up your key points and close your presentation by stating your most important message. And now for the 'wow' factor. Do you want to leave your audience laughing, or even crying? Do you want applause, or even cheering? Or do you want to make your mark by ending with a question left wide open or appealing to your audience to commit to a course of action?

Avoiding the Seven Deadly Sins of Presenting

Thorough preparation is key to making a successful oral presentation. Unfortunately things can go wrong. Here are some classic mistakes to avoid. Try thinking of them as the seven deadly sins of presenting:

- ✔ **Cramming too much into your visual aids:** You don't want to make your slides, OHPs or PowerPoint screen look so busy that your audience can't take in the information. Aim for no more than 7 or 8 lines of text a slide, OHP or PowerPoint screen.

- ✔ **Using excessive jargon:** You run the risk of losing your audience, or trying to appear a 'smart Alec.' Keep the language simple; if you must use jargon, check beforehand if your audience is likely to be familiar with it.

- ✔ **Failing to proofread your visual aids:** Always check any visual aids you're going to be using for spelling and grammatical errors as these distract your audience from your message and undermine the impact of your presentation.

- ✔ **Reading from your script:** Don't be tempted to read from a script, as this suggests you don't know your subject well, and it stops you from engaging with your audience because you're not maintaining eye contact.

✓ **Speaking and not being heard:** Mumbling or speaking too quickly, too quietly, or in a monotone voice is a no-no. Practise beforehand and get feedback, and if needed ask for advice on how to project your voice.

✓ **Distracting your audience:** Pacing up and down, swaying back and forth, jingling coins in your pocket, and other repetitive gestures can be very distracting for your audience. So practise in front of a mirror and watch your mannerisms.

✓ **Patronising your audience:** Always avoid talking down to your audience or showing them a lack of respect. Give time to finding out what and how much your audience is likely to know about your presentation topic.

Chapter 6

Starring in Role-Plays

· ·

In This Chapter

▶ Understanding what goes into role-plays

▶ Knowing how to tackle the exercises

▶ Preparing yourself for stardom

· ·

*T*aking part in a role-play exercise is likely to be one of your
most memorable tasks on your Assessment Centre. Now
is your chance of holding centre stage. In a role-play exercise
you're given the principal role and an excellent opportunity
for discovering how you interact with others. Being in the
spotlight means you've nowhere to hide, the attention is
focused entirely on you.

In this chapter, we set out to show you how to make the most
of your starring role by explaining the different forms role-
play exercises take and how you approach them so that you
can give a performance of a lifetime.

Recognising Role-Play Exercises

Role-play exercises, also often referred to as Interview
Simulations, are designed to simulate those frequent occasions when you find yourself working with a few other people,
or, most commonly, one other person. Role-play exercises
differ from group exercises (refer to Chapter 4) in that you
alone direct the action without the support of others.

A role-play exercise gives you the opportunity of displaying
your interpersonal skills, such as communicating effectively,
listening and empathising.

Whether you take part in a role-play exercise depends very much on the target job. For example, if you're applying for a sales job or a job that involves carrying out interviews, then you have a good chance of being invited to take part in a one-to-one role-play on your Assessment Centre.

Most role-plays are face to face, carried out in a traditional office set-up, in which you would be seated at a desk. Or, in the less common operational set-up, such as a shop assistant talking with a customer, you're standing up. However, you may also come across a role-play exercise just using the phone, for simulating jobs in call centres, such as customer service advisers and telesales staff.

Although we refer to these exercises as *role-plays*, it's important that you recognise that *you* aren't being asked to role-play. Yes, you're being asked to take on a certain job role and you're given responsibilities and goals to achieve, but you have to understand that you're not an actor, you're there simply to be yourself. The assessors' job is to assess the 'real' you, the behaviours you display during the role-play, not your acting ability! So, the only person who is role-playing is the person or persons you're interacting with in the exercise. This is why role-play exercises are often called Interview Simulations, to avoid any possible confusion.

One-to-one role-play exercises

In a one-to-one role-play exercise you're given a written brief describing the situation and the task, and the person you're due to meet, and what you're expected to achieve. You're given about 15 to 30 minutes to study the brief and to prepare for the meeting. The meeting itself is generally scheduled to last about 20 to 45 minutes, but 30 minutes is most common.

Here's a typical example of a brief for a one-to-one role-play exercise.

Roz Banner: Instructions for Participant

The Situation

This exercise is designed to help assess your interpersonal skills and your ability to conduct a performance meeting.

You are asked to assume the role of a newly appointed Production Manager for Bulk Packaging. Your task is to conduct a performance meeting with the Stores Supervisor, Roz Banner, who is one of your team members.

Roz Banner has been with Bulk Packaging for the past 6 years and has worked in a number of different departments during this time, but has only been in her current position for 6 months. You have been with the Company for a few weeks, having started on 9 March, and to date you have only had a few brief words with Roz in your first week with Bulk. For the last week you have been on a skiing holiday in France and have therefore had little time to get to know your team. You are aware of a number of important issues that need to be dealt with fairly promptly and one such issue relates to Roz Banner.

Your predecessor, Nicky Read, has left you a note and a file on Roz that highlights a performance problem needing to be addressed. He explained that he was unable to deal with this matter before he left because of time restrictions and felt the matter should be dealt with as soon as possible. The contents of this file are included in your instructions and they contain recent hand-over notes and a letter of complaint from a customer. Furthermore, during your first week with Bulk you personally witnessed Roz losing her temper and responding in a rather abrupt way towards some of the people in your area.

Your Task

This exercise allows you 30 minutes to prepare for the interview (during which time you may make notes if you wish) and 30 minutes for the interview itself.

By the end of the interview you are required to have made some progress on the way ahead.

The performance meeting is intended to:

1. Inform Roz about her performance.

2. Maintain Roz's level of motivation.

3. Highlight areas for development.

4. Discuss the way forward.

5. Discuss any issues Roz wishes to raise.

For the purpose of this exercise, today's date is 2 April.

PLEASE DO NOT TURN OVER UNTIL TOLD TO DO SO

During a one-to-one role-play, the interaction is between you and the role-player, with the assessor observing and recording the way you develop your relationship with the role-player and how you handle any particular challenges that may come up. Try thinking of a one-to-one role-play as if it's a game of tennis. The dialogue between you and the role-player passes backwards and forwards 'across the net'. When the role-player asks a question or makes a particular point, you alone have the responsibility of responding, which puts pressure on you and the ball back into your court. Compare this situation with a group exercise where there's a shared responsibility. A comment by one of the group can be taken up and returned to the sender by any member of the group who chooses.

Multiple role-play exercises

Multiple role-play exercises are much less common than one-to-one role-plays. However, if you're asked to take part in a multiple role-play exercise on an Assessment Centre you need to know what makes this type of exercise different from the more traditional one-to-one role-play.

The purpose of a multiple role-play exercise is to see how you cope with challenges created by the interchanges between two or even three role-players. For example, you may find yourself:

- ✔ Intervening in a conflict situation between two or more people.

- ✔ Responding to people from different cultural backgrounds.

- ✔ Tackling a rapidly changing situation.

- ✔ Dealing with a number of unrelated issues at the same time.

You're more likely to be presented with these types of scenarios if you're being assessed for an operational role, such as a police officer, security guard, fire and rescue officer, or a team leader or supervisor.

The preparation time for a multiple role-play exercise is typically 15 to 30 minutes, similar to one-to-one role-play exercises, although in some scenarios it can be as little as 5 minutes. However, the running time for a multiple role-play is generally shorter. This is because having more than one role-player requires a more complex scenario and it's difficult for the exercise designers to script a multiple role-play if it runs for too long because you can't be sure what behaviours each person taking part is going to display during the exercise. Usually multiple role-plays last from 5 minutes up to about 30 minutes.

A multiple role-play can be quite stressful because more people are taking part. Work on staying calm and thinking clearly. Try to get to grips with the needs of the different parties and assess the demands of the circumstances facing you so that you can decide how best to fulfil the requirements of your brief.

Here's a typical example of the sort of brief you can be given for a multiple role-play exercise.

Shopping Centre Challenge: Instructions for Participant

Introduction

This is an exercise to assess how you're going to deal with a changing situation. Below are a number of pieces of information that you need to read through before beginning the exercise.

Background

You are a shift manager responsible for safety and security at one of Europe's largest shopping centres and you've just arrived to start the late shift. The early shift manager, Dan O'Grady, who has now left for the day, didn't have time to hand over to you in person. Instead, he left you a note.

Your Task

1. You have 5 minutes to read through Dan's notes before you meet the people involved. As shift manager it's your responsibility to deal with the situation as you see fit. You won't be able to ask for advice from your own manager although you do have your team available

to help you. Sam Woods (one of your operations staff) can update you on events as they're happening in the shopping centre. You can assume that the map of the shopping centre is correct and all exits and areas are clearly marked.

2. You have up to 20 minutes to deal with the situation.

For the purposes of this exercise, the time is now 3:00 p.m.

Note: Please do not throw away any written work that you do during this exercise.

Time: You now have 5 minutes to prepare. The exercise then starts immediately. The exercise lasts for up to 20 minutes.

PLEASE DO NOT TURN OVER UNTIL TOLD TO DO SO

Note from Dan O'Grady to the Late Shift Manager

Sorry I wasn't able to speak to you personally, I've got to accompany my wife to an antenatal class. There are a couple of things you need to know about what's happening today:

1. Gemma Stone (the famous author) is due to arrive at the Blaze Bookstore on Level 1 at 3:00 p.m. for a book signing for her latest novel. She has to leave the centre at 3:45 p.m. sharp, for another engagement.

2. Gemma's PR Manager Max Stafford wants to see you as soon as possible, although I've got no idea what it's about. I've told Max that you'll be available from 3:05 p.m. Max is coming to find you.

3. There's a protest planned for 3.15 p.m. outside the Real Coffee Court on Level 0 (see attached floor plan) about the exploitation of cheap labour by the coffee growers in Africa, so there are loads of people around.

4. I've asked Sam Woods to come and see you in 5 minutes to brief you on the current situation because I saw Sam arriving early for the shift.

Have a good shift.

Dan

Most of the skills described for a one-to-one role-play also apply in a multiple role-play but additional skills may be required, as the task could also involve:

> ✔ Mediating between people in a dispute.
>
> ✔ Empathising with people holding different views.
>
> ✔ Acting decisively under pressure.
>
> ✔ Taking charge and giving clear instructions.

Popular Scenarios

Role-play exercises simulate one of two organisational environments: internal or external. The scenario depends on whether the person or people you're meeting are internal or external to the organisation you're representing.

Internal role-plays

Internal role-plays simulate a meeting with one or more people within your organisation, such as your boss, a colleague, one of your subordinates, or members of your team.

A subordinate

If you're asked to take part in an internal one-to-one role-play, then a meeting with one of your subordinates is the most likely context. The purpose of this type of meeting is usually to carry out a performance review, a disciplinary review or a counselling session. In meetings with subordinates you're the one who makes the decisions, but you must do more than simply show you're the person in charge. You're expected to discuss with your subordinate and agree on a mutually beneficial outcome, which means exerting a positive, motivational influence over the role-player.

Your boss

In a role-play exercise, it's much less common to be asked to attend a meeting with your boss, but such a scenario does occasionally take place. If this happens you're typically given a goal that you need to achieve. You may be presented with a scenario in which you have to make a difficult request of your boss, for example, moving to a new project or asking for extra resources and you need to convince your boss that you have a strong case.

A colleague

Meeting a colleague is another popular scenario for an internal role-play and it could be for any number of reasons. For example, you may need to gain your colleague's support or co-operation on a project that you're responsible for, where your colleague was previously unhelpful.

Members of your team

You may be asked to carry out a meeting with members of your team, such as a briefing session before setting about a task or operation. For example, you may be a police inspector briefing your officers before a drugs-busting operation.

External role-plays

External role-plays often simulate meetings with a customer, prospect, supplier, or a representative of a business or organisation, such as the press or an independent agency.

A customer

External role-plays simulating a meeting with a customer are quite common, particularly for jobs that require a lot of customer contact, such as sales jobs or service jobs. Usually the scenario is one where you're visiting a customer to talk about a customer complaint or some other aspect of the service your company provides. This type of scenario tests your negotiating skills to see how well you can maintain a good relationship with the customer without having to make unnecessary concessions.

A prospect

You may find yourself being assessed for a sales job and it's quite likely that you're going to be asked to carry out a role-play in which you call on a prospect to progress a sales opportunity. In such a scenario you have the opportunity to display your full range of sales skills: establishing rapport; identifying the need; proposing a possible solution; handling objections; and closing.

Behaviour breeds behaviour

An interaction between you and a role-player goes as follows. Note *how* the role-player responds is based on your approach:

> You: 'So why do you think your sales figures are down?'

> Role-player: 'I don't know, but I don't think you appreciate just how tough it is out there at the moment.'

Now you have a choice:

✔ **You can go softly, softly:**

> You: 'I do, which is why I want to help you to explore how we can overcome these challenges and get you back on track.'

> Role-player: 'Well, it would be good to have some help, as I want to reach my target.'

✔ **Or, you can go all guns blazing:**

> You: 'I just think you're making excuses, as it hasn't stopped others from hitting their targets. You're clearly not trying hard enough and you need to make more effort; otherwise, you've got no future here.'

> Role-player: 'Well, if that's your idea of how to motivate someone, perhaps I'd be better off moving to another team.'

A supplier

Being asked to take the role of supplier is common if you're being assessed for a job in Purchasing or Procurement, such as a Chief Buyer. In the role-play scenario, you meet one of your suppliers and typically have to negotiate terms prior to signing an order.

A member of the press

If you're applying for a job in a senior position such as a member of a board of directors, a spokesperson or a public relations officer, all requiring you to interact with other organisations or institutions, then you may find yourself taking part in a role-play where you're facing the press and being interviewed under pressure. The task of the assessor is to see how you respond to challenging questions in a tough situation. This type of role-play exercise happens infrequently because there are fewer jobs around needing this skill set, but you need to be aware of the possibility of coming up against this type of exercise.

Role of the Role-Player

To perform your best in a role-play exercise, understanding the way a role-player is behaving is going to help you in your own performance. Role-players can be members of staff from the organisation, such as line managers or HR staff; occasionally assessors also take on the job of the role-player, although it's generally thought unwise to try to do the two jobs at the same time. Some organisations like to use professional role-players, often actors between jobs. Role-players are usually given specific training aimed at familiarising them with the exercise being used and what behaviours they need to display so that the assessor can observe and record your handling of the situation.

Role-players usually work to a script, but because they can't know what you're going to say, they need to be able to ad-lib and steer the interaction in a particular direction. One of the golden rules of role-playing is that the role-player needs to follow the principle 'Behaviour breeds behaviour', allowing your behaviour to direct the role-player's response. For example, at certain critical stages in the discussion, you have to decide how to press your point. You may choose a 'softly, softly' approach, or you may decide to go in 'all guns blazing'! It's going to be no surprise to find that the role-player responds differently to the two approaches.

In a number of key stages during the role-play, you have to decide on your next step. The behaviours you display at each stage are assessed in relation to the behaviours required for success in the target job, which may or may not be the 'softly, softly' approach.

Common Competencies Being Assessed

Your performance is assessed against a set of competencies linked to the activity. (For more about competencies take a look at Chapter 2.) The most common competencies you're

likely to meet in a role-play exercise are the following,
together with a definition of each competency:

- **Planning and Organising:** The ability to establish efficiently an appropriate course of action for self and/or
others to accomplish a goal.

- **Interpersonal Sensitivity:** Awareness of other people and
environment and own impact on these. Actions indicate a
consideration for the feelings and needs of others (but
not to be confused with 'sympathy').

- **Leadership:** Motivates, enables and inspires others to
succeed, utilising appropriate styles. Has a clear vision of
what is required and acts as a positive role model.

- **Flexibility:** The ability to modify own behaviour, adopting a different style or approach to reach a goal.

- **Persuasive Oral Communication:** Able to express ideas
or facts in a clear and persuasive manner. Convinces
others to own expressed point of view.

- **Listening:** Able to pick out important information in oral
communication. Questioning and general reactions indicate 'active listening'.

- **Stress Tolerance:** Stability of performance under pressure and/or opposition. Makes controlled responses in
stressful situations.

- **Diversity Awareness:** Treats all individuals with respect,
responds sensitively to differences and encourages
others to do likewise.

- **Customer Service:** Exceeds customer expectations by
displaying a total commitment to identifying and providing solutions of the highest possible standards aimed at
addressing customer needs.

Most of these competencies relate to how you might behave
during the face-to-face interaction. Your Planning and
Organising ability will be assessed on the basis of how you
prepared for the interaction and how well you structured your
approach to the meeting. Customer Service and Diversity
Awareness could be assessed if the context of the role-play
creates the opportunity to observe such behaviours. Your
Stress Tolerance is more likely to be assessed in a pressurised
scenario such as a Multiple Role-play Exercise.

Behaving Effectively

Achieving stardom in a role-play exercise requires you to use the right behaviours and in this section we describe the sorts of things that can maximise your chances of success.

Having a well-prepared plan

A key factor contributing to a successful role-play exercise is having a well-prepared plan. You have to be clearly focused on what you're trying to achieve and your preparation is all-important. You need to set out clear goals and have a struc-tured plan that will help you to reach the outcome you're seeking. Figure 6-1 shows you how a face-to-face meeting is planned.

• Introduction and explain purpose of meeting	(5 mins)
• Discuss current performance	(10 mins)
- His views and things he wishes to raise	
- My views and suggestions for improvement	
• Agree areas for improvement	(5 mins)
• Identify actions	(5 mins)
• Summarise and close meeting	(5 mins)

Figure 6-1: A plan of a face-to-face meeting.

Building the relationship

Enjoying a good relationship with the other person (or per-sons) is a fundamental part of a role-play exercise. Each of the different scenarios poses its own challenges, but the basic skills that you need in building relationships are the same across all the scenarios. The following sections describe things you need to do to build a successful relationship.

Developing rapport

Most role-play exercises place you in a situation where you've never met the person before, which often reflects the reality of the situation. So at the beginning of your meeting you need to spend a little time developing rapport before diving into the business at hand. Building rapport is a fairly universal practice in most cultures, although be wary of those individuals who detest small talk and want to get straight down to business.

Your brief and how things go during the first 30 seconds give you a good idea of how you're going to continue the meeting. If the brief offers you personal details about the person you're meeting, such as her family or hobbies, then you can start off by showing an interest in the person by asking polite questions about her family. Similarly, if the person is described as being warm and friendly, then your attempts to establish rapport are likely to be well received. On the other hand, if the brief describes the person as 'driven' and 'businesslike' then you're likely to be wasting your time and hers by making small talk and worse still you may even irritate her.

Creating an impact

First impressions are important. How you behave can strongly influence how you're seen by the other person. For that reason, you need to create a positive impact on the person you're meeting. If the role-play scenario is about visiting a client you need to act confidently by offering to shake hands, maintaining eye contact and smiling. And don't forget to introduce yourself!

Using 'active listening'

After the discussion begins, make sure you're listening to what the person is saying. Show that you're interested by making eye contact and paying attention to what the other person is talking about by saying 'yes', 'really' or using similar forms of acknowledgement; and if necessary restating or clarifying what has been said. 'So you're looking for a supplier who can . . . ;' 'Does that mean . . . ?'

Positive behaviours serve to strengthen the relationship between you, but be careful not to overdo it; otherwise you may be seen as toadying and manipulative.

Tuning in to non-verbal behaviour

Non-verbal behaviour, or body language, shows a person's true emotional state, which can often be at odds with what the person is actually saying. To interpret non-verbal behaviours you need to recognise the signs. Here are a few key signs to look out for:

- ✔ **Eye contact:** The amount of eye contact you display shows how confident you're feeling. The more intense the eye contact, the greater the level of confidence. However, your level of eye contact usually decreases when you're thinking of what to say next and increases when you're listening. A person may break off eye contact when she's being less than truthful, so you need to monitor the role-player's eye contact if you're asking searching questions and you have reason to suspect the role-player is withholding something important.

- ✔ **Hand gestures:** You generally find that you use fewer hand-to-face gestures when you're feeling confident. Dishonesty is often signalled by hand gestures covering the mouth (to hide the wry smile) or playing with an ear lobe, as if to prevent the person hearing her own lie! Look out for the stroking of her chin, sometimes accompanied by the forefinger on the cheek and the tilting of her head to one side, all of which signal that the person is thinking about what you're saying. Other useful hand gestures to look out for include 'steepling' of the fingers (confidence), strumming on the desk (boredom), pointing (aggression), rubbing the back of the neck (frustration), or tugging at one's collar (nervousness).

- ✔ **Body posture:** If the role-player is sitting with her arms folded across her chest and her legs crossed and angled towards the door, it signals that she's feeling uncomfortable and would probably rather not be there! During the role-play try adopting an 'open' posture with arms and legs unfolded, hands resting on the table or your lap, showing how relaxed you are, inviting the role-player to get in the same mood.

Making your point

Role-play exercises give you the opportunity of being the 'star of the show', but to shine means being prepared to stand up and say what you have to say loud and clear. Your brief spells out the details of the situation and expected goals, but only you can make it happen, and the role-player is there to present the challenges you need to overcome in reaching your goal.

Being willing to speak up and make your point and not 'folding under pressure' are essential for a successful outcome to the role-play exercise. Aim to highlight the advantages and benefits of the ideas that you're putting forward when selling your views to the role-player, emphasising what's in it for her and where appropriate, the organisation. A note of caution: Don't get into the situation where making your point at all costs means running the risk of 'winning the battle but losing the war.'

Don't bludgeon the role-player into submission in order to get your point accepted. Although you may be achieving a short-term victory, you do so at the expense of losing the goodwill existing between you and the role-player. The risk is greatest where you appear to be the person 'holding all the cards', the senior person or the customer, and you're perceived as having the stronger hand.

Handling resistance

Meeting resistance from the role-player is inevitable because this is a key part of her role. During your preparation time you need to set out a strategy for overcoming any resistance from the role-player. Try preparing arguments that counter the role-player's objections, assuming you can anticipate what objections the role-player is likely to raise. Another strategy you can use is switching the role-player's attention to another point by saying: 'Okay, but can we come back to that in a minute, as I'd like to talk about . . . '. This buys you thinking time and may even result in the role-player forgetting what her objection was in the first place, particularly if the objection was being used to conceal something or divert you from a more important issue.

Experienced salespeople often ignore an objection and wait to see if the prospect raises the objection again and only then do they treat the objection seriously.

Expecting the unexpected

Look out for the unexpected. Watch the role-player carefully during the role-play to detect if she's hiding any essential information and testing your ability to spot what isn't immediately obvious. Examples of this strategy include suddenly presenting a personal problem as a reason for underperforming in the job, an unanticipated customer complaint, or a last-minute requirement demanded in a negotiation.

The assessor is likely to be assessing your listening and empathy skills. To do this the role-player adopts behaviours hinting that all is not well: non-verbal signs such as a glum facial expression, a sad tone of voice, a slouching body posture and saying things like: 'Well it's difficult to focus on my objectives at the moment', sending out a strong message that something is amiss. Or, you're being assessed to see how you cope with a surprise event, such as a meeting with a customer for a regular account review and immediately you come into the room you're on the receiving end of a blast of anger because of a major service failure.

When you come up against the unexpected you need to stay calm, listen carefully, show empathy and respond sensitively while looking for the right solutions to resolve the problems and challenges in front of you.

Balancing individual and organisational needs

When looking for solutions to the challenges that you're facing during the role-play exercise, it's easy to find yourself focusing on the needs of the individual more than the needs of the organisation, or vice versa. Achieving a sensible balance between the two is more likely to bring about a successful outcome. For example, if the role-player tells you a pitiful story about personal problems, you clearly need to show some sympathy for the circumstances, but never allow personal problems to excuse poor performance.

Adopting behaviours showing a total disregard for the person's plight and insisting that she 'pulls herself together' and achieves her business targets isn't a good strategy. Neither is succumbing to agreeing that, under the circumstances, failing to achieve her targets is not important. Instead, you need to find a compromise aiming to achieve a 'win-win' outcome, so that the organisation can see some commitment to achieving its goals and the individual feels that her problems are being acknowledged and she's getting help. Achieving this balance is tricky and you're going to need to use a range of skills to arrive at a successful outcome.

Summarising the outcome

End the role-play by summarising what you've agreed and make sure that you've made a record of the agreement for future reference. Your summary needs to include any action you're going to take and the date of your next meeting to review progress.

Avoiding Ineffective Behaviours

Succeeding in role-play exercises doesn't just rely on you displaying effective behaviours. It also requires that you avoid ineffective behaviours that can damage your prospects of achieving a successful outcome.

Becoming angry or aggressive

Stop and take hold of the situation when you feel the pressure rising. Sometimes conflict between you and the role-player can spill over into anger or aggression. If you suspect things are going to be tricky, then try:

- ✔ Taking deep breaths before entering the room.
- ✔ Having a prepared response in case you're on the receiving end of an outburst.

Should an outburst occur quite unexpectedly, stay calm and listen to what the role-player is saying. If you need to calm the person down, try:

- ✔ Responding in a slow and measured tone.

- ✔ Saying something positive and avoiding put-downs.

- ✔ Avoiding inflammatory remarks such as 'With due respect . . .' (usually conveys the exact opposite); 'You're not listening to me . . .' (accusatory and argumentative), and 'I'm trying to be reasonable . . .' (implying that the other person is being unreasonable).

- ✔ Avoiding using aggressive body language such as hitting the table with the palm of your hand or your fist, or pointing or wagging your finger.

Getting frustrated

There may come a point in the role-play when you don't seem to be making any real progress and you're starting to get frustrated. If this happens, take a step back and ask yourself why this is happening. Some possibilities are:

- ✔ You're asking too many closed questions which result in short and uninformative answers, so you're struggling to understand the relevant issues in the scenario and this inevitably adds to the pressure. If you find this happening to you, try asking more open questions, or some follow-up questions to get a fuller picture of what's been happening.

- ✔ You're in the position of asking the other person (in this case the role-player) what she thinks is a good way of tackling the problem, and she's saying she doesn't know because her brief tells her that she has to wait for you to come up with the ideas – so you've both hit a brick wall! At this point try offering one idea and then asking the role-player if she has any other ideas. If neither of you can think of anything, suggest that she gives the problem some thought and comes back to you with ideas within the next few days. The important thing is that you commit to some form of action.

Starting to panic

Getting into a panic when you're feeling under pressure, such as in a multiple role-play, saps your energy and stops you thinking clearly. Stopping yourself from panicking is a must, because your stress tolerance is one of the competencies that the assessor is probably going to be assessing. It's important to give the assessor the impression that you're on top of the situation, even if all around you are showing signs of losing control.

If you want to impress the assessor and have a calming influence on the role-player, then you have to give out the right impression, regardless of how you're genuinely feeling. Staying calm can be achieved by taking slow, deep breaths; speaking at a measured pace; keeping your heart rate under control; accepting failures; staying positive; and expecting to succeed.

Gearing Up for the Role-Play Exercise

Performing well in role-play exercises is all about having a clear set of objectives and a suitable plan, coupled with the skills to execute the plan and getting yourself in the right frame of mind to achieve it. Once you have this focus there are some things you can do before and during the Assessment Centre to support this aim.

Before the Assessment Centre

If you know you're going to be doing a role-play exercise as part of your Assessment Centre, then try to find out beforehand if it's a one-to-one or multiple role-play, and whether it is set in an internal or external context. Knowing the type of role-play that you're going to be taking part in is helpful for matching your preparation to the task ahead.

Preparing for a role-play is much like taking part in a rehearsal. Try visualising yourself interacting with the role-player and responding to any challenges that you're expecting to face.

During the Assessment Centre

We've already covered some of the key things you need to do when preparing for a role-play exercise – in the section 'Recognising Role-Play Exercises' earlier in this chapter. However, keep one important point in mind: Make sure you use your preparation time well.

Remember the saying 'He who fails to plan, plans to fail'? Over the years we've noticed many participants on Assessment Centres failing to prepare properly for role-play exercises. After 5 to 10 minutes of reading the brief and making a few notes, which are often little more than a script of what they're intending to say, they start looking round the room totally bored. It's almost as if the participant doesn't see the need to prepare, relying instead on her ability to make it up as she goes along, or she thinks that you only need to prepare for more formal group meetings. Make sure you don't fall into the same trap!

Match your role-play plan to the sample plan we gave you earlier in this chapter. Make sure you set out a structured plan for achieving a clear set of goals. And think about the obstacles and challenges that you're likely to face during the course of the meeting and how you're going to overcome them.

If you prepare well for a role-play exercise and take account of the issues we've raised in this chapter, then it's more than likely that your role-play exercise is going to be a positive experience and you have every chance of enjoying an Oscar-winning performance!

Chapter 7

Shining in Fact-Finding Exercises

. . . .

In This Chapter

▶ Looking into fact-finding exercises

▶ Going about the exercises in the right way

▶ Getting ready to succeed

. . . .

*F*act-finding exercises are a powerful tool for assessing your ability to analyse information while 'thinking on your feet' and coming up with a sound decision supported by the facts. You're unlikely to come across fact-finding exercises on an Assessment Centre as often as other types of exercises, but if you're invited to take part in a fact-finding exercise, regard it as a great opportunity to shine under the spotlight.

In this chapter we explain how fact-finding exercises are structured and how to tackle them, the behaviours you need to show during the exercise, and how best to prepare for the exercise so that you end up being one of those to shine!

Fathoming Fact-Finding Exercises

Most Assessment Centre exercises are designed to simulate as far as possible the target job. However, fact-finding exercises are different in that the purpose is to assess your ability to use your analytical skills in a two-way setting. Fact-finding exercises are best suited for candidates seeking jobs where they need to demonstrate an inquisitive mind, such as a researcher, police officer, coroner, fire investigator, loss adjuster – or even tax inspector! In a fact-finding exercise you're asked to investigate a set of circumstances and gather information through wide-ranging questioning, allowing you to decide between two possible courses of action.

Fact-finding exercises usually follow a rigid four-phase structure, giving the exercises an artificial feel. The following sections outline these four phases.

Phase 1: Planning and preparing

At the start of the fact-finding exercise you're given a brief description of the circumstances around an event and have just a short time, often as little as 5 minutes, for preparing your questions to find out more about the situation.

Don't be surprised or put off by the shortness of the description of the situation, which can be as brief as the following:

> *You're the newly appointed sales director of Cosmos PLC and you've been asked by Jan Karlsson to make your first key decision, which is whether or not to dismiss Blake Sutherland.*

At this point of the exercise you need to quickly think about what questions you're going to be asking, in readiness for phase two of the exercise.

So that you don't overlook any suitable questions, you may find it helpful to use Rudyard Kipling's poem 'I Keep Six Honest Serving Men' as a prompt:

> *I keep six honest serving men*
> *They taught me all I knew;*
> *Their names are What and Why and When*
> *And How and Where and Who.*

By using this approach you can quickly come up with a list of about six or more questions for starting you off, such as:

✔ **What** has happened? What does Cosmos PLC do? What is the relationship between Jan Karlsson and Blake Sutherland?

✔ **Why** is Blake Sutherland's dismissal being considered?

✔ **When** did the incident (whatever it is) happen?

✔ **How** did the incident (whatever it is) happen?

✔ **Where** did the incident (whatever it is) happen?

✔ **Who** is Jan Karlsson? Who is Blake Sutherland? Who else is involved in the incident?

 Every minute counts. Listing your questions and then leaving enough space in between for writing your answers is a good way of making the most of the time you're given for your investigation.

Phase 2: Questioning and interpreting

In the second phase of the fact-finding exercise you have about 15 to 20 minutes to question someone called the Resource Person who has all the relevant information about the situation that you need to know. The Resource Person is totally impartial and has no involvement in the circumstances of the event whatsoever. The Resource Person's task is simply to give you the information you need in an objective and disinterested way, but only in response to specific questions from you.

You're likely to find that the answers to your preliminary questions prompt you to think of further questions as you become aware of more ways of looking at the situation. Always listen carefully to how the Resource Person phrases his answers, as these can give you clues about other facts that he's holding. For example in response to the earlier question 'Why is Blake Sutherland's dismissal being considered?', the Resource Person may say something like: 'One of the reasons is that Blake was rude to a customer', pointing out that more than one reason exists for considering dismissing Blake Sutherland. You clearly need to ask follow-up questions about the reason you've been given, but you can also start exploring the other reason(s) as well.

As you go on with your questioning during the second phase, you're busy trying to find out what the Resource Person's answers mean and getting a picture of what you've found out so far, leading you onto the next phase of the exercise.

How you use the time during the second phase is usually up to you. You can decide whether to use all your time asking questions, or you may want to stop asking questions and start reviewing the information you've already collected. However, it's usually best at this stage to ask as many relevant questions as you can think of; it's not unusual for strong candidates to ask as many as 25 to 45 questions depending on the circumstances and the style of questioning.

Phase 3: Evaluating and deciding

In the third phase of the exercise, which usually lasts about 5 to 10 minutes, you're busy weighing up the arguments for and against the decision you're about to reach.

You may think that drawing up a list of the 'fors' and 'againsts,' to see if the weight of evidence supports one side more than the other, is the best method for reaching your conclusion. However, be careful about being swayed by the *number* of arguments without taking into account the *importance* of those arguments. For example, there may be five reasons against dismissing Blake Sutherland, but the one reason for his dismissal may be so significant that it outweighs the number of arguments against the case.

During the third phase of the exercise you present your decision to the Resource Person and give the reasons for your decision. The usual practice is for you to deliver your decision informally, keeping in mind that the Resource Person has no part to play in the situation and is totally impartial. The Resource Person may often summarise your decision and reasons before moving on to the fourth and final phase.

Phase 4: Reviewing and justifying

In Phase 4, the Resource Person tests the soundness of your decision by offering you other relevant information that you failed to uncover in Phase 2. After giving you the extra information he may ask: 'Does this have any bearing on your decision?' You now have the opportunity to review your original decision. Clearly the Resource Person's question has no right or wrong answer and whether the new information has a bearing on your decision is determined by the significance of the new information in relation to the facts you've already uncovered.

The purpose of Phase 4 is to give the assessor the opportunity of observing and recording how you test the new information against the information you've already received, how well you justify your position, and how you respond to being challenged and put under pressure.

Common Competencies Being Assessed

Your performance is assessed against a set of competencies linked to the activity. (For more about competencies take a look at Chapter 2.) The most common competencies you're likely to meet in a fact-finding exercise are the following, together with a definition of each competency:

- ✔ **Planning and Organising:** Having the ability to establish efficiently an appropriate course of action for self and/or others to accomplish a goal.

- ✔ **Problem Analysis:** Effectiveness in identifying problems, seeking pertinent data, recognising important information and identifying possible causes of problems.

- ✔ **Judgement:** The ability to evaluate data and courses of action and to reach logical decisions. Has an unbiased, rational approach.

- ✔ **Decisiveness:** Readiness to make decisions, state opinions, take action or commit oneself.

- ✔ **Persuasive Oral Communication:** Ability to express ideas or facts in a clear and persuasive manner. Convinces others to own expressed point of view.

- ✔ **Stress Tolerance:** Stability of performance under pressure and/or opposition. Makes controlled responses in stressful situations.

✔ **Listening:** Ability to pick out important information in oral communication. Questioning and general reactions indicate 'active listening'.

Not all seven competencies in the list are necessarily going to appear during your Assessment Centre. However, if you're facing a fact-finding exercise, you're assessed against some of them, or competencies like them.

Keeping track of what competencies are being assessed at each phase of the fact-finding exercise is important for tackling the exercise successfully. Table 7-1 shows the four phases of a fact-finding exercise and which competencies are most probably being assessed.

Table 7-1   Typical Competencies Assessed at Each Phase of the Fact-Finding Exercise

Phase	Competencies
1. Planning and preparing	Planning and Organising Problem Analysis
2. Questioning and interpreting the facts	Problem Analysis Judgement Listening
3. Evaluating the facts and coming to a decision	Judgement Decisiveness Persuasive Oral Communication
4. Reviewing and justifying your decision	Judgement Decisiveness Persuasive Oral Communication Stress Tolerance

Behaving Effectively

Shining in a fact-finding exercise requires you to use the right behaviours and in this section we describe the sorts of things that will maximise your chances of success.

Thinking on your feet

Being able to think on your feet is the most important skill in a fact-finding exercise, because seeking out and gathering all the relevant facts is crucial in making an informed decision.

Thinking on your feet may not come naturally to you, but try out the following:

- ✓ Ask questions quickly to create momentum and get your adrenalin flowing.

- ✓ Listen carefully to the answers to your questions, because the answers give you clues about further areas of investigation.

- ✓ Use follow-up questions to delve deeper into the circumstances to get a clearer understanding of the situation.

- ✓ Explore the breadth of the situation by approaching it from different perspectives so you're covering every angle.

Taking brief notes

Taking brief notes is essential for remembering the answers to your questions. You may be asking 25 questions or more, so having all the information at your fingertips is important for when you come to review the information you've collected. Unless you're skilled at shorthand, you won't have the time to write detailed replies to your questions, because this slows you down and uses up the limited and valuable time you have for questioning. Your best tactic is to use key words for recording the essential points to your answers. Although don't forget to write clearly so that you're sure of being able to read your own handwriting!

Weighing up the information

After you've gathered all the facts, you need to review what you've found out so you can reach a well-considered conclusion. Fact-finding exercises are designed so that the problem you're considering has no obvious right answer, so your conclusion needs to be based on how you set about testing out your facts.

In the business world, deciding whether to recommend firing someone, closing a business facility, or stopping an investment programme are big decisions with potentially serious consequences and it's important that you show sound judgement. To help you reach your decision, you need to weigh up the pros and cons of each of your options, reviewing both the quantity and quality of the various arguments. While doing this, you need to also consider the wider implications of your decision and how it's going to impact on the:

- ✔ Individuals directly involved in the situation.
- ✔ Other individuals in the organisation.
- ✔ Organisation's reputation in the market.
- ✔ Organisation's commercial situation.

Coping with the pressure

You need to be well prepared for the final phase of the fact-finding exercise because this is where your ability to cope with pressure is going to be tested. At this point in the exercise the Resource Person puts pressure on you by giving you more and more facts previously unknown to you that may contradict the decision you've made. If you managed to gather all the significant information you needed in Phase 2, Phase 4 of the exercise is unlikely to be daunting. But if you didn't succeed in uncovering important chunks of the relevant information, you may now find that your decision is being seriously challenged. Being able to think on your feet is critical.

Having been presented with new information you certainly shouldn't feel compelled to change your decision. Neither should you be determined to stick to your decision at all costs. The key to successfully handling Phase 4 of the exercise is to take a balanced view and objectively reassess your decision in the light of all of the facts. What you must not do is change your decision because you think it's going to please the assessor.

Avoiding Ineffective Behaviours

Shining in fact-finding exercises doesn't just rely on you displaying effective behaviours, it also requires that you avoid ineffective behaviours which can damage your prospects of achieving a successful outcome.

Jumping to conclusions

In the earlier section 'Phase 2: Questions and interpreting,' we said that some candidates are likely to ask 25 to 45 questions to help them come to an informed decision. You may be amazed to discover, though, that other candidates can ask as few as six questions before making a decision!

Freezing in the headlights

Some candidates just panic when they're presented with the task of investigating the circumstances of an event and have very little information to go on. To avoid getting into this type of situation you need to plan carefully and prepare a few well-chosen questions to help you get started. When you've used all your prepared questions but can't think of any follow-up questions, pause, review your notes, and try thinking of other areas that need exploring. You can usually stop and start as often as you want during the questioning phase. Don't panic, but do watch the time and make sure you're using your time effectively.

Being prejudiced and having preconceived ideas

One of the worst things that can happen to you in a fact-finding exercise is losing your capacity for being objective. Never allow personal prejudices and preconceived ideas to rule your interpretation of the information you've been given. When candidates display this type of behaviour you can almost hear them thinking: 'Don't confuse me with the facts, my mind is made up!' It's important to keep an open mind and to make sure your analysis of the situation and the decision you come to is free of prejudice at all times.

Asking ineffective questions

Don't waste time asking questions that aren't going to lead anywhere. Here are some examples:

- ✓ **Closed questions:** These questions invite 'yes', 'no' or brief factual answers and are best used for confirming, explaining or ending a subject. Closed questions often start with 'Do', 'Did', 'Has', 'Have', 'Was'. For example: 'Was he angry?', 'Do you know him?', 'What time did he leave?'. Avoid these types of questions if you're looking for a more detailed or expansive answer.

- ✓ **Multiple questions:** Multiple questions happen because the candidate suddenly thinks of another aspect of the situation that is worth exploring and adds another question onto the original question. For example: 'How many projects is he working on and are they all in the same field, or do they cover different fields?' The problem with multiple questions is that they can confuse the Resource Person and this can slow down his response, wasting valuable time. Sometimes the candidate and the Resource Person forget what's being asked and a useful piece of information gets overlooked.

- ✓ **Leading questions:** Leading questions are particularly unhelpful in a fact-finding exercise because they can push the Resource Person into giving an answer that the candidate expects or wants to hear, at the risk of missing out on more relevant information. Often leading questions are asked in an attempt by the candidate to confirm what the candidate thinks may be the 'right answer'. For example, 'Presumably the CEO wants Peters sacked for being rude to an influential customer?', when the CEO may not want Peters sacked, or may have different or additional reasons for wanting him sacked.

- ✓ **Irrelevant questions:** Although we've stressed the value of asking as many questions as you can fit into the time available, you clearly don't want to ask questions simply for the sake of it. You need to make sure that your questions are relevant by asking yourself if they meet the 'Relevance Test,' which is: 'Is this question going to help me to make an informed, rounded and rational decision?.'

Gearing Up for the Fact-Finding Exercise

Performing well in fact-finding exercises is about having a suitable plan, coupled with good questioning and listening skills and the ability to objectively evaluate the information you collect, so you can present a sound decision which can be defended under cross-examination. With this focus in mind here are some things you can do before and during the Assessment Centre to help you shine.

Before the Assessment Centre

Practising the relevant skills before taking part in the fact-finding exercise is going to pay dividends. What you put into the exercise is hopefully what you're going to get out: namely, that sought after job.

Planning and preparing

Find a short article (say no more than 40 words), such as the opening paragraph to a news story, and set yourself a time limit of five minutes to write down as many questions as you can think of relevant to the subject matter. When your time is up, review your list and now read the full article to see how well your questions anticipated some of the facts and issues covered in the story. Are there any gaps or obvious things you missed? For example, some candidates overlook questions about people, while other candidates overlook questions concerning business issues.

Having at least six or so prepared questions and using Kipling's 'I Keep Six Honest Serving Men' can help you approach the situation from different perspectives (look back at the earlier section in this chapter 'Phase 1: Planning and preparing').

Questioning and interpreting

Try fixing up a 15-minute question time with someone who's an expert in a field that you know very little about. It can be a hobby such as beekeeping or fly-fishing, or an unusual career such as a circus performer. Spend five minutes preparing your initial questions and 15 minutes asking the person about his job or hobby. Don't forget to make notes, and at the end of the 15 minutes go over your questions, asking the person to point out any obvious gaps in your questioning.

Evaluating and deciding, and reviewing and justifying

'Evaluating and deciding' and 'reviewing and justifying' are the two phases of the fact-finding exercise that are difficult to practise in a truly meaningful fashion, because they're very much dependent on what has gone before. However, have a go at practising by taking part in a debating session where you have to weigh up the facts about a 'Yes/No' scenario and identify the key arguments in favour of or against a particular position. You may also find it helpful to watch TV programmes such as *Question Time*, where contentious issues are being debated and notice how those taking part put forward and give reasons for their particular point of view.

During the Assessment Centre

In 'Fathoming Fact-Finding Exercises' earlier in this chapter, we covered how to tackle the different stages of a fact-finding exercise during the Assessment Centre. Stay focused and keep cool and calm throughout. Remember to display suitable competencies at the right time to impress the assessor and fill you with confidence. And best of all, after following the advice in this chapter you're highly likely to find yourself glowing with success!

Chapter 8

Achieving in Analysis Exercises

In This Chapter

▶ Examining analysis exercises

▶ Appreciating the different formats

▶ Watching your behaviours

*A*re you one of those lucky people born with an analytical mind? If someone gives you a problem, you have no trouble finding ways of solving it. But if you're not so lucky we're here to help. As part of your assessment it's more than likely that you're going to be asked to do an analysis exercise because they're an excellent way of finding out how well you handle and analyse data, solve problems and make decisions. These skills are a key requirement in most jobs, ranging from relatively straightforward tasks, such as deciding how and when to order and arrange new stock for your shop – through to more complex situations, such as working out how to break into the Brazilian coffee growers' market.

In this chapter we talk about the different forms that analysis exercises take and how to set about doing an exercise, making sure you achieve the task in hand.

Analysing Analysis Exercises

Analysis exercises (sometimes also called case-studies) are for measuring the full range of your analytical skills. On an Assessment Centre, case-studies are often used because they deal with real-life situations and are an excellent way of simulating the target job and giving you the opportunity of experiencing the types of challenges you can face in the actual job.

For example, you're applying for the job of a business analyst. You're given a case-study where you're working for a client named Riley Games, specialising in the production of video games. Your task is to test the market potential of five new games being considered for development. You're asked to recommend just one game for development, say why you're choosing that particular game, and give your reasons for rejecting the other four.

An analysis exercise is a solitary activity, in that you're working on your own and coming to your own decisions.

To carry out an analysis exercise, you're given a brief containing a lot of information, from a range of sources and in different formats: graphs, tables, charts, reports, and so on. You have to go through the information, deciding what the key issues are, and use your findings to make recommendations or come to a decision.

Analysis exercises are about taking logical steps: reviewing the available data, picking out the important pieces of information, evaluating the various options, and coming to a clear decision or recommendation supported by logical and rational reasoning.

Outlining Analysis Exercise Formats

How you carry out an analysis exercise can vary according to the demands of the exercise. For example, you may be asked by your manager to produce a detailed written report on the pros and cons of moving your operation to a new office, giving the reasons for your decisions. In another situation you're asked by your director to present your analysis and recommendations verbally to stakeholders on changes in the organisation, much like giving an oral presentation (refer to Chapter 5). Alternatively, you've been assigned to a project team and are responsible for analysing the status of a current project and need to discuss your findings and recommendations with the team, similar to the format of a group discussion (refer to Chapter 4).

Appreciating that there are different ways of carrying out an analysis exercise is important for knowing what behaviours you're expected to display in each type of scenario.

Analysis exercise written reports

Written reports are the most favoured format for an analysis exercise because they give you an excellent opportunity for displaying your full range of analytical skills, as well as your written communication skills. Here's a typical example of a candidate brief for producing a written report.

Introduction

In this exercise you are to take the role of an Independent Management Consultant. Amanda Styles, the Managing Director of Parts 4 Printers Ltd, has invited you to look at the status of the business and to submit a written report on how the Company should proceed over the next 3 years.

Your Task – The Report

The information that follows represents a summary of the facts that you have been able to gather in readiness to write your Report.

You will have 1½ hours to analyse the material on the following pages, form your judgements and write the Report.

You may feel that to carry out this task you have to make additional assumptions. This is permissible provided that an adequate explanation of the reasons for such assumptions is given.

Note: Please do not dispose of any written work that you may create during this exercise.

Time: You have 1½ hours to complete the Report.

Writing a report that fulfils your brief means taking a planned and structured approach, telling your readers what they need to know in the right level of detail. For the person reading the report it should be like reading a story, with a beginning middle and end – guiding the reader to the same conclusions that you've reached (or at least to understand how you reached your conclusions). When writing a report it's important to include the following sections:

✔ **Executive Summary:** Giving an overview of the content.

✔ **Aims:** Saying what you're trying to achieve.

✔ **Main Body:** Describing the conclusions you've reached, supported by your reasoning and what you're planning to do.

✔ **Summary:** Highlighting your decisions.

✔ **Appendix:** Showing your detailed analysis of how you reached your conclusions, including graphs, charts and tables if needed.

Often the main body of the report is the hardest to put together. Using your brief as the basis for structuring your report helps you decide on the content of the main body of the report. For example, your brief asks you to write a report on the following:

> Three locations have been identified for an office relocation taking place in six weeks time. Write a report taking account of:
>
> 1. The pros and cons of each of the three locations.
>
> 2. Which site you're recommending for relocation and why.
>
> 3. Who else is going to be involved in the relocation project to make sure the removal takes place within the deadline.

Here your brief sets out three issues to be discussed in the main body of your relocation report: arguments for and against; decisions/recommendations; and reasoning behind your decision/recommendations. It's sensible to structure your report including one section on each issue.

However, if you're asked to write a report around a single issue (to decide whether to launch a new product for example), you need to think about how you're going to break the product launch down into logical steps. For example, discuss the product options available; the pros and cons of launching each product; your decisions/recommendations with supporting reasons; and, how best to carry out your decisions/recommendations, if you do decide to launch.

Typically an analysis exercise lasts for between 1 and 2 hours. As fulfilling all the requirements of the report takes time, you need to split your time appropriately between analysing, decision making and writing. It's up to you to decide how much time you're going to spend analysing the information compared to actually writing the report.

Analysis exercise presentations

Instead of producing a written report, you may be asked to present a report orally. The following example shows a typical candidate brief for producing an oral presentation. (For more about oral presentations refer to Chapter 5.)

Introduction

In this exercise you are to take the role of a Senior Consultant for Bennett Enterprises. The company is looking to implement a Change Programme to increase synergies between departments.

The Board will meet you tomorrow to hear your conclusions and to ask you some questions on your ideas. They have 40 minutes for the meeting and have asked that you take 20 minutes to brief them so they can then spend the remaining 20 minutes clarifying their understanding.

They expect you to cover the following points:

1. An assessment of the current situation within Bennett Enterprises, based on the information available.

2. Your recommendations about the scope, structure and priorities of the Change Programme.

3. Your justification for making these recommendations, together with suggestions about how these would be implemented.

You may feel that to carry out this task you have to make additional assumptions. This is permissible, so long as you provide an adequate explanation of the reasons for any such assumptions.

If you're being asked to present your report orally, it's highly likely that the job you're applying for requires excellent presentation skills – and doing an oral presentation best simulates the target job. In this situation, by the end of the 1 to 2 hour period, you're expected to have prepared your presentation, which you go on to deliver afterwards.

Alternatively, you may be asked to make an oral presentation of the main points of your report as well as producing a written report. You complete your analysis and report within the 1 to 2 hour period as before and then you're usually given extra time for preparing a presentation (for example, 30 minutes) before you go on to delivering your presentation (20 minutes, including questions). The extra time gives 'your manager' (typically the assessor) the opportunity of asking questions about any areas that aren't clear, or points you haven't covered in the report.

Presenting your report orally is a great way of demonstrating different behaviours, such as getting your ideas across clearly, making a positive impression, influencing, being flexible in your approach, and responding to challenges. Go to Chapter 5 to find out how these behaviours are linked to this task.

Analysis exercise group discussions

You may be asked to take part in an analysis exercise group discussion. This format is most likely being used because it's the best way of simulating what happens in the target job, for example analysing your current department's performance and then meeting up with other department heads to decide how best to implement a change programme. In an analysis exercise group discussion, you're usually given an hour or so to analyse the situation and make notes individually. You're then given about an hour to meet a group of other candidates to decide how best to take forward the issue you're discussing.

The purpose of an analysis exercise group discussion is to allow you to show how well you display the following behaviours as well as your analytical skills:

✔ Persuading others to your point of view

✔ Challenging other peoples' thinking

✔ Changing your opinions to fit in with the group's views

See Chapter 4 to find out how these behaviours are linked to this task.

Common Competencies Being Assessed

Your performance is assessed against a set of competencies linked to the activity. (For more about competencies, take a look at Chapter 2.) The most common competencies you're likely to meet in an analysis exercise are the following, together with a definition of each competency:

✔ **Attention to Detail:** Total task accomplishment through concern for all areas involved, no matter how small.

✔ **Planning and Organising:** Ability to establish efficiently an appropriate course of action for self and/or others to accomplish a goal.

✔ **Problem Analysis:** Effectiveness in identifying problems, seeking pertinent data, recognising important information and identifying possible causes of problems.

✔ **Judgement:** Ability to evaluate data and courses of action and to reach logical decisions. Adopts an unbiased, rational approach.

✔ **Decisiveness:** Readiness to make decisions, state opinions, take action or commit oneself.

✔ **Written Communication:** Ability to express ideas clearly in writing, in good grammatical form, in such a way as to be clearly understood.

✔ **Commercial Awareness:** Ability to understand the key business issues that affect the profitability and growth of an enterprise. Takes appropriate action to maximise success.

✔ **Strategic Perspective:** Takes account of a wide range of longer-term issues, opportunities and contingencies. Identifies the means of implementing plans in line with the vision and direction.

Not all eight competencies in the list are necessarily going to appear during your assessment. However, if you're taking part in an analysis exercise, the Assessment Centre is likely to be assessing some of these competencies. Also, if you're asked to do an oral presentation or take part in a group discussion, you may want to look at other competencies listed in Chapters 4 and 5.

Keeping track of which competencies are likely to be assessed in different aspects of an analysis exercise will increase your chances of a successful outcome. Table 8-1 shows the different aspects of an analysis exercise and the competencies being assessed.

Table 8-1	Typical Competencies Assessed for Each Aspect of an Analysis Exercise	
Aspects of the Analysis Exercise	*Competencies*
Report structure and clarity	Attention to Detail
	Planning and Organising
	Written Communication
Analysing options	Problem Analysis
	Commercial Awareness
	Strategic Perspective
Making recommendations and giving reasons	Judgement
	Decisiveness

Behaving Effectively

During an analysis exercise you're going to be showing a wide range of behaviours, particularly if the analysis exercise is linked to an oral presentation or a group discussion. Don't forget: Whatever behaviours you display they're all going to be closely observed and recorded by the assessors on the Assessment Centre.

Managing your time well

Balancing your time between reading, analysing and weighing up the facts when writing a report can be difficult to get right. To make sure you get the balance right, be clear in your mind what you're trying to achieve, the information you need, and how long it's going to take you to write your report.

When putting together a report for an analysis exercise, try allowing a specific time for each activity. For example, if you're given two hours in total, you can divide your time as follows:

- ✔ **20 minutes** to read the information

- ✔ **50 minutes** to analyse and make decisions

- ✔ **45 minutes** to write the report

- ✔ **5 minutes** to check the report

Once you've made a plan, you're ready for action. Don't make the mistake of drawing up a plan and then never using it – you'll have wasted at least 5 minutes of your precious time if you don't use it! Also remember it's there for a reason. Plans help you to balance time between tasks – otherwise you might end up spending most of your time analysing the issue and not writing up your understanding in sufficient detail for the Assessor to read in the report, meaning you lose precious marks.

If you have a lot of information to get through, you can avoid getting bogged down and using up valuable time by skim-reading most of the material first. Skimming alerts you to the relevant or interesting sections of your information, which you can then go back to and read in detail. However, it may just be possible to read all the information in detail within your timeframe. It's up to you to judge how best to approach this task.

Deciding what information is missing

In an analysis exercise you're usually given a number of options to choose from, each with some appeal, making it harder for you to decide what course of action to take and what recommendations to make. But you may not be happy about suggesting a particular option because you're missing out on some important information and would rather wait until you had all the facts. However, if you try to avoid making a decision while waiting for the information you're unlikely to achieve your goal within the timeframe.

If you find yourself in the situation of not having all the information you need, weigh up the information you do have and base your decision or recommendations on what you know. Then make a note saying what extra information you would ideally have liked to have had prior to making your decision. This shows the assessors that you recognise where important information is missing but that you're still willing to deal with the uncertainty and make tough decisions.

Analysing the pros and cons

Analysing your options is a key approach to solving a problem. You can do this by drawing up a table of your options, listing the advantages and disadvantages, benefits and risks, or pros and cons. You can begin analysing your options while reading through the information, so that by the time you've finished reading you've made a list of the key points that you need to include in the report. Table 8-2 shows an example of a table listing the pros and cons relating to two options.

Table 8-2   The Pros and Cons for Each Option

	Pros	*Cons*
China	The site is located in a brand new state-of-the-art industrial park.	Needs adequate Corporate Social Responsibility policies and actions to be eligible for this plot of land.
	Planning approval has already been obtained for the new site.	Waste management practices may need to be reviewed.
India	Site is already occupied by a plastics manufacturer.	Transport links aren't sophisticated – distribution has been a problem for the existing manufacturer.
	The site is close to sources of raw materials.	Higher purchase price than the China site.

Giving reasons for decisions

You'll naturally get some credit for stating a decision or rec-ommendation, but this will be limited, unless you provide rea-sons as to why you've made this choice.

An analysis exercise rarely has a right or wrong answer, which makes it harder for you to choose between your options and even more crucial that you can explain to the assessors why you've chosen one option over another.

Nearly all options have benefits and risks attached to them. It's your job to decide which of your options offers the most benefits with the least damaging risks.

Try to avoid focusing entirely on the positives attached to your preferred option and ignoring the risks. If you do, the assessor is likely to think that you're not aware of the risks and may think that you've made an ill-considered decision. To make sure the assessor understands how you've come to your decision, openly mention the risks and disadvantages of your chosen option, saying how the risks and disadvantages impact on the option, and how you're going to overcome them. Doing so shows the assessor you've arrived at your decision by a well-rounded decision-making process.

Remembering other effective behaviours

Remember that in addition to being evaluated on your analytical skills, if you have to give an oral presentation or take part in a group discussion you're going to be assessed on the skills and behaviours linked to those tasks as well. For more information on effective behaviours when delivering an oral presentation, go to Chapter 5. If you think you're going to be taking part in a group discussion, head to Chapter 4.

Gearing Yourself Up for the Analysis Exercise

Analytical thinking, effective decision making and good communication skills are essential in most jobs so you need to be able to demonstrate these skills during the exercise. Therefore, planning your approach to tackling the exercise is going to give you an edge while on the Assessment Centre and greatly add to your chances of success.

Before the Assessment Centre

You can get some preparation in before the Assessment Centre by looking at the ways you've gone about solving problems on previous occasions.

Dig out an old report you wrote when you were at school, university or in a previous job. If you can't find one, then think about how you would have approached such a task. Consider:

✔ The level of detail of your analysis.

✔ The emphasis you took when resolving the issue (for example, financial or commercial issues versus people issues).

✔ The clarity of your report.

✔ The feedback you received in relation to the output.

Thinking about these aspects of writing a report is going to help you see what you need to concentrate on when doing the analysis exercise for real.

To polish up your analytical skills take a newspaper or magazine and cut out all the articles on the first 5 to 10 pages (depending on the length of the articles) and give yourself one hour to read them. Then taking on the role of editor, spend the next hour thinking how you're going to arrange the articles for printing. Write down the order in which the articles are going to appear and your reasons for placing them in that order. If possible, ask a friend or colleague to look at what you've come up with and give your reasons for arranging the articles in that particular way. And don't forget to ask your friend or colleague for feedback on how your publication can be improved.

During the Assessment Centre

Before beginning your analysis exercise, draw up a plan of how you're going to use your time and keep it by you throughout the exercise to make sure that you're using your time wisely. Write your objectives at the top of your plan, as these will provide you with a clear point of focus. See the earlier section in this chapter 'Analysis exercise written reports' for tips on what to include in your plan.

An analysis exercise isn't about testing your ability to copy information from one place to another; it's about testing your understanding. Try including only the key messages supporting your decisions/recommendations, and good luck!

Chapter 9

Performing in Planning and Scheduling Exercises

· ·

In This Chapter

▶ Figuring out planning and scheduling exercises

▶ Knowing how to tackle them

▶ Taking the steps to success one by one

· ·

*P*lanning and scheduling exercises are among the least well-known Assessment Centre exercises. But if you're applying for a job as a project manager, logistics manager, resource scheduler, team leader, project co-ordinator or conference and events organiser, a planning and scheduling exercise is right up your street. Planning and scheduling exercises are mainly used for assessing candidates for middle management jobs and below, where the skills of planning timetables and making the best use of resources to carry out the activity are all important. You're less likely to be doing a planning and scheduling exercise if you're being assessed for a senior position, unless there's a strong requirement for project planning or project management. This is because this type of assessment exercise focuses on planning and implementation, which are usually the responsibilities of staff at a lower level of the organisation, such as first-line managers and administrative assistants.

In this chapter we explain how planning and scheduling exercises are structured and the steps you need to take to put in a peak performance!

Introducing Planning and Scheduling Exercises

A planning and scheduling exercise is about analysing information for a project, putting a plan together to achieve what you're being asked to do, using the available resources to allow you to put your plan into action, and delivering your plan within a fixed timeframe.

Planning and scheduling exercises are designed as individual exercises, so you're asked to complete one on your own. The exercises can be complex, because you're likely to be asked to decide the order in which the various activities take place, identify those activities that are dependent on other activities and personnel, and decide which activities can run in parallel.

If you're asked to do a planning and scheduling exercise, you're given a brief describing a specific task and a fixed amount of resources: time, personnel, equipment, facilities and budget. Your challenge is to decide how you're going to use your resources to fulfil your brief effectively. Here's an example of an extract from the Instructions for the Participant for a planning and scheduling exercise:

The Firm Brochure

Instructions for the Participant

Introduction

This is an exercise to assess how you would handle an administrative scheduling task, which involves a number of facets and details. For the purposes of this exercise you can assume that all aspects of the work that you are required to co-ordinate with other people will happen on time.

Background

You are a recently appointed Trainee for a medium sized Accountancy Firm called Beadle, Hart & Myles. Six months ago they acquired a smaller firm, Myles & Partners, since when they have had to restructure and reorganise the expanded firm. They now wish to create an updated brochure to reflect the expanded practice and the new services they can offer their clients. You have been given responsibility for organising the production of this brochure, in time for a forthcoming regional exhibition. This exhibition represents the Firm's first opportunity to market itself as the newly merged firm and it is therefore essential that a quality brochure be produced on time, through a well-managed process. As this group of staff is not used to working together as a team, your role as a co-ordinator is important to the project's success. Unfortunately, you are having to work under a tight timeframe, as the accountants have been under considerable pressure managing the recent change and it coincides with some clients' year-end, so this task has been 'left to the last minute'.

The overall objective is to ensure that all the actions that need to take place to produce the brochure are scheduled into the diary. Thus the question, 'What needs to take place, by when and by whom?' can be answered at any stage in the project's process. This process has a number of complexities. The people you need to co-ordinate, the activities you need to schedule, and the time and availability constraints, are described in more detail on the following pages.

Your Task

Assuming that today is 18 December, you need to work out the most time-efficient way of scheduling the activities listed above, to ensure that the brochure is produced in time for the regional exhibition, which starts on 9 March.

You can use the diary sheet provided, both to assist your calculations and write your final answers. Please write in pencil. It is important to note or indicate any calculations you have used in coming to your conclusions, on the extra paper provided.

Note: Please do not dispose of any written work that you may create during this exercise.

Time: You have 1 hour to complete this task.

PLEASE DO NOT TURN OVER UNTIL TOLD TO DO SO

The rest of your brief gives you more details about the resources available to you, and a template for recording what you're proposing. Generally, your output in a planning and scheduling exercise takes the form of a timeline or project schedule, rather than writing a narrative-based report, as in an analysis exercise (refer to Chapter 8).

A Gantt chart (also known as a bar chart) is a much loved and much used project management tool. If you're expecting to be doing a planning and scheduling exercise then you may find it helpful to do a little background reading about Gantt charts. They aren't complicated and plenty of helpful information about them is available on the Internet.

You can see an example of a typical timeline or project schedule in Figure 9-1.

Week	1	2	3	4	5	6	7	8	9	10	11	12
Planning meeting	■											
Obtain testimonials	■	■	■	■	■	■						
Write first draft		■	■	■								
Plan graphic design			■	■								
Arrange photos				■	■							
Review drafts					■	■						
Arrange layout						■						
Check first proof							■					
Correct proof							■					
Check second proof								■				
Printing									■	■		
Brochure delivered											■	
Exhibition runs												■

Figure 9-1: Example of a typical project schedule presented in timeline format.

Given the nature of planning and scheduling exercises, it's often the case that a single best answer is possible or just a few equally valid answers. Either way the assessor will compare your proposed solution with a 'model answer' and the closer it matches, the better you score.

The time allowed for a planning and scheduling exercise can vary, but you usually have between 30 and 60 minutes to analyse the information and produce your proposed schedule for the task.

Six Steps for Project Planning and Implementation

Almost everyone makes a plan for a future event at one time or another: in your private life, or in your work, where it can be a major part of your job or just one of a number of aspects of the job.

Planning and scheduling is about using resources effectively. Producing a schedule is a useful way of establishing the most suitable solution for meeting a particular need or project.

Projects can come in all shapes and sizes, such as:

✔ A major construction job (for example, a bridge, road, tunnel)

✔ Managing the merger of two companies

✔ A company relocation

✔ A product launch

✔ Arranging a conference or event

✔ Carrying out a major staff recruitment campaign

✔ Designing and building a new product

Whatever the differences in the size and complexity of a project, the general approach to planning and implementing the project is fairly consistent, as the following steps show:

1. **Define the objective and target date for completion.**

2. **Identify all associated tasks and resources required.**

3. **Put the tasks into an appropriate sequence.**

4. **Estimate time required for each task with start and finish times.**

5. **Carry out tasks in sequence (or in parallel if appropriate).**

6. **Review progress against the plan at each stage of the project and revise if necessary.**

Note that Steps 1 to 4 have to be completed before the project actually begins as they're integral to the project planning process, whereas Steps 5 to 6 are to do with implementing the plan and happen as soon as the project is under way.

Not every task or activity that you'll be assigned in a job warrants being called a project, but there are likely to be many occasions when you'll still need to use the skills involved in project planning, if you are to ensure a successful outcome.

Common Competencies Being Assessed

Your performance is assessed against a set of competencies linked to the activity. (For more about competencies take a look at Chapter 2.) The most common competencies you're likely to meet in a planning and scheduling exercise are the following, together with a definition of each competency:

✔ **Planning and Organising:** Ability to establish efficiently an appropriate course of action for self and/or others to accomplish a goal.

✔ **Problem Analysis:** Effectiveness in identifying problems, seeking pertinent data, recognising important information and identifying possible causes of problems.

✔ **Judgement:** Ability to evaluate data and courses of action and to reach logical decisions. Adopts an unbiased, rational approach.

✔ **Attention to Detail:** Total task accomplishment through concern for all areas involved, no matter how small.

In a planning and scheduling exercise you need to show the assessor your ability for planning and organising and to do so successfully, you also need to demonstrate your skills in analysing problems, exercising sound judgement and attending to detail.

Applying problem analysis to your project helps you to understand the facts, spot relationships in the data, and recognise
potential problems that can arise when implementing the
plan. You then need to exercise your judgement to identify
possible solutions, weigh up the different options, including
costs and benefits, so that you can make an informed choice.
You also need to show attention to detail to make sure that
none of the minor aspects of the task are overlooked. If you
can harness all these skills you're likely to produce a well-
thought-out plan that can be carried out successfully.

Behaving Effectively

You can do a number of useful things to make sure that your
approach to a planning and scheduling exercise increases the
likelihood of a successful outcome.

Following the rules

As with any Assessment Centre exercise – read the instructions carefully. But this is critical when it comes to planning
and scheduling exercises, because as the saying goes: 'the
devil is in the detail'. The instructions make it very clear
about what you can and can't do, providing you with some
clearly defined boundaries. Although you may feel that the
rules restrict your options when it comes to putting your plan
together, you mustn't be tempted to ignore them.

You may find it helpful to highlight key points in the brief with
a coloured pen, so that you don't overlook any complex
details when working on your plan. Highlighting the important
bits of the brief helps you in your planning, and also alerts the
assessor to the fact that you've noted key points in the text,
and you may well get credit for it, even if your plan isn't as
good as it might have been.

Recording your thoughts

In planning and scheduling exercises you're usually given a lot
of factual information (maybe four to eight pages of text) and
before you can start to structure your plan you need to read
and understand what is being said. As you get to grips with

the facts, note down any thoughts that come to you that may impact on your plan. This makes sure that you don't forget or overlook any significant information and allows the assessor to see how you came to your conclusions.

An assessor can only give you credit for what you're actually seen to be doing during the exercise. But like in some exams, in planning and scheduling exercises you're given credit for your workings out, even if the final result isn't accurate.

Reviewing your final solution

If you have time, check your final solution, to see if you can improve your plan in any way, and to make sure that you haven't overlooked a key instruction. If you find that you've made a mistake then try to put it right in the time you've got left. This may involve revising your plan, or if time allows, creating a completely new version. Don't be afraid to ask for a new template or diary for a fresh attempt, if you need to.

Avoiding Ineffective Behaviours

A few things can go wrong when tackling a planning and scheduling exercise, as with any other Assessment Centre exercise. Here are a couple of common pitfalls to watch out for and to avoid.

Creating confusion

If you finish your plan, then think of ways it can be improved and then produce a second version, make it absolutely clear which version of your plan is your final version. Handing in both versions won't do any harm, as this shows you had the time to review and revise your final solution. But you won't impress the assessors if they think you aren't sure which is best, and they have to work it out for you. So make sure you label your number-one choice boldly and clearly.

Overlooking dependencies

You need to make sure your plan lists the various activities in the right sequence, and the biggest mistake you can make is to schedule an activity in advance of something that the activity depends upon. For example, if your project is to make a cup of tea, then the steps are:

1. Boil the kettle

2. Put the tea bag in the cup

3. Add boiling water

4. Add milk

5. Let the tea bag brew for a short time

6. Remove the tea bag

Now it's obvious you can't do Step 5 before Steps 2 and 3, but unfortunately such dependencies in a planning and scheduling exercise aren't always as clear as this, particularly if the project is elaborate and complex.

When describing the actions in your project that need to be taken step by step, ask yourself: 'Are there any steps that need to happen before this one?'

Preparing for Action

Performing well in planning and scheduling exercises is all about being able to analyse a set of information relating to a situation and preparing a structured, sequential plan to achieve a specified objective. With this requirement in mind, this section covers some things you can do before and during the Assessment Centre to help you successfully achieve this aim.

Before the Assessment Centre

If you know you're going to be facing a planning and scheduling exercise, then you may find it helpful to prepare yourself by doing some research and practising producing a project plan.

Obviously, simply reading this chapter is a step in the right direction. You need to pay particular attention to the information in the sections 'Behaving Effectively' and 'Avoiding Ineffective Behaviours'. Beyond this, you can do the things outlined in the following sections to get yourself geared up for your planning and scheduling exercise.

Reading up on project planning

You can find countless references to project planning on the Internet, and loads of books on project management or time management, giving you a lot of tips on how to produce an effective project plan. Almost any book on the subject will do – the basic principles of good project planning are very straightforward.

Don't be put off by some of the project management terminology, such as 'critical path analysis' (CPA), or 'project evaluation review technique' (PERT). And don't be misled into thinking you need the planning skills of a military genius such as Field Marshall Montgomery to cope with the challenge, when all you really need is to follow a series of logical steps to ensure you produce a well-thought-out plan.

Many large, complex projects can look very daunting but remember that even the biggest projects are really just a series of small ones, as is well illustrated by the question: 'How do you eat an elephant?' Answer: 'One bite at a time!'

Practising producing a project plan

Fortunately you have many opportunities for practising producing a project plan, in both your work and personal life. For example, at work you may have been given the task of writing an important report, reorganising some aspect of your department, or analysing an internal system or process. At home you may be planning an exotic holiday, arranging a big 21st birthday party, or even planning to move house.

Take one of these projects and give yourself 30 to 60 minutes (based on how long you think you're going to be given on the Assessment Centre) to work through the first four steps of the project planning and implementation process described in the earlier section 'Six Steps for Project Planning and Implementation'. Note that steps 5 and 6 of the process aren't part of the planning and scheduling exercise on the Assessment Centre but of course in real life you need to carry them out to finish your project successfully!

During the Assessment Centre

Because a planning and scheduling exercise isn't an interactive exercise, you're not likely to be under as much pressure as in some of the other Assessment Centre exercises where you're working with a role-player or doing a group activity. However, if you're one of those people who suffer from exam nerves then you may find a planning and scheduling exercise quite challenging. Apart from being well prepared through having practised this type of task (as suggested in the previous section), make sure you do the following during the Assessment Centre:

- ✔ Read the instructions carefully and note all relevant details, as explained in the earlier sections 'Following the rules' and 'Recording your thoughts.'

- ✔ Make a rough plan of the amount of time you're going to spend on each part of the task and monitor your progress to make sure that you've enough time to do each step.

- ✔ Create a logically structured, step-by-step plan. See the earlier section 'Overlooking dependencies' for details on what a logical plan looks like.

- ✔ Go over your first attempt at the project plan and ask yourself if it can be improved? Go to the earlier section 'Reviewing your final solution' for finding out how to revise your plan.

- ✔ Stay calm, don't allow yourself to get into a panic – remember the 'elephant': Just take things one bite at a time!

If you follow the above advice and the other suggestions made throughout this chapter, then you should be as well prepared as you can be to produce a peak performance on a planning and scheduling exercise.

Chapter 10

Managing In-Basket or Inbox Exercises

● ●

In This Chapter

▶ Recognising in-basket and inbox exercises

▶ Looking into your in-basket or inbox

▶ Multitasking effectively

● ●

*W*hat image springs to mind when you hear the expression 'Up to your eyeballs'? Are you picturing yourself sitting at your desk snowed under a pile of work, and wondering where to start? The chances are that you're familiar with this situation. But what is it that makes it easy for some people to rise to the challenge while others are left struggling?

Candidates can find themselves facing this same challenge when they're asked to take part in an in-basket or inbox exercise (sometimes also called an in-tray exercise). Although the intention isn't to intimidate, an in-basket or inbox exercise can have that effect. The thinking behind an in-basket or inbox exercise is to measure your ability to manage a stretching workload, embracing a wide range of tasks; this is better known as multitasking.

In this chapter we explain the differences between an in-basket and an inbox exercise and then tell you how to go about the exercise in the best possible way to help you get that target job.

In-Basket or Inbox?

In-basket or inbox exercises are often used on an Assessment Centre and are especially suited to candidates who will be required to work alone. The exercises are popular because you get the opportunity for some hands-on experience of tackling typical issues for that target job. But what is the difference between an in-basket and an inbox exercise?

- ✔ **In-basket:** The in-basket exercise is a paper-based exercise. This is the traditional format of this type of exercise and simulates office-based working practices before the widespread use of computers.

- ✔ **Inbox:** The inbox exercise is a computer-based exercise, recognising that most businesses and organisations use computers for carrying out their operations and for communicating by email.

The exercises are designed to reflect everyday life in the workplace. To start the exercise your desk is piled high, (or your inbox is full) with items demanding your attention: a customer complaint, requests for information, your opinions around internal policies and procedures, a staffing problem, and so on. In an in-basket exercise these items can take the form of memos, notes, letters or reports and vary in length and detail. In an inbox exercise these items can take the form of emails, notes, letters or reports and also vary in length and detail. However, in an inbox exercise you may also receive 'fly-in' emails – these are emails that aren't in your inbox when you start the exercise, but instead they fly in at some point during the exercise.

Most in-basket and inbox exercises leave it to you to decide 'how to action' each of the items on your desk or on the computer screen: for example, welcoming a new client by writing a letter, arranging a meeting, or delegating the issue to somebody else.

The following example shows a brief for an in-basket exercise.

Objective

This exercise is designed to give participants an opportunity to develop skills in personal organisation and management. The media are a fictitious 'in-basket' and subsequent performance evaluation. Feedback is usually by a colleague/senior manager within the client organisation.

Instructions for the Participant

After an initial briefing you will work privately on the in-basket exercise.

The Situation

For the next 1.5 hours you are to assume the role of Simon Dainton who has been made acting General Manager of 'Organic R Us' Foods Ltd. The appointment follows the shock announcement that Alex Dryden, the previous General Manager, has been taken seriously ill and they are unsure when he might return.

Today is Sunday 1 December. Your appointment has coincided with the annual Corporate Strategy Meeting that is to commence this evening in Glasgow. Your attendance at this meeting is imperative, and it is due to last for the whole of the coming week. You have gone into the office today to ensure that all runs smoothly in your absence. This is the first chance that you have had to take stock of the matters arising at 'Organic R Us' Foods. It is now 1 p.m. and you must leave the office by 2:30 p.m. in order to catch your flight to Glasgow in time for the Managing Director's opening address. While at the meeting there will not be any opportunity to contact staff at 'Organic R Us' Foods.

The Company

'Organic R Us' Foods Ltd is part of the Johnson-Frederick Group which also includes The Farmers Fayre and Chocalicious confectionary and sweets. 'Organic R Us' Foods specialise in organic produce and supporting local farms. The products are sold primarily through retail outlets, although business through 'trade outlets' (hotels, cafes and company canteens for example) is increasing.

The majority of the Company's retail outlets are small chains which also deal with Farmers Fayre and Chocalicious products too.

The In-Basket

The material in your In-basket is as left by Alex Dryden earlier in the week, with some additions from Lisa Jones, the secretary.

Write the action to be taken either on each item or clip a note (stationery provided) to the relevant item.

You can write memos, notes, letters, plan meetings, make decisions, request information and so on.

As you will not be back in the office until Monday 9 December and are not contactable in the interim, you must make sure your instructions for each of the items are clear. You should also ensure you leave the in-basket in the state you expect Lisa to find it when she comes into the office on Monday 2 December.

If this was an example brief for an inbox exercise then the context could still apply but you'd be asked to take different actions when responding. For example you wouldn't be expected to 'clip a note' to the relevant item but you would be able to attach a document to your response email. Note that the exercise doesn't set any specific tasks. However, some in-basket and inbox exercises might ask you to complete certain tasks such as:

- ✔ **Assign a priority to each item such as High/Medium/Low**

- ✔ **Provide a summary of the issues in items 2, 5 and 6**

- ✔ **Make a clear decision for items 3, 4 and 7**

When you're doing the in-basket or inbox exercise you need to know how you set about deciding which items to mark high, medium or low priority. Go to the section 'Setting priorities with a matrix' later in this chapter to find out how to prioritise your in-basket or inbox items.

In-basket and inbox exercises often vary according to the number of items you're dealing with and the time you're given for the task. Some exercises can have 10 items and last for an hour, other exercises can have 15 to 20 items and last one and a half to two hours respectively. However, the size and scope of the in-basket or inbox exercise should match the target job, and you have to bear in mind that the higher the level of job you're applying for, the longer and more complex the exercise is likely to be.

Tackling the Task Before You

You need to use your time wisely in an in-basket or inbox exercise and that means deciding on your approach quickly, leaving the majority of your time to tackle the items. Following are some key tips to help you decide on an appropriate approach.

Setting priorities with a matrix

You're given a fixed amount of time to deal with the items in your in-basket or inbox. This compels you to think about prioritising, so that you start by tackling the most urgent and important items first. To do this you need to find a way of identifying the items that are important or urgent. One way of doing this is by using a priority-setting matrix. Figure 10-1 shows what a priority-setting matrix looks like.

Each item in your exercise will contain information about when it was sent, who it was sent by and the issue in the item. You must use this information to judge how important it is on a scale of 1 to 10 in terms of urgency and importance. You can then use the matrix in Figure 10-1 to see what might be an appropriate approach to tackling that item.

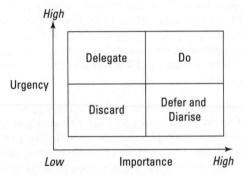

Figure 10-1: A priority-setting matrix.

Having reviewed each item against the priority-setting matrix you then:

- ✔ **Do** the most important and urgent items first; deciding how you're going to respond to each item.

- ✔ **Defer** those items that are important but not so urgent; deciding for how long the items can be put on one side and recording the items in your diary, to remind you when to take action on them (you can do this later in the exercise).

  ✔ **Delegate** the urgent but less important items to someone else; deciding who that person is (assuming that the level of urgency doesn't demand an immediate response) and give clear instructions to the person you've nominated.

  ✔ **Discard** (or ignore for now) those items that aren't important or urgent; often junk mail or items that have been copied just for information.

Tackling paper-based in-basket exercises

When you're tackling an in-basket exercise you're physically sorting through paper-based items. A paper-based in-basket exercise can offer some advantages over the inbox exercise format, as we explain in the next section.

Seeing the bigger picture

One of the most useful aspects of an in-basket exercise is that you can instantly see the size of your task. You can see how many pieces of paper there are in front of you and how much reading and writing you're going to be doing. This visual overview can help you quickly get to grips with how you're going to be organising your time. Also, when working through the items, it's encouraging to see the pile getting smaller and smaller as you go.

Laying out the paper-based items in front of you allows you to quickly get an impression of who you are, what you do, the type of correspondence you receive, and the likely importance of each item. Although some of these advantages can also apply to an inbox exercise, it's more difficult in an inbox exercise to view all the information at the same time and you have to rely on your memory for a lot of the detail of the items that are out of view.

Sorting items into themes

Another advantage of dealing with paper-based items is that you can physically sort through the items and put them into themes. For example, you can sort items according to the type of response they need, such as letter, memo or phone call; or who the item is from; or the subject of the item. Sorting the items into common themes means that you don't waste valuable time hunting for items that need to be dealt with soon and all the relevant information you need is in one place.

Dealing with electronic inbox exercises

When you're doing an inbox exercise, you're sitting in front of a computer or at a laptop and the items that you're dealing with are presented in email format. An inbox exercise is made to look and feel as if you're using Microsoft Outlook, Yahoo or Google mail. Inbox exercises are designed to simulate the increase of technology and the tendency to communicate via email. Figure 10-2 shows you a screenshot of an inbox exercise.

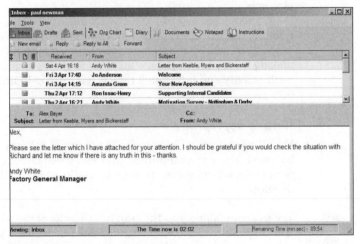

Figure 10-2: Screenshot of an inbox exercise.

Adapting to 'fly-in' emails

'Fly-in' emails (see the earlier section in this chapter 'In-Basket or Inbox?') are a feature of inbox exercises. You could find that you get one fly-in email 20 minutes after starting the exercise and then another one with only 10 minutes of the exercise left. This causes a change to your current circumstances, as you have new information to read, digest and respond to. Fly-in emails are a good way of assessing your ability to cope with new information and also how you go about rearranging, prioritising and deciding how to respond to the new item in your inbox.

Using the functions on offer

Computers offer some great benefits that cut out a lot of the effort attached to writing letters, memos, and so on; such as the ability to copy and paste text, accessing and updating addresses, and being able to send/forward the same information to several people in one go.

There are a number of email functions that can speed up the processes in an inbox exercise, such as sorting emails into groups and prioritising them using tools such as coloured flagging systems, or being able to paperclip items together. Highlighting items in your inbox can help you to decide which emails to tackle first, and the paperclips remind you to look at the content of previous emails. Having easy access to this information can help you when responding to a later email, or vice versa.

Keeping track of the time is important in both in-basket and inbox exercises. Computers usually have an inbuilt clock making it easy to check how much time you're spending on each activity and how much time is left for you to finish the exercise.

Writing appropriately

Your first contact with a new colleague or client may well be by email. The way you phrase your email can impact on the recipient, and determine how your relationship is going to develop.

Try to avoid falling into the trap of using the same sort of 'email-speak' you use with friends, when addressing your manager, or someone that you don't know personally, in the context of an inbox exercise. Emails can be very disarming, leading you to express yourself in a way that you're unlikely to do if you're meeting someone face to face. For example, it's easy to forget to use appropriate and courteous greetings such as 'Dear . . .' or 'Hi . . .,' or closing your email with 'Best wishes' or 'Kind regards.' You're unlikely to open or close a letter without such courtesies, so why ignore them in emails?

Also try to avoid being too blunt in an email simply to speed up the process. Phrasing things bluntly may cause offence and you may come across as being aggressive or pushy. Don't forget to consider the impact your email can have on the recipient.

Common Competencies Being Assessed

Your performance is assessed against a set of competencies linked to the activity. (For more about competencies take a look at Chapter 2.) The most common competencies you're likely to meet in an in-basket or inbox exercise are the following, together with a definition of each competency:

> ✔ **Planning and Organising:** Ability to establish efficiently an appropriate course of action for self and/or others to accomplish a goal.

> ✔ **Delegation:** Effective allocation of decision making and other responsibilities to the appropriate person, inside or outside the team.

> ✔ **Organisational Sensitivity:** Capacity to perceive the impact and implications of decisions and activities on other parts of the organisation.

> ✔ **Judgement:** Ability to evaluate data and courses of action and to reach logical decisions. Adopts an unbiased, rational approach.

> ✔ **Problem Analysis:** Effectiveness in identifying problems, seeking pertinent data, recognising important information and identifying possible causes of problems.

> ✔ **Decisiveness:** Readiness to make decisions, state opinions, take action or commit oneself.

> ✔ **Strategic Perspective:** Takes account of a wide range of longer-term issues, opportunities and contingencies. Identifies the means of implementing plans in line with the vision and direction.

> ✔ **Initiative:** Actively influencing events rather than passively accepting, sees opportunities and acts on them. Originates action.

Not all eight competencies in the list are necessarily going to appear during the in-basket or inbox exercise. However, the assessors are likely to be assessing at least some of them or competencies like them.

The competencies you display during in-basket and inbox exercises relate to *how* you tackle the task (the 'Process'), while other competencies being assessed are about *what* you do with the different items in your in-basket or inbox (the 'Content'). Table 10-1 shows you what competencies are being assessed when looking at your approach to process and content in an in-basket or inbox exercise.

Table 10-1	Typical Competencies Assessed in Your Approach to In-Basket and Inbox Exercises
Approach	**Competencies**
Process ('How')	Planning and Organising
Delegation	
Content ('What')	Problem Analysis
Judgement	
Decisiveness	
Organisational Sensitivity	
Strategic Perspective	
Initiative	

Behaving Effectively

You can adopt a number of behaviours to help you to tackle this type of exercise swiftly and effectively. Read on!

Looking before you leap

Don't be tempted to charge into the in-basket or inbox exercise and start replying to letters or emails the minute the task begins. Although an in-basket or inbox exercise can be challenging and every second counts, if you go rushing into the exercise you miss the opportunity of getting an overview of what the items are about, and which items you need to tackle first. You may discover too late that the key item is the one at the bottom of the pile or list! Give yourself enough time at the beginning of the exercise to grasp the following:

- ✔ Who you are in the organisation
- ✔ What your job role is
- ✔ Who you report to
- ✔ Who makes up your team and what they do
- ✔ What the items are about and which ones need responding to first
- ✔ How long you have to finish the exercise

There are likely to be other points that you need to take into account but the key to the whole exercise is getting an overview of what's in your in-basket or inbox and how best to approach the task in hand. Always remember 'less haste, more speed!'

Making things stand out

Making sure that you've read and understood all the items in your in-basket or inbox – you know how and who to respond to, and in which order – is hugely important for finishing the exercise successfully.

To heighten your chances of success start the exercise by reading the items in turn and highlighting the key information in each item. You can also make notes about who needs to know this information and how you're going to respond.

Checking priorities

In-basket and inbox exercises are all about multitasking. You have to decide which items you're going tackle first and how long you're going to spend on each item. To do this successfully you need to prioritise each item; see the earlier section 'Tackling the Task Before You'. You can use the priority-setting matrix given in Figure 10-1 or simply mark each item as being high, medium or low priority. Also take into account when you received the item. For example, how long the item has been in your in-basket or inbox without any action being taken. If none of the items in your in-basket or inbox is urgent, you may decide to spend time taking action on the older items. There's no single right way of setting priorities – it's a matter of choice. Once you've decided which items need prioritising, you can label them (for example H, M, L) or in the case of an inbox exercise, ask the computer to flag items according to your level of priority.

Whatever your approach to setting priorities, you need to recognise that priorities can and do change. As you progress in the exercise it's likely that certain items you initially gave high priority to have to be reassessed in the light of the content of later items. For example, you've earmarked your reply to your manager about financial information for a Board meeting as high priority. However, when reading a later item from a customer detailing a serious complaint, you decide that this new item takes higher priority, and that responding to your line manager is now medium priority.

Giving a new priority to items as you go along allows you to make informed decisions about which items to tackle and in what order. This helps you to make sure that by the end of the exercise you've responded to all the high-priority items and most, if not all, of the medium-priority items. Only then tackle low-priority items if time allows.

Looking for links

In-basket and inbox exercises often include items that are linked in some way. For example, a request for a meeting in one item may clash with an appointment in another item. Alternatively, information that you read in one item may be important in helping you to respond to a later item.

Reading all the items before you start responding to them helps you to pick up on links between items. Looking for links saves time and duplication of effort. Linking later items to earlier items and getting an up-to-the-minute picture of the situation means you're not sending out unnecessary and incomplete replies.

Tuning into your audience

Items in your in-basket or inbox can come from anyone in the organisation, from your line manager, colleagues and members of your team. The way you respond and the level of detail in your response can vary according to the person you're writing to or emailing. You're likely to respond to a colleague in less formal language than the language you would use when responding to a more senior person in the organisation, such as your line manager or a director of the company. Equally, responding to a member of your team or someone in a junior position may mean giving a more detailed or supportive response, such as guidance on handling the task in hand.

Think about how your boss (or previous boss) speaks to you when delegating tasks and what sort of language she uses? Does your boss speak in different ways to members of your team or a senior colleague?

If this happens to be the first job you're applying for, then think about when you were at university, college or school and how you spoke to friends or fellow students versus the way you addressed a person in authority, such as the principal or one of the lecturers.

Using all available resources

To help you carry out the in-basket or inbox exercise, you're often given additional resources, which are detailed in your brief. Here are some examples of the types of resources available to you:

- ✔ **A diary.** This is for planning your time. It allows you to set up and attend meetings, monitor your availability and note deadlines for completing tasks. A diary is useful for checking if events or meetings clash and have to be rearranged. In some in-basket and inbox exercises you may also be given access to other peoples' diaries, allowing you to arrange meetings for other people and checking when they're free.

- ✔ **An organisational chart.** This helps you to understand the set-up of the organisation and 'who is who' in each department. This is particularly useful when you're delegating, responding to or forwarding items to other people in the organisation, making it easy to check out the person's status, job title and responsibilities within the organisation.

✔ **Information from a predecessor.** If the target job is a managerial position you may also be provided with information from the person previously in the job. This information can include short descriptions of each team member, detailing job title, working style, and perceived strengths and weaknesses. This information can help you when delegating tasks, as you can match the task to the right person with the appropriate skills and experience, or to a person who is ready for professional development.

Watching the clock

Keeping track of how you're using your time is vital to finishing the in-basket or inbox exercise successfully. You need to make a rough plan of how you're going to divide your time between the various activities. Given that time is a key factor in an in-basket or inbox exercise, you need to keep an eye on the clock so that you can adjust your plan as time goes on. For example, you may start your 60-minute exercise with the following plan:

✔ **10 minutes** to read and digest the information

✔ **25 minutes** to tackle the four high-priority items

✔ **15 minutes** to tackle the four medium-priority items

✔ **5 minutes** to tackle the two low-priority items

✔ **5 minutes** to revisit earlier items

If during the exercise you find yourself spending 35 minutes on the high-priority items, you have to then adjust the amount of time you're spending on the other items. For example, 12 minutes on the medium-priority items, 3 minutes on the low-priority items, and you have to abandon the idea of revisiting the earlier items. You may also decide not to respond to the low-priority items to ensure you have enough time to respond appropriately to the other items.

Always check the time at frequent intervals. This allows you to finish as many items as possible at the right level of detail and keeping within your timescale.

Avoiding Ineffective Behaviours

Thorough planning is essential to doing a successful in-basket or inbox exercise. However, you need to avoid certain behaviours if you want to ensure your plan is implemented effectively. Here are some classic mistakes to steer clear of.

Being superficial

Try to avoid falling into the trap of responding to each item very briefly in the hope that you're going to be able to respond to all the items in your in-basket or inbox. The chances are that by adopting this approach you're only going to supply limited detail in your replies, which may not always be appropriate. Remember, the assessor will mark you on what you've actually done and not on what you intended to do. Take a look at the following:

> 'I'll email John next week to give him the necessary information about whether to go ahead with the outlined proposal.'

The assessor is likely to give the sender minimal credit for this response, whereas she's likely to view the following more favourably:

> 'Hi John, Thanks for the information that you sent me yesterday. I have read the outlined proposal and think that this looks like a sound approach. I agree with you that this matter ought to be progressed soon. If you have any queries about how to do so then please get in touch, otherwise please keep me posted on how the proposal is going. Regards, Alex'

The second response has a lot more content and shows the assessor that you've responded in time to meet John's request, that you believe the approach is a good one, that you're offering John further help, and that you wish to be kept informed on the progress of the proposal. The assessor is able to give you credit for these actions as appropriate.

Being overly detailed

While you shouldn't be too brief in your responses you also need to take care that you're not being too detailed. It's essential when responding to the items in your in-basket or inbox that you balance your responses according to the time you have available. When you're responding to high-priority items it's likely that your response is going to be quite detailed. However, try to avoid spending so much time on high-priority items that you jeopardise your chances of getting credit for responses to the medium and low-priority items.

To try and determine what the right balance should be, think about how you would behave within your normal working environment if you knew you had a prescribed amount of time to get a number of tasks done. You'd probably start by deciding which are the most important tasks. Next you might complete these to a level that allows the respondent to progress them in your absence, allowing you to check up on the progress on your return. You might then turn your attention to the next most important tasks and ensure that you complete these to a sufficient level until your return, or you could delegate these tasks to another qualified individual who has availability. Finally, you'd tackle the remaining tasks, perhaps by sending a holding response, informing the relevant people that you'll deal with this on your return. For one or two tasks you may decide that these can easily be left until your return and therefore you leave them without any response at all.

Here's an example of an overly detailed response:

> *'Hi John, I'm taking over from Dan. It would be nice to get together sometime so I can better understand your role and responsibilities. I propose that we do this face to face and give ourselves enough time to get properly acquainted. Thanks for the information that you sent me yesterday. I've read the outlined proposal thoroughly. I would like to know more information about the background of this client to better understand the culture and priorities of the organisation so that I can suggest some tweaks to the proposal. However, I do think that this approach is going to work as it is. I suggest that you progress this matter; maybe you could email the client first to set up a meeting where we can both be present to outline this approach? It's just a thought. Anyway, feel free to action this in my absence and then send me a summary of what is happening in the meantime, so that we can discuss the matter on my return. Shall we get together on the 20th? Alternatively, if that isn't any good, why don't we do the 21st or 23rd? Looking forward to meeting you in person. Regards, Alex'*

Although you may think that the sender's response is too wordy and contains some information that isn't relevant, the key is to respond to the item appropriately. How you respond depends on the importance of the content, to you and the organisation, and the urgency of the matter. For example, in the previous text, you could propose a date and ask the recipient to suggest a suitable date and to liaise with your secretary rather than suggesting several different dates.

Never-ending paper shuffling

Although never-ending paper shuffling sounds like a topic clearly aimed at the paper-based in-basket exercise, avoiding 'paper shuffling' is an activity that applies equally well to the computerised inbox exercise.

Don't keep picking up an item: reading it, thinking what action you're going to take on it, putting it down – only to go through the whole process again a short time later. Dithering is going to cost you time and only serves to distract you and upset your train of thought. Aim to be decisive in your task and get yourself into the habit of 'picking up' each item no more than two or three times at the most. By doing this you're likely to get through the pile of items much more quickly, as well as forcing yourself to take a more critical and considered approach to dealing with each item.

Gearing Yourself Up for the Exercise

In the following sections we talk about ways to prepare yourself for an in-basket or inbox exercise to ensure you perform at your best.

Before the Assessment Centre

In-basket and inbox exercises are hard to prepare for, because it's nigh on impossible to know ahead of the exercise what the content of the items in your in-basket or inbox are going to be, what behaviours you need to show, and what behaviours are likely to be assessed. Your best way of preparing for the exercise is by practising prioritising (see the earlier section 'Setting priorities with a matrix') and also practising your written communication skills (see 'Writing appropriately', earlier in this chapter).

If you know you're going to be doing an inbox exercise then it's a good idea to spend some time sharpening your computer skills and getting fully acquainted with the many options in the email system you're using. It's unlikely that the inbox exercise is going to be using an identical system to Microsoft Outlook, for example, but the more familiar you are with how your system works, the easier you're going to make it for yourself on the day. To find out more about electronic inbox exercises, see 'Dealing with electronic inbox exercises' earlier in this chapter.

Multitasking is the 'name of the game' when it comes to in-basket and inbox exercises. To prepare yourself for the exercise, think back to an occasion when you had to do a multitude of tasks at the same time, such as organising a big wedding. It's vital for the success of the event that you get all the details right and contact all the right people in time for the big day. If some things got missed, for example you forgot that some of your in-laws' family are vegetarians, then think about what you could have done differently to make sure that the wedding turned out to be an absolutely perfect day!

During the Assessment Centre

You may possibly be given time before your inbox exercise begins to get some practice in using the electronic system. Such sessions are usually quite short, maybe 10 to 20 minutes, but it's important to take up the opportunity if it's on offer. Make sure you use this time wisely by looking at the important features of the system and asking any questions that you may have about how the system works.

Yes, we've said it before but it's worth saying again: It's crucial that before launching headlong into responding to the items in your in-basket or inbox, you spend time digesting the information and deciding on the right approach to tackling the task. A few minutes spent doing this is likely to make the difference between succeeding at an in-basket or inbox exercise, or not.

Part III

Excelling at Non-Exercise Assessment Centre Activities

'Before we start on the psychometric tests, I hope you're not feeling too nervous.'

In this part . . .

*A*ssessment Centres invariably incorporate other activities in addition to the simulation exercises covered in Part II, so in this part we describe some of those additional elements.

Interviews and psychometric tests are almost certainly the most commonly used assessment tools, so in each case we describe how they might feature within an Assessment Centre. We cover their different formats and what you need to do to excel at them.

Assessment Centres often include one or more sessions in which you get an opportunity to introduce yourself, to hear about the organisation, or to receive some feedback relating to your performance. We describe the sorts of things that can arise and provide some guidance about dealing with them.

Chapter 11

Responding Effectively in Interviews

In This Chapter

▶ Appreciating the different types and techniques of interviews

▶ Knowing how to tackle competency based interviews

▶ Preparing yourself for the interview

*N*early everyone at some time or other in life faces an interview, and it is without doubt the most common assessment method used in job selection – featuring 99 per cent of the time. One of the reasons for the popularity of the interview is that it provides an excellent opportunity for the person carrying out the interview to get to know you and check that your face fits.

Assessment Centres often include an interview alongside one or more of the simulation exercises described in Chapters 4 to 10. The interview differs from these simulation exercises because this is your chance to talk about the 'real' you and for the assessor/interviewer to explore certain aspects of your background and experience.

In this chapter you'll find out how the interview process works, both from the perspective of the person being interviewed and from the person(s) conducting the interview. We talk about the different types of interview you can meet on an Assessment Centre, and the different approaches an interviewer can use when carrying out an interview. We also tell you about the highly popular competency-based interview and how it works. Finally, we provide you with some advice on how to behave during the interview and suggest how you can prepare in advance to give you the self-confidence to maximise your chances of success.

Staffing the Interview

The style of an interview can vary based on a number of factors but one that can have a significant impact is the number of people involved in conducting the interview.

One-to-one interviews

The majority of interviews are conducted on a one-to-one basis and this is what you're most likely to encounter on an Assessment Centre. The interviewer manages the process, so follow his lead. All good interviewers recognise that their task is to learn all about you and this is made easier if they can help you to relax by creating an environment with minimal stress. So an effective interviewer will tell you what's going to happen and will guide you at each stage of the interview, enabling you to concentrate on answering his questions and building your relationship with him.

In a one-to-one interview, your relationship with the interviewer is especially important for a successful outcome. Try to get on the interviewer's wavelength. You can do this by responding to his body language and manner of speaking. For example, some interviewers display a more formal, 'matter-of-fact' style and they're likely to prefer you to respond in a similar way. Other interviewers may adopt a more informal and casual style, showing warmth and friendliness, and are happy for you to do the same.

An important difference between one-to-one interviews and other types of interviews, is that the person conducting the interview shoulders the entire responsibility for managing the process. The success of the interview can depend as much on the interviewer as on the person being interviewed, as the interviewer takes charge of:

 ✔ Opening the interview

 ✔ Putting you at ease

 ✔ Asking questions

 ✔ Listening to your answers

 ✔ Making notes

> ✔ Asking follow-up questions
>
> ✔ Ensuring all intended areas are covered
>
> ✔ Explaining the next steps
>
> ✔ Closing the interview

Now we recognise that it's difficult to expect you to have any sympathy for the interviewer – especially when you're the one on the receiving end of a grilling, but it may help you to keep in mind that you aren't the only one under pressure!

By helping the interviewer do his job, you're likely to be help-ing your own cause. You can both find yourselves responding to each other positively and moving onwards with the inter-view confidently and purposefully.

Two-to-one interviews

Occasionally you find yourself facing two interviewers rather than one. In a two-to-one interview nothing much changes from your point of view, apart from the fact that you may need to develop a relationship with both interviewers, depending on how they conduct the session.

There are a number of reasons why two interviewers might be working together. First, it may be so that one interviewer takes notes while the other concentrates on asking the ques-tions and thinking about your answers and suitable follow-up questions. Second, the two interviewers may have agreed beforehand that each covers certain aspects of the interview and they're both going to be playing a part in asking ques-tions. For example, you may find that a line manager is paired up with an HR manager, with the line manager asking ques-tions about your technical skills and the HR manager explor-ing your people skills. Third, it may be the policy of the organisation of having two interviewers 'double-marking' the interview, to cut out any likelihood of bias or prejudice occur-ring and making sure the interview is carried out fairly and objectively.

Whatever the reason for using a two-to-one approach, you need to make sure that you're interacting with both interview-ers, by maintaining eye contact, particularly when they're each asking you questions in turn and engaging you in discussion.

Panel interviews

Panel interviews are becoming less and less common and rarely take place on Assessment Centres, mainly because they're difficult to organise and require more staff. However, panel interviews are still quite popular in the public sector, and for some senior roles in the private sector.

If by chance you're invited to a panel interview, you can expect to be facing a row of three to eight people. The chairperson usually introduces himself and may ask the other panel members to do the same. It's usual for the chairperson, who is managing the interview, to invite the different panel members to put questions to the person being interviewed.

You may find a panel interview quite intimidating. So here are few helpful tips to keep you feeling calm and collected:

- ✔ Take a deep breath before going into the interview room.

- ✔ Be sure to smile and say 'Good morning/afternoon'.

- ✔ Follow the chairperson's lead on how to behave – you may be greeted with a handshake. And if there are only a few people on the panel you may feel it's fine to shake hands with them as well, but this is less likely if the panel is larger.

- ✔ Listen carefully if and when the panel members introduce themselves. You may pick up who are the more influential panel members, but don't discount anyone.

- ✔ Make eye contact with the person asking the question but try to look around and engage with the other panel members – try giving the impression that you find them all interesting, not knowing who holds the power!

- ✔ Be prepared for questions coming at you from all sides; so don't get flustered, take your time to think about your answer and remember, although a brief pause may seem like it's lasting forever it's really only a few seconds.

- ✔ Hang onto your poise and dignity and try to show an air of confidence.

In general the behaviour you display in a panel interview shouldn't be any different from your behaviour in any other type of interview.

Panel interviews are more likely to contain people with little or no interview training who may ask questions which seem irrelevant. Answer all questions politely and try to provide them with evidence that you can do the job.

Taking the Structured Approach

Another key factor that has a bearing on how an interview is carried out is whether the interview uses a *structured* or *unstructured* approach.

You're unlikely to meet an unstructured interview on an Assessment Centre but it's worth giving you a brief explanation, because it's good to know! Unstructured doesn't mean disorganised or chaotic. It simply means that a structured and consistent process isn't used within the interview.

On an Assessment Centre the interview is more than likely to be structured, using a standardised and consistent approach. This ensures that each candidate is treated in exactly the same way and is interviewed honestly and fairly and free from prejudice or bias. Also the data from a structured interview can easily be integrated with the data collected from the highly structured assessment process used with the simulation exercises.

There are two different types of structured interview in general use, the *situational interview* and the *behavioural description interview*, with the behavioural description interview being the much more popular of the two.

You're unlikely to be told if the interview is structured or unstructured. In most cases you're only going to get an understanding about the type of interview being used, once the interview gets under way. It really isn't that important to know whether the interview is unstructured or structured, because your aim is to do as well as you can in the interview, regardless of the methodology being used. Your job during the interview is to respond to the questions clearly and confidently, with well-thought-through answers that show you at your very best.

Situational interviews

In a situational interview you're given a series of scenarios, each similar to the sorts of situations you can meet in the target job. For each scenario you're asked what 'would you do in that situation' and the interviewer notes down your answers, which are later marked by comparing your answers with a range of responses collected from people who are already doing that job.

Don't be surprised if the interviewer comes across as rather distant in a situational interview; this type of interview is naturally rather formal because of its regimented approach.

Situational interviews can feel a bit artificial because you're being asked to give answers to hypothetical questions in imaginary situations that you may never have experienced. Here's a typical example from a situational interview:

> *As sales director you've noticed a steady decline in the performance of one of your sales people over the last four months. You've already mentioned this to the sales manager but you haven't noticed any improvement in the situation; indeed things seem to be getting worse. What would you do in this situation?*

Given the wholly theoretical nature of the question, it's perfectly reasonable for your answer also to be theoretical and you have the opportunity of saying what you think you're likely to do in that situation, even though you've never actually done it!

Bring with you to the Assessment Centre a few prepared examples of how you're likely to handle certain situations that may come up in the target job. You can get some useful pointers about the job content from the original job description, or possibly from the job advertisement if you can get hold of it (refer to Chapter 3). You may also have been told ahead of the interview about the skills or competencies needed by the successful job holder, giving you a good idea of the sorts of situations that you're likely to meet in the actual job. For example, if 'teamwork' is mentioned, think of the sorts of scenarios that can occur while working in a team in the target job.

Behavioural description interviews

Behavioural description interviews (sometimes called behavioural event interviews), and best known as *competency based interviews* (CBIs), are unquestionably the most popular form of structured interview. The competency based interview is markedly different from the situational interview in that you're being asked to describe situations or events that you've actually experienced and you talk about how you handled those situations. A competency based interview is rooted in reality, in contrast to the highly theoretical situational interview.

On Assessment Centres, the competency based interview is the principal approach used in job interviewing, so we're going to focus on the competency based interview for the rest of this chapter.

Highlighting Competency Based Interviews

The competency based interview (CBI), as the name suggests, looks at how capable you are of doing a particular job in relation to what are called competencies. Competencies are the skills and behaviours that show how well you're performing in your job. In a competency based interview, the interviewer asks you to describe a job situation that you've actually experienced and then delves deeper, asking for more specific details.

If you've never experienced a competency based interview before, then it can seem rather strange the first time round. This is because a competency based interview is in sharp contrast to the more traditional interview where you've been used to describing your work experience in general terms and the interviewer isn't asking for a lot of detail. Indeed you may have been unwilling to talk a lot about yourself, for fear of sounding arrogant or being boring.

When you're in a competency based interview, be ready to go into specifics and don't be shy about talking about yourself rather than being lost within the team. Remember, although there is no 'I' in 'team', neither is there a 'we', but there *is* a 'me'!

The key principle behind competency based interviews is that past behaviour predicts future behaviour. Competency based interviews work on this theory, meaning how you behaved in your last job is a good indicator of the way you're going to behave in the target job, and a reliable way of testing your suitability for the post you're applying for. The interviewer asks you for specific examples about specific events, relevant to the knowledge, skills and abilities needed in the target job you're being assessed for. So get yourself ready to:

- ✔ **Provide specific detailed examples:** You need to go into specific details, as the interviewer wants to fully understand the examples you're describing. Avoid talking in vague generalities.

- ✔ **Provide relevant examples:** Try to give examples that are in a similar setting or as close as possible to situations you're likely to meet in the job for which you're being assessed. The closer the similarity, the more powerful the example is in showing your capability and suitability for the target job.

Competency based interviews follow a specific three-step process that we describe in the following sections. To see an example of the three-step process in action, take a look at the example in the later section 'Step 3: Describing what happened'.

Origins of the competency based interview

The idea of competency based interviewing was developed by industrial/occupational psychologists back in the 1970s in response to the need to merge interview data with the data collected from an Assessment Centre. Because Assessment Centres have always assessed candidates in relation to a set of competencies, it's necessary for an interview to be designed in such a way that it provides an output on the same basis.

To help you remember the three-step process, you can use either of the following acronyms:

- ✔ **STAR: S**ituation or **T**ask (Step 1), **A**ction (Step 2), **R**esult (Step 3).

- ✔ **CBI: C**ircumstances (Step 1), **B**ehaviour (Step 2), **I**mpact (Step 3)

Step 1: Describing the context/scenario

In a competency based interview, the first thing you're going to be asked to do is describe a specific situation or task from your past experience, which is relevant to an important aspect of the target job. The interviewer is looking for you to give a detailed description and it may help you to think of describing the situation as if you're telling a story: with a beginning, middle and end. This gives the interviewer the chance of understanding all the circumstances of the scenario you're describing. The type of question the interviewer asks is:

> *'Can you tell me about an occasion when you were given responsibility for planning a project?'*

Try to avoid talking in general or vague terms, as the interviewer is only going to ask you to be more specific.

When you're being asked this type of question, don't be afraid of taking a little time to think of a suitable example. The interviewer is going to prefer that you pause and think while gathering your thoughts, rather than feel compelled to give an instant response that comes out as a confusing ramble.

Step 2: Describing what you did

After describing the scenario (explained in the preceding section) the interviewer asks you to say what part you played in the situation.

Focusing on talking about what *you did* is important. You may have been working as part of a team but making the most of your contribution is vital in this situation. This is contrary to the fact that highlighting your ability to work as part of a team is generally encouraged – now is the time for telling the interviewer, 'this is what I did'. Make sure you're talking in the first person, especially when describing the part you played in the situation.

Don't be diffident or self-effacing – or let modesty or reserve hold you back. Be proud of your achievements, but do be careful about coming across as arrogant.

Step 3: Describing what happened

Finally, the interviewer asks you to explain what happened as a result of your actions, or 'what impact did your actions have on the situation', or 'what was the outcome?'

There are a number of possible aspects to this type of question. For example, you may be asked to place some quantifiable value on the outcome, such as 'what was the sale worth to the organisation?', or to provide some qualitative evidence such as 'how did other members of the team or other people in the organisation react to your decision?'. And you may also be asked, 'what did you learn from this situation?'.

Even if you feel you didn't handle the situation all that well at the time, you can still show the interviewer that you got something from the experience. This can be important, because the interviewer may be looking for evidence of your ability to bounce back and learn from difficult challenges or setbacks.

Here's an example of the three-step process used in a competency based interview.

> **Question:** Tell me about a difficult customer complaint that you've had to deal with.
>
> **Circumstances:** 'I took this call from an angry customer who was complaining about having to wait to speak to one of our customer service representatives for over 15 minutes. He was phoning to ask why he'd been charged £25 on his account for being £10 overdrawn for just one day. The customer was very abusive and shouted at me about our poor, slow service and wouldn't give me a chance to let me answer his questions.'

Action: 'I decided that I had to let him get things off his chest but I also knew that I had to let him know that I was listening to him, so I acknowledged his comments without trying to agree with him, by saying: 'I can understand how you're feeling sir', and 'I can appreciate that sir'. After a couple of minutes of ranting, he began to calm down, although he was still clearly angry at what he thought was an excessive penalty charge. I asked for his account details and just as I was accessing his account, our system went down. I explained to him what had happened and he became extremely annoyed again, complaining that he'd had to wait to be put through and now he wasn't able to get things sorted out. I apologised and said I would look into his problem and I promised to call him back as soon as possible to save him having to call us again. He reluctantly agreed. When our system came up again, I made it my top priority to look into his account and I found that he'd gone overdrawn like this on three previous occasions in the last 6 months and he'd been warned about a likely charge in future when he'd phoned to query penalty charges previously. I called him back and explained the situation and he started to get angry again, so I cut in and explained that as this problem was within my authority I was going to reimburse the charge to his account for the inconvenience he had experienced, but stressed that if this occurred again the charge would have to stand. I suggested that he may like to amend the dates of any outgoing direct debits where he could, to avoid the problem happening at this time of the month in the future.'

Result: 'The customer thanked me for being understanding and said he was going to take my advice about amending the dates of one or two of his direct debits to avoid this monthly problem. He complimented me on remembering to call him back and said that it was fortunate I had, because he'd seriously been thinking about switching his account, but my calling back had changed his mind.'

Common Competencies Being Assessed

Competency based interviews are suitable for assessing almost any competency, except specific aptitudes such as numerical reasoning ability and certain technical skills such as written communication. The most common competencies you're likely to meet during a competency based interview are the following, together with a definition of each competency.

- ✔ **Planning and Organising:** Ability to establish efficiently an appropriate course of action for self and/or others to accomplish a goal.

- ✔ **Leadership:** Motivates, enables and inspires others to succeed, utilising appropriate styles. Has a clear vision of what's required and acts as a positive role model.

- ✔ **Persuasive Oral Communication:** Ability to express ideas or facts in a clear and persuasive manner. Can convince others to own expressed point of view.

- ✔ **Problem Analysis:** Effectiveness in identifying problems, seeking pertinent data, recognising important information and identifying possible causes of problems.

- ✔ **Teamwork:** Willingness to participate as a full member of a team of which heis not necessarily leader; effective contributor even when team is working on something of no direct personal interest.

- ✔ **Commercial Awareness:** Ability to understand the key business issues that affect the profitability and growth of an enterprise; takes appropriate action to maximise success.

- ✔ **People Development:** Develops the skills and competencies of others through training, coaching and other development activities related to current and future roles.

- ✔ **Customer Service:** Exceeds customer expectations by displaying a total commitment to identifying and providing solutions of the highest possible standards aimed at addressing customer needs.

- ✔ **Strategic Perspective:** Takes account of a wide range of longer-term issues, opportunities and contingencies.

Identifies the means of implementing plans in line with the vision and direction.

✔ **Openness to Change:** Proactively supports change and effectively adapts own approach to suit changing circumstances or requirements.

✔ **Integrity:** Ability to maintain social, organisational and ethical norms in job-related activities.

✔ **Flexibility:** Ability to modify own behaviour, such as adopting a different style or approach to reach a goal.

✔ **Quality Standards:** Sets high goals or standards of performance for self, others and the organisation. Dissatisfied with average performance.

✔ **Initiative:** Actively influences events rather than passively accepting; sees opportunities and acts on them. Originates action.

✔ **Listening:** Ability to pick out important information in oral communication. Questioning and general reactions indicate 'active listening'.

✔ **Interpersonal Sensitivity:** Has an awareness of other people and environment and own impact on these. Actions indicate a consideration for the feelings and needs of others (but not to be confused with 'sympathy').

✔ **Impact:** Makes a good first impression on other people and maintains that impression over time.

✔ **Stress Tolerance:** Stability of performance under pressure and/or opposition. Makes controlled responses in stressful situations.

If you encounter a competency based interview, then it's quite likely that the interviewer(s) are going to be assessing about four to six competencies, mostly by questioning, but some by direct observation of how well you respond to the questions. For example, some of the competencies being assessed indicate your level of ability in relation to general skills, while others are focusing on more specialised skills. Other competencies the interviewer(s) may be looking out for are about your attitudes and values, which can be more difficult to observe in simulation exercises. Finally, as the interview is interactive, it will clearly provide direct evidence of some of your interpersonal skills. Table 11-1 shows how the competencies can be viewed within these four different categories.

Table 11-1	Typical Competencies Assessed by Category Groupings in a Competency Based Interview
Category	*Competencies*
General Skills	Planning and Organising Leadership Persuasive Oral Communication Problem Analysis Teamwork
Specialised Skills	Commercial Awareness People Development Customer Service Strategic Perspective
Attitudes and Values	Openness to Change Integrity Flexibility Quality Standards Initiative
Observed Behaviours	Persuasive Oral Communication Listening Interpersonal Sensitivity Impact Stress Tolerance

Behaving Effectively

Coming across well in the interview and making a positive impact is critical for a successful outcome. Your behaviour is going to be closely scrutinised by the interviewer(s) so here are a few tips for making you stand out.

Making a good first impression

As with all interviews, it's important that you make a good first impression. Research shows that interviewers can be strongly influenced by your behaviour in those first few minutes. Try paying careful attention to the following tips:

⍽ Make sure you're dressed appropriately, taking into account the organisation's dress code. If you're in any doubt about the dress code, err on the side of caution and to go for a smart dress or suit that goes with the formality of the occasion.

✔ Introduce yourself confidently. Give your name clearly, accompanied by a firm handshake, and a smile.

✔ Wait to be offered a chair before sitting down. This gives the interviewer a chance to show who's in charge of the interview. But when you're sitting down, sit up straight and avoid slouching or hunching.

✔ Respond to small talk from the interviewer, smile and keep eye contact, all of which help to build rapport and show you're feeling confident.

✔ Be prepared for the interview to move on to the serious stuff. Try to stay calm and relaxed and behave naturally.

Try not to let those first precious minutes of the interview overpower you. Use them as your first opportunity for showing the interviewer that you're a confident and capable person. This is your big chance to take centre stage and you need to grab it with both hands!

Listening attentively

Listening carefully in an interview is plain common sense. In a competency based interview it's especially important. With some competency based interviews you're told in advance what competencies are going to be assessed during the interview, and you may have the interviewer saying 'I'd now like to move onto Planning and Organising . . .'

At other times you may have no idea what competencies are going to be assessed in the interview. In this case you need to listen very carefully to how the question is worded, and particularly how any follow-up questions are expressed, to try to work out what competencies the interviewer is examining. This is important because once you know what the interviewer is looking for you can give answers showing your capabilities in that area. Assuming your answers are reasonable and relevant to the target job, you're likely to get good marks, rather than being marked down for failing to provide good evidence of that particular competency, even though this may be due to a lack of clear focus in the interviewer's questioning.

Getting on the right track

Having carried out many competency based interviews, we've noticed that the sooner the person being interviewed gets on the right track by giving specific detailed examples of job experiences, the easier the interview becomes for both the interviewee and the interviewer. In contrast, if you fail to start off on the right foot, you're going to be like the golfer who's developed a bad swing – finding it more difficult to correct your approach.

Although it's fair to say that it's the interviewer's job to help you get on the right track, unfortunately some interviewers aren't as good at this as they ought to be, so you may need to help yourself. Make sure you're going into enough detail and you're talking about specific examples of things you've done in the past, relating to the competencies being assessed.

Always respond to the interviewer's questions by giving examples that are similar to the sorts of situations you may meet in the target job. Try to give examples that are significant rather than trivial; work-related examples are preferable to any relating to your private life. Also make sure you're focusing on recent examples, as these are better indicators of your current ability and future potential. All these factors are likely to give more weight to your examples.

Putting your failings positively

Sometimes the interviewer asks questions about your failings. If this happens your best line is to admit to any failings and to try putting a positive spin on them. For example, you may face a question such as: 'We all occasionally fail to convince someone to accept a point of view we feel strongly about. Tell me about the last time this happened to you.'

The key thing to notice about the question is that the first part of the question makes it very difficult, if not impossible, for you to suggest that you've never experienced such a failure. So the trick here is to make sure that your answer shows that you did all that could reasonably be expected in the situation you're describing, and that your failure was due to circumstances beyond your control. You can also put yourself in a strong position if you can explain how you learned from the situation and applied that learning to a subsequent situation where you were successful.

If you adopt a positive approach, then hopefully the interviewer is going to heed the words of Alexander Pope when evaluating your answer: 'To err is human, to forgive, divine.'

Avoiding Ineffective Behaviours

Performing well in interviews doesn't solely rely on you displaying effective behaviours; it also requires that you avoid ineffective behaviours that can damage your prospects of achieving a successful outcome.

Sitting in painful silence

Some of the questions you're asked may leave you struggling to come up with a suitable answer, perhaps because you can't think of a good example. If this happens you don't just sit there in silence, causing the interviewer to be unsure as to what's going on. Did you hear the question? Don't you understand it? Are you trying to think of an example? Or worst of all, have you got nothing worth saying?

No fire in the belly!

We were once asked to sit in on a panel interview to appoint someone into a senior finance position, and one particular candidate stood out for all the wrong reasons. He was sitting in a slouched position with one arm draped over the back of the chair, displaying an unbuttoned jacket and a loose tie hanging around his neck, and casually waving his other arm around while speaking in a sleepy and relaxed tone. Despite giving good answers to the questions and confirming his strong technical ability, the panel members doubted if anything would ever make him show the drive and determination that they expected from someone in that job. Needless to say the candidate was rejected!

The candidate just didn't seem to have any fight in him. He looked as if he'd switched off his 'fight or flight response'. This is when the body produces adrenalin in order to heighten the ability to perform under pressure or adversity.

If you find you're struggling to think of a good example, try responding with something like: 'That's a tough question, let me see if I can think of a suitable example.' Usually the interviewer is going to be sufficiently sympathetic to agree to this and say: 'Yes it is, so do take a few moments to think of an example.' This allows the interviewer to know what's happening and it buys you some valuable thinking time.

Clearly you mustn't overdo or take advantage of this request by taking too long to think of an answer (20 to 30 seconds at the most). Pausing after every question is likely to make the interviewer anxious about the time that's been given for the interview and may not be able get in all the questions he needs to ask.

Appearing too laid-back

Don't allow yourself to appear so calm and relaxed that you come across as being laid-back. Looking just too relaxed can send out a message that you're a bit casual and the interviewer may decide that you don't really care and nothing is likely to stir you into action.

Talking hypothetically

Giving textbook answers to questions isn't going to impress the interviewer. Don't talk about what you *would do* in a situation or describe the textbook theory of how a situation ought to be handled. Avoid giving theoretical answers at all costs. If you do, all it shows the person interviewing you is that you're a good talker!

Remember, in a competency based interview the interviewer is looking for specific examples of what you've actually done in the past, so that he can determine your ability to do the job in relation to certain competencies.

Telling blatant lies

Yes, everyone is guilty of that little white lie from time to time or embellishing the truth, but telling blatant lies is quite another thing. Apart from the fact that being untruthful is unethical, never lie during the interview, as not only are you deceiving the interviewer but you're unlikely to be doing yourself any favours. First, if it's later discovered that you told a blatant lie during a job selection interview, you may be dismissed. Second, if you're appointed to the job because you said you had certain skills and abilities and this was found to be untrue, then you're going to be under severe pressure to perform and your lack of ability may prove to be embarrassing, even leading to being demoted or dismissed.

Be aware that one of the reasons for the popularity of competency based interviews is that it's very difficult to make up specific examples of previous job experience without running the risk of being found out, because it's the interviewer's job to probe deeper and deeper to get a true picture of your capabilities.

Preparing for Action

Performing well in interviews is all about having a clear set of objectives and a suitable plan, coupled with the skills to execute the plan and getting yourself in the right frame of mind to achieve it. Once you have this focus you can do certain things before and during the Assessment Centre to support this aim.

Before the Assessment Centre

Try to find out before your Assessment Centre if your interview is going to be a structured interview, and to be more exact, a competency based interview.

Knowing the competencies in advance

If you know you're having a competency based interview you've very likely to have been told what competencies are going to be assessed. If not, do ask so that you can do the necessary preparation for your interview. If you're unable to find out then try working out from any information you have about the job, such as a job description or the job advertisement, what competencies are going to be looked for by the interviewer.

Fortunately, this isn't rocket science. All you need to do is to pick out references to the sorts of skill-based situations you're going to need in the target job. For example, the advertisement says: 'The successful applicant needs to be able to work in a project team and be able to build relationships with various stakeholders. You also need to be able to convince potential clients of the value of our solutions.' From this brief description you spot competencies like: Teamwork, Persuasive Oral Communication, Commercial Awareness and relationship building (possibly project leadership).

Preparing behavioural examples

Once you know what competencies are likely to be assessed, set about preparing two or three different examples showing your typical behaviours in those competencies and how your behaviour serves to demonstrate your capability for the target job.

Structure each behavioural example following the three-step process we describe in the section 'Highlighting Competency Based Interviews' earlier in this chapter. Your interview is going to cover no more than four to six competencies in a 40 to 60 minute timeframe (approximately 10 to 15 minutes for each competency). If you don't know for certain what competencies the interview is going to cover, you're going to need to prepare a few more examples to make sure you're fully prepared.

Sometimes thinking about an example in detail can reveal evidence of your capability in relation to several different competencies. If appropriate, you can use the same example in response to a different question, although you need to try to use different examples to show your breadth of experience.

Preparing for tough questions

Take a look at Rob Yeung's excellent book *Answering Tough Interview Questions For Dummies* (Wiley). It gives you lots of tips on how to handle hundreds of tricky questions and goes into much more practical detail about the interview process than we have time for in this chapter.

During the Assessment Centre

After following all the advice we give you in this chapter you're going to be well prepared for your interview. Make sure you know exactly where the Assessment Centre is and allow yourself plenty of time to get there. Here are one or two more general tips:

- ✔ Don't be late, stick to the timings.

- ✔ Take all the documents you need to the interview: CV, lists of questions you may want to ask, a portfolio of your work, and pen and notepaper.

- ✔ Switch off your mobile phone so it doesn't ring during the interview!

Keep smiling and looking confident, and make sure you enjoy being the centre of attention; after all, it's your big day.

Chapter 12

Perfecting Your Approach to Psychometric Tests

In This Chapter

▶ Understanding what psychometric tests measure

▶ Distinguishing different types of psychometric tests

▶ Familiarising yourself with test questions

*P*sychometric tests have been around in one form or another for centuries and in basic terms they're standardised attempts at understanding what goes on in your head compared with others. In the context of the world of work and the job market, psychometric tests are a very useful way of matching the individual to the job and to the organisation. For this reason they're often used alongside business simulation exercises on an Assessment Centre.

In this chapter we describe some of the different types of psychometric tests and explain what the tests are measuring. We show you what the questions look like by giving you plenty of examples, so that when you're faced with your test you thoroughly understand what's expected of you and how best to answer the questions – making sure you come out of the test with top marks.

Studying Common Psychometric Tests

Psychometric tests are designed to find out what makes you tick and in a job assessment are used for measuring:

- **Your ability:** Whether you can do the job.
- **Your personality:** How you're going to do the job.
- **Your motivation:** Whether you want to do the job.

Imagine that you're applying for a job as a fund manager in a large hospital where you're continually being asked to make tough decisions. Psychometric tests are a useful tool for finding out your suitability for the job: whether you have the *ability* to make tough decisions, whether you have the right *personality* for making tough decisions involving other people, and whether you've got the *motivation* to cope with making tough decisions on a daily basis.

When taking part in a psychometric test, your performance is compared with the performance of other candidates taking the same test, and the results are used to assess your 'fit' for the job in question. For this reason it's important to make sure that the psychometric tests are administered, interpreted and scored in a fair and consistent way, as we explain in the following sections.

In the later sections of this chapter we go into more detail about what the different types of tests measure and give you example questions, so that you can get to grips with the different types of tests and the reasoning behind them. For a detailed overview of psychometric tests and for lots of practice questions, try Liam Healy's excellent book *Psychometric Tests For Dummies* (Wiley).

Administration

To make sure that everything is fair and square, psychometric tests are usually carried out at a fixed location, under supervised examination conditions, that is, during an Assessment Centre. This ensures a standardised and consistent approach, allowing the candidates taking part an equal chance. All candidates are given the same amount of time and have the same opportunity for asking questions such as whether the test is timed or what they should do if they can't answer a question – is it better to guess a response or not?

With the introduction of the Internet, many organisations and test providers have started using online tests. This reduces the time, effort and cost of getting all the candidates together in one location at the same time. Online psychometric testing is especially popular in large countries such as the US, where distance between candidates can be vast.

Unfortunately the lack of invigilation allows candidates to cheat when sitting online tests – by asking someone else to take the test for them. This has led many organisations to take counter measures, such as asking candidates to resit a particular test at a later stage of the recruitment process, perhaps during an Assessment Centre. This gives the person managing the recruitment process the opportunity for comparing the first and second set of scores, and alerting them to anything suspicious.

Interpretation and scoring

Your test scores are compared to what's known as a *norm group*. Test publishers often produce a series of norm groups, each with a different profile, covering demographic and work-related characteristics, such as career or job role, industry sector, educational level, ethnicity, age range and gender. The recruitment agency or employer picks out an appropriate norm group for the job you're applying for, and your answers are looked at in comparison to the norm group.

When you're given your test score, you're likely to be graded from A to E or given a percentile (a percentage of the norm group who scored below you). This tells you where your result lies in comparison to the norm group average – if you're higher than average, average, or below average.

Performing at Ability Tests

Ability tests measure your powers of reasoning: that is, what you're capable of – in other words, what you can do intellectually, which is indicative of your intelligence.

There are two forms of intelligence: crystallised and fluid. *Crystallised intelligence* is acquired through experience of situations and gaining new knowledge and skills. *Fluid intelligence* is linked to your reasoning abilities. Ability tests seek to tap into separate parts of your intelligence, such as verbal, numerical, abstract, mechanical and spatial.

Ability tests aren't the same as IQ tests. IQ tests measure your intelligence using a formula related to your age. IQ tests are primarily used for measuring a child's intellectual ability for educational purposes and are rarely used for measuring adult intellect in a work setting.

The ability test is designed to match the job you're applying for. For example, if you're applying to be a data analyst, your future employer is going to want to know how well you work with numbers, and may only ask you to sit a numerical ability test. However, other jobs may require you to show ability in a range of areas and so you're asked to do a number of different ability tests.

In an ability test you're presented with a set of questions, each question having one right and several wrong answers. You can get two types of ability tests: speed and power.

- ✓ **Speed tests** ask you to complete a large number of questions, all at the same level of difficulty, in a fixed timescale. For example, answering 60 questions in 30 minutes under pressure. Speed tests are for examining the accuracy of your answers.

- ✓ **Power tests** look at the quality of your answers and therefore ask a smaller number of questions that get progressively harder and more complex. Power tests can sometimes be untimed or allow you enough time to answer all the questions, say 15 questions in 60 minutes.

Some tests set a maximum time to complete the test and in some tests the timeframe is given for guidance only. Ask your administrator whether the timeframe of your test is fixed or unfixed.

In the following sections we describe the four most common types of ability tests and give you examples of the sorts of questions they include.

Verbal ability tests

Verbal ability tests look at your ability to comprehend language and use it to communicate with others. Good communication skills are essential in most jobs and it's highly likely that you're going to come across a verbal ability test at least once in your working life.

There are several types of verbal ability tests, each looking at different aspects of communication: your spelling, grammar, comprehension and critical thinking ability. Some jobs need you to be good at spelling and grammar, for example a secretary, while other jobs like a chief executive need you to be good at verbal reasoning.

Verbal ability tests are for examining your communication skills, so the questions are set to test the skills that you use on a daily basis. Figure 12-1 shows a sample of verbal ability test questions.

If you get stuck during a spelling test, practise writing the word out to see how you would spell it if you were including it in a letter or email. This can help, because often your gut feeling is right first time round. If the test questions ask you to 'fill the gap' or replace one of the existing words, try saying the sentence in your head, each time replacing the word with one of the answers. This helps you to 'hear' which response sounds right.

You can improve your verbal ability slowly over time by reading widely but make sure that your reading matter is well written and of a good standard. For spelling and grammar specifically, the Internet is a good source for tips on improving and testing your abilities in these areas. Try these:

- ✔ www.askoxford.com/betterwriting/classic errors/?view=uk

- ✔ www.webgrammar.com/

- ✔ http://owl.english.purdue.edu/handouts/ grammar/

Verbal Ability Test

Spelling

1. Circle the correct spelling from the list of words:

a. bizzarre

b. bizzare

c. bizarre

d. none of them

2. Identify the incorrectly spelt word in the sentence:

The restaurant was immeadiately closed after the terrible tidings.

a. restaurant   b. immeadiately   c. terrible   d. tidings.

Grammar

3. Write the statement below in a grammatically correct form, or if already correct, write 'correct'.

I would of caught it but I didn't see it.

....

Comprehension

4. Choose the answer that makes two separate phrases from the words below.

Reading . . . Worm

a. earth   b. hole   c. book   d. glasses

5. Circle the missing word from the list below.

The price of a luxury car. . . to stay about the same.

a. always   b. never   c. tends   d. more or less

6. Which answer means the same as the word below?

Inane

a. weird   b. senseless   c. boring   d. strange

Verbal Test

7. Based on the following text, decide whether the statements below are True (T), False (F) or Impossible to say (I).

With one foot grounded in time-honoured traditions and the other fervently striding into the entrepreneurial e-age, India embraces diversity as passionately as few other countries on earth can.

Boasting a population of one billion people – and growing – India is as vast as it is crowded and as sublime as it is squalid. It's a country of contrast, with plains that are flat and featureless and mountains that are towering and spectacular and the people are as easy going as they are tenacious. Perhaps the one thing that encapsulates India is that it is a place to expect the unexpected.

a. India has varied landscapes. ( )

b. India embraces diversity more than other countries do. ( )

c. India has plenty of space for its growing population. ( )

Answers:

1. c   2. b   3. I would have caught it but I didn't see it.

4. c   5. c   6. b   7. a: T   b :I   c: F

Figure 12-1: A verbal ability test examining your communication skills.

Numerical ability tests

Numerical ability tests are used for measuring your ability to answer mathematical questions correctly. Nearly all jobs need you to be able to work out simple sums, such as addition or division. However, there are a range of jobs where you need more complex numerical skills such as accountancy or banking and where you have to manage financial information like turnover, profit and profit margin. Figure 12-2 shows the kind of questions you're likely to be asked in a numerical ability test.

As with verbal ability tests, you can get two types of numerical ability test: speed and power. See the earlier section 'Performing at Ability Tests' for checking out the two types of tests.

Honing your numerical ability skills is slightly easier to work on than improving your verbal ability because a lot of practice material is readily available to help you. The Internet is a good place to start looking for suitable practice exercises.

A good way of practising your mathematical skills is to do a few old GCSE maths papers. GCSE maths papers have all the types of questions that you can expect to face when sitting a numerical ability test, such as percentages, ratios, algebra, addition, multiplication, subtraction, division and probability. Before attempting the papers you may want to read about basic mathematical principles to make sure you understand how to answer these types of questions. You can find information on basic principles on the Internet (www.bbc.co.uk/skillwise) or alternatively, get hold of a copy of Mark Zegarelli's book *Basic Math & Pre-Algebra For Dummies* (Wiley).

When you're doing a numerical ability test, focus on the questions you can do, and don't agonise over the questions that you don't understand or can't work out. Also remember to focus on the numbers – rather than the text!

Abstract ability tests

Abstract ability tests look at your ability to solve problems creatively. This type of test usually comes in the form of pictorial questions (see the example questions in Figure 12-3) which require you to see links or relationships between objects, where the relationship isn't immediately apparent.

Numerical Ability Test

1. 3 x 3 x 3 = ?
a.27   b. 9   c. 3   d. 12

2. 178 ÷ 2 = ?
a.84   b. 86   c. 89   d. 91

3. (136 ÷ 2) x 4 = ?
a.268   b. 276   c. 270   d. 272

4. −25–30 –25?
a. −80   b. −60   c. 80   d. 60

5. 2 x 1 x ? x 1 = 2
a. 1   b. 2   c. 3   d. 4

Numerical Critical Reasoning Test
Below is a set of actual sales won compared to sales targets. Each staff member is set an appropriate sales target at the beginning of the year. Commission is then paid to each staff member according to the income above target.

	Salary	Commission	Target	Actual
Sarah	£22,000	10%	£150,000	£120,000
Jamie	£20,000	20%	£120,000	£150,000
Michelle	£18,000	10%	£110,000	£140,000
Anna	£15,000	10%	£100,000	£50,000
Kate	£12,000	20%	£100,000	£100,000

1. Who is the worst performing seller?
a. Jamie   b. Anna   c. Sarah   d. Kate

2. What would Michelle's sales need to be in order to earn a bonus of £5,000?
a. £100,000   b. £120,000   c. £140,000   d. £160,000

3. How many people are going to get a bonus this year?
a. 1   b. 2   c. 3   d. 4

Numerical Ability:
1. a   **2.** c   **3.** d   **4.** a   **5.** a

Numerical Reasoning
1. b   **2.** d   **3.** b

Figure 12-2: Sample questions in a numerical ability test.

Abstract ability tests make it difficult for you to draw on past experiences to help you in answering the questions. In many ways therefore an abstract ability test is a sure-fire way of measuring your intellect, because you have to rely on your raw analytical reasoning ability.

Try looking for patterns and how the pattern links to the 'odd one out' or 'the next one in the sequence'. Remember this is a visual exercise so take into account the following aspects of the test when trying to answer questions testing your abstract abilities:

- ✔ Shape
- ✔ Size
- ✔ Colour
- ✔ Number
- ✔ Position

Practice makes perfect. To perform well in this type of test you need to get some practice in. Do a few practice papers and then check your answers (check out www.practice tests.co.uk/Reasoning4.html). It's important that you understand why you do or do not have the right answer, because the more you understand how patterns occur, the better you're going to be at solving problems.

Mechanical and spatial ability tests

You're more likely to meet mechanical and spatial ability tests if you're applying for a job as an engineer, in production, manufacturing or design. Mechanical tests look at physical and mechanical properties of objects such as mass, volume, weight, heat, light and speed. Spatial tests look at your ability to visualise objects and to show how the objects work. Figure 12-4 shows you some specimen mechanical and spatial ability test questions.

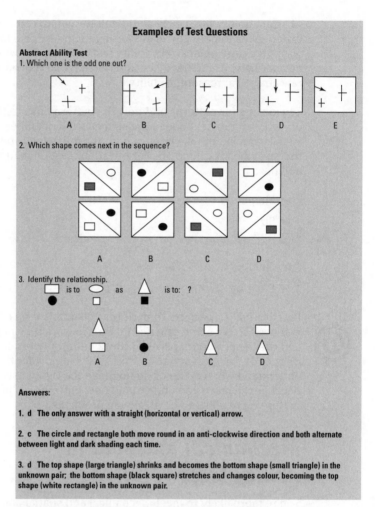

Figure 12-3: Examples of abstract ability test questions.

The types of questions you get in a mechanical and spatial ability test are very similar to topics you covered physics or design and technology lessons at school. As you may remember from such lessons, some people seem to have a natural ability for these subjects whereas others find this type of thinking much harder. If you're looking to improve your mechanical and spatial ability skills you're going to need to put in quite a bit of effort!

Practising can definitely help develop your skills. For example, physics GCSE papers can help those of you sitting a mechanical test. Get hold of a copy of *Psychometric Tests For Dummies* by Liam Healy for heaps of practice questions.

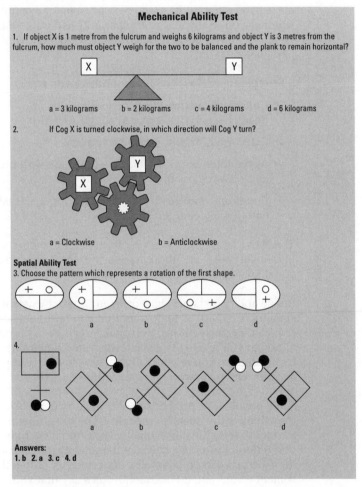

Figure 12-4: Examples of mechanical and spatial ability test questions.

Answering Personality Questionnaires

The type of person you are governs how you apply your natural abilities in everyday situations. Although psychologists are still hotly debating what 'personality' is exactly and what makes you different from the next person, for example whether you're shy and retiring or jolly and outgoing, psychologists have, nevertheless, managed to identify five main personality traits:

- ✔ **Openness:** How involving of others you are.

- ✔ **Conscientiousness:** How concerned you are with meeting deadlines and delivering to a high standard.

- ✔ **Extroversion:** How outgoing you are.

- ✔ **Agreeableness:** How concerned you are with being liked and pleasing people.

- ✔ **Emotional stability:** How you react under stressful or emotionally charged situations.

These five characteristics vary from person to person and personality tests are about measuring which characteristics you display compared with other people.

Unlike ability tests, no right or wrong answer exists in a personality test, and it's important that you try to get across the real you. Because of this, personality tests aren't timed and although you're usually given a suggested timeframe, about 30 to 40 minutes, you're generally allowed to take as much time as you want in answering the questions.

Some people fall into the trap of trying to put across what they think is the 'ideal' personality. The big problem here is that there *is* no ideal personality type. You need to be aware that different jobs suit different personalities. When applying for a job you can do yourself a disservice by pretending to be someone you're not. For example, let's say that you've succeeded in getting a job as a client representative, which requires an outgoing person to interact and get along with clients on a daily basis. However, as you're naturally shy and retiring, it doesn't take you long to find out that you're not really enjoying the job that much. This is because you're having to act in a way that isn't you.

To avoid any tendency to think about the 'right' answer – go with your gut instinct. Read the question and answer instinctively. This way your answer shows your 'natural' behaviour in that situation.

There are two different ways of viewing your personality; one is according to *type* and the other looks at your *traits*:

- ✔ **Type questionnaires** get you to decide whether you're one type or another type and they force fit you into a particular category, for example, whether you're extrovert or introvert.

- ✔ **Trait questionnaires** allow for much greater variation. For example, a trait questionnaire asks you to what degree you're introvert or extrovert.

The sample questions in Figure 12-5 illustrate both types of personality test questions.

Type Personality Test
1. I challenge people if I think I'm right.
a. Agree   b. Disagree

2. Circle the word that describes you best.
a. Relaxed   b. Tense   c. Anxious   d. Calm

Trait Personality Test
1. I always want to be invited to parties.
a. Strongly agree   b. Agree   c. Don't know   d. Disagree   e. Strongly disagree

2. I happily take risks.
a. Strongly agree   b. Agree   c. Don't know   d. Disagree   e. Strongly disagree

Figure 12-5: Examples of type and trait questions in a personality test.

Some personality questionnaires also include questions measuring your motivational behaviour. For example, a traditional personality questionnaire asks you about your typical behaviour when working in a team, but motivational questions look to find out to what degree you enjoy or dislike having to work in a team. Motivational questions ask whether you 'need', 'want' or 'like' certain work aspects.

Questions about how motivated you are also help to show your suitability for the job. If you're applying for a job where you spend 80 per cent of your time working in a group and you're not a natural teamworker, then this is unlikely to be the job for you. You may be better off in a job where group work takes up only 50 per cent of your time. Finding a job that fits means job satisfaction – an important reason for being in the right job, especially when you're going to be spending a large chunk of your life working.

Handling Situational Judgement Tests

Showing good judgement is an essential skill for performing successfully in the majority of jobs. A number of decisions that employees make often require them to use their own judgement when dealing with complex business issues. For example, you're required to deal with a challenging client, overcome unexpected setbacks, or manage conflicting priorities. Situational judgement tests (SJTs) are a valuable way of assessing an individual's capacity for making judgements and recently we've seen a marked increase in the popularity of SJTs being used alongside traditional psychometric tests.

In a situational judgement test you're given a number of business scenarios simulating the target job. Each question presents you with some background information about a particular scenario, followed by a number of different actions that you can take in response to the scenario. You then have to decide on the effectiveness of the responses. Most SJTs ask you to rate the effectiveness of each action, or to rank the actions in order of effectiveness. You can see two examples of situational judgement test scenarios in Figure 12-6.

Situational Judgement Test Scenarios

Question 1
You've recently attended an internal training course delivered by your manager. While talking to the other participants after the course, several of them are critical of how your manager delivered the course. Your manager is unaware of this feedback and you feel that the course was delivered adequately.

Rate the effectiveness of each of the actions below on the following scale:

1 = Very ineffective, 2 = Ineffective, 3 = Effective, 4 = Very effective.

a. Tell your manager that you personally think the course went well and don't mention the feedback from the other participants.
b. Tell the other participants that they should speak to your manager about how they feel about the course if they feel strongly about it.
c. Tell your manager about the feedback from the other participants, without mentioning anyone by name.
d. Don't mention any feedback about the course to your manager.

Question 2
A new initiative has recently been introduced. Customers are given comment cards allowing them to give feedback on services they're receiving. A number of customers have commented on how long it's taking for the comment cards to be dealt with. You're fully aware that customers aren't happy with the slowness of the response, especially at peak times.

Rate the effectiveness of each of the actions below on the following scale:

1 = Very ineffective, 2 = Ineffective, 3 = Effective, 4 = Very effective.

a. Arrange a customer meeting to get a clearer idea of what they want to be improved and sort out solutions.
b. Find out which team members are good at delivering customer service and make sure that they're the staff responsible for dealing with customer feedback.
c. Tell your team members that the feedback is slow because you're understaffed and encourage them to be quicker when dealing with customers, supported by suitable training as needed.
d. Arrange a team meeting and tell staff about the customer feedback, asking your staff if they have any helpful suggestions.

Figure 12-6: Examples of situational judgement test scenarios.

When preparing for a situational judgement test try thinking back to any difficult or complex situations you've had to deal with in the past. How did you deal with the issues and what could you have done differently? Ask family, friends or colleagues about challenging situations they've had to face and how they responded to the situation and what was the outcome. Giving some thought to the consequences attached to different actions is going to help you in preparing for a situational judgement test.

Scenarios in a situational judgement test can vary in length, with most tests including 20 to 30 short scenarios (two to four sentences in length). Other SJTs may have more lengthy scenarios, where more in-depth information about the situation is given. After completing the test your answers are compared with a set of ideal answers and you're scored on this basis. In some cases SJTs may also ask you to indicate how likely you would be to take each action, which will demonstrate how you would typically behave in this situation.

Situational judgement tests can take the form of a written test, or you may be asked to do an online test, or in some cases a video-based SJT, in which the scenarios unfold in front of you.

Completing 360° Feedback Questionnaires

A 360° feedback questionnaire, as the name suggests, gives a rounded picture of how others view you, by bringing together a series of answers from other people's perspectives. If you're taking part in a 360° feedback process, you're asked to fill in a standard questionnaire about yourself and to nominate a number of other people to fill in the questionnaire with details about you. It's usual to nominate your line manager, team members, direct reports and a few of your customers or suppliers.

Typically 360° questionnaires are used in a developmental context to give performance-related feedback from a range of sources about the individual concerned. Sometimes an organisation may ask an employee to fill in a 360° questionnaire highlighting the employee's strengths and where any professional development needs lie.

The 360° approach can also be used for carrying out an assessment for a target job, for example when someone is applying for a promotion. However, organisations need to take into account and to be wary of the quality of the data in a 360° questionnaire, because sometimes data can be biased, prejudiced or, worse still, malicious deceit. There's greater scope for having control in a 360° exercise if all the respondents are known to the organisation, so that the organisation can explain to those taking part why they're taking this particular approach.

It's important that your answers in a 360° questionnaire are completely honest and that you nominate people who know you and have a thorough understanding of how you work and ideally are working with you currently. The data you get out of the 360° questionnaire can be a rich source of feedback that hopefully complements any other tests or exercises you're doing. You can use the data in the 360° questionnaire for building up a true picture of where your strengths lie and where you may need to make improvements.

Figure 12-7 shows you a portion of a 360° questionnaire.

Example of 360° Items

Please assign a rating to each item using the following 1–5 scale:

1 = Strongly agree
2 = Agree
3 = Neither agree or disagree
4 = Disagree
5 = Strongly disagree

Items
1. Willing to get to the heart of issues through careful probing and listening.
2. Demonstrates integrity by honouring commitments and promises.
3. Shares ideas and best practices with other departments and individuals.
4. Invests time and energy in self-development and growth of others.
5. Delivers what is promised on time.

Figure 12-7: Types of questions found in a 360° questionnaire.

Psyching Yourself Up for the Test

Feeling anxious isn't going to help you perform at your best so it's important that you try to minimise any anxiety in advance of the day. Your best way of doing this is to be well prepared.

Before the day

Make sure that you know what types of psychometric tests you're going to be doing and what the tests are measuring. Knowing the answer to this question helps you to focus your preparation accordingly. Once you're clear on the type of test and what's being measured, you can help yourself by doing some practice questions. This helps in reducing any anxiety you may be feeling when sitting the tests for real.

For tests like verbal ability or numerical ability tests, which you can prepare for in advance, start by sourcing appropriate information from the Internet (try visiting test publishers' websites, such as www.shl.com or www.opp.eu.com), or books that give you lots of practice questions.

Personality tests don't have a right or wrong answer. Try to answer the questions instinctively, making sure that you're getting across the real you.

On the day

You're well prepared and now all you need to do is make sure you're at your best to perform. Have something to eat to fuel your brain, and drink plenty of water to keep yourself hydrated, making you feel wide awake and alert.

Too much coffee isn't going to keep you alert; instead you experience a buzz, followed by a lethargic slump – and you don't want that to happen in the middle of your test!

Also make sure you let the administrator know of any last-minute problems you may have, such as forgetting your glasses/watch or if you're suddenly feeling unwell.

Chapter 13

Tackling Other Activities

- -

In This Chapter

▶ Starting off confidently

▶ Distinguishing yourself in other assessment activities

▶ Making the most of information sessions coming your way

- -

*A*ssessment Centres are highly structured and methodi-
cally organised events. As well as the exercises and
activities we describe in Chapters 4 to 12, yet more goes on at
an Assessment Centre that we want to tell you about. In this
chapter we focus on those activities that feature on the
Assessment Centre but that aren't generally part of your
assessment – but which if well handled, will enable you to
deliver the 'complete performance'.

We start by emphasising how important it is to get off to a
quick start, and what you can do to boost your confidence
from the outset, giving you the momentum to propel yourself
forward and carry you through the event.

Some of the activities we describe may be completely new to
you, so we give you some useful tips on ways of tackling the
activities and making them work for you.

Finally, we offer you guidance on how to make the most of any
information sessions that organisations build into the event,
and the best behaviours to display in order to stand out,
while at the same time creating a promising impression.

Getting Off to a Quick Start

Feeling nervous before a big event is quite natural, so don't be surprised if this is how you're feeling before the Assessment Centre begins. Indeed a few nerves can be a good thing, keeping your adrenalin flowing in anticipation of performing at your peak. A total absence of nerves can be a sign of complacency or the fact that you aren't ready for action. However, if you're feeling nervous, you'll probably find that once the Assessment Centre begins you quickly become engaged in the event and your nervousness disappears.

Making a positive impact and starting as you mean to go on is the name of the game. As any top athlete or sports star can tell you, maintaining your momentum after a good start is a lot easier than recovering from a poor start. So make sure you're ready to perform from the minute you walk through the door.

Controlling your nerves upon arrival

When you arrive at the Assessment Centre you need to check in at reception, where you're shown or directed to the main room for the Assessment Centre. It's likely that you'll be greeted by one of the administrators and offered some refreshments before the Assessment Centre begins and you may be introduced to some of the other participants or left to introduce yourselves.

This period of anticipation is when you're likely to be most nervous, so try to relax as much as possible and behave naturally. Here are a few tips for controlling your nerves:

✔ **Putting things into perspective.** In such situations the tendency is to get things out of proportion and to see everything as much more important than it really is. If what you fear happens, is it really going to be that bad? Tell yourself, 'I may get the job or I may not, but either way this is a valuable experience and I can take a lot away from it.'

✔ **Trying to relax by breathing deeply and slowly.** Breathe in for a count of five and out for a count of five. Getting oxygen to your brain helps you to think more clearly.

✔ **Avoiding stimulants like tea or coffee.** Caffeine won't help you to relax and worse still it can add to your anxiety. You may also need to make frequent trips to the loo, which may not come at the best time! Taking sips of water or having soft drinks is better and avoids getting dehydrated and having a dry mouth when introducing yourself or chatting to people.

✔ **Employing a calming ritual.** Taking a short walk, thinking pleasant thoughts, and a brief bout of meditation and visualising your successful outcome of the Assessment Centre are positive things to do. So do them.

Making an impactful introduction

Most likely you and your fellow participants are going to be invited to make your own introductions so it's up to you to make the most of your first appearance on the scene. On an Assessment Centre it's the usual practice for introductions to go round the room with participants giving some essential facts about themselves, including:

✔ Your name.

✔ Where you're from, for example your university or company, or if it's an internal Assessment Centre, your department.

✔ What you're currently doing, for example your university course, or your job title.

✔ If you've ever attended an Assessment Centre or Development Centre before (head to Chapter 1 to find out the difference between the two).

✔ Other interesting facts about yourself.

Sometimes you may be asked to give other details about yourself such as where you're from, your leisure activities, or what you hope to get out of the event.

Although you can't predict with any certainty what you're going to be asked to say when introducing yourself, try to have a few items prepared just in case so you have one less thing to worry about when the Assessment Centre begins.

Your introduction rarely forms part of the assessment process, so if you come across as a bit nervous, or make a less than impressive introduction for whatever reason, don't let this undermine your confidence. Try not to forget, though, that this is your first opportunity of making an impact, so squash any nerves and do the best you possibly can.

Most Assessment Centres favour a fairly informal approach to making introductions. You're most likely to be invited to introduce yourself from where you're sitting. Sometimes though you may be asked to stand up and introduce yourself or asked to go to the front of the room to make your introduction. It's possible for the assessors to be asked to introduce themselves as well, and this can be your first chance of finding out who's who and their level of seniority, so listen carefully to all the introductions.

 When it's your turn, be sure to speak clearly and at an even pace and don't forget to make eye contact with your audience. Chapter 5 is invaluable for giving you useful tips on making an oral presentation.

After the introductions you're likely to be given some general information and advice about making the most of your Assessment Centre (see Chapter 17). Next you're given your timetable telling you exactly where you need to be and when. At this stage the administrator is likely to ask if anyone has any questions before filling you in about your first task.

 If you're uncertain about anything relating to your assessment, now is the time to ask. It's much better to ask and find out what you want to know than to sit there in silence for fear of looking silly and possibly being put at a disadvantage by not knowing. Take note of the Chinese proverb:

> *'He who asks is a fool for five minutes, but he who does not ask remains a fool forever.'*

Tackling icebreakers

To help you to settle into the event before your assessment starts for real, some Assessment Centres begin with an icebreaker. You'll be relieved to know that an icebreaker definitely isn't part of your assessment! An icebreaker may take the form of:

✔ An addition to the introductory session in which everyone says three things about himself, of which one is pure fiction. The rest of the group votes on which one of the three is the lie.

✔ A group task (at this stage a group task is generally less daunting than an individual task) in which the group members have to discuss a hot topic such as, 'What can we do to protect the environment?' for, say, 10 minutes.

✔ An activity in which you're given a worksheet entitled 'Find someone who . . .' with a number of boxes containing items such as 'is a vegetarian', 'reads Harry Potter books', 'goes to the gym regularly', and so on. The idea is to get one name in each box, encouraging participants to mix and get to know one another quickly.

Icebreakers are usually very short but are a great way of letting you find out more about your fellow participants. But the overriding purpose of an icebreaker is simply to help you overcome your nerves and relax, so that you can be sure of showing yourself at your best.

Being a bit too relaxed or too casual may give out the wrong signals; you don't want to be thought of as being totally uninterested in what's going on around you. But don't get overexcited either, like using bad language or making a joke in poor taste, or being offensive towards another participant.

The key to tackling an icebreaker successfully is to enjoy being involved in the activity and entering into the spirit of the task (you don't want to come across as being serious or boring) but at the same time showing that you know what is acceptable and proper behaviour for the occasion.

Making Your Mark on the Assessment Activities

Once the introductory phase of the Assessment Centre is out of the way, you move on to the main part of the event where you're going to be engaged in a range of assessment activities relating to the target job. We describe these activities and exercises in detail in Chapters 4 to 12. But you may also be asked to carry out a number of other activities that we talk about in this chapter.

Participating in business games

Business games come in a variety of shapes and sizes, but their purpose, like any other Assessment Centre exercise, is to provide a realistic simulation of the demands of the target job, as the basis for assessing your suitability for that role.

Business games have much in common with case-studies and analysis exercises (refer to Chapter 8), although the content and the way the task is carried out makes a business game a little different from an analysis exercise. Head to Chapter 8 for pointers that can apply to business games.

A business game is designed to simulate a sophisticated business environment where you take part in a sizeable project or a series of related business tasks. The activity generally lasts for the whole of your time on the Assessment Centre. While you're involved in the task, events unfold around you as the day passes. Business games are often carried out between competing teams and are sometimes controlled by computer programs to manage the environment and these features further justify the reference to the term business 'game'.

Typical scenarios for business games can include:

✔ **The Corporate Announcement:** A major company announcement is scheduled for the end of a hectic trading period. Each participant is given a senior management role and a series of key events occur during the course of the game, which will have a bearing on the content of the Chairman's announcement to the staff and shareholders.

These unforeseen events can include things like a sudden fall in demand, industrial action, an environmental problem, increased competitor activity, or a delay with a product launch. The participants need to respond to these events as they unfold, in order to protect the company's position and to ensure the company continues to prosper.

✔ **War and Peace.** This game is set in the time of the Cold War between NATO and the Warsaw Pact in the period after World War II. The participants assume various diplomatic roles from key countries within the two alliances. Discussions are punctuated by Reuters' news bulletins, which have a bearing on the various treaties and agreements. Participants are expected to achieve specified objectives, which often need to be redefined and they need to evaluate situations and respond appropriately. This type of game is clearly more appropriate for personnel within the MOD or the Diplomatic Service and games such as this are used at the Royal Military Academy at Sandhurst to assess and develop participants' skills in the areas of strategic planning, decision making, communicating, influencing and negotiating.

✔ **The Competitive Tender.** Two or more sales teams compete for a lucrative sale, involving making a series of sales visits to explore the need before writing a sales proposal. This is followed by each team making a presentation to the Board and finally negotiating on price, with the winning team being given the order.

Business games aren't a regular feature of an Assessment Centre because they can be complex to stage, but if you're invited to take part in a business game you usually know in advance and are asked to do some introductory reading as preparation for the event.

The behaviours you display in a business game are much the same as you display in other simulation exercises such as a group discussion, role-play, analysis exercise, and an oral presentation that we describe in Chapters 4–10. You may also find that you're expected to manage your workload and business activities entirely by email, as if you're taking part in an inbox exercise. (Refer to Chapter 10.)

Business games can be big-time events. The scale, complexity and number of business activities add towards the uncertainty of the outcome, just as in real life! So be prepared for the unexpected happening and stay alert to the changing circumstances as the scenario unfolds.

Undertaking outdoor activities

You're only likely to take part in an outdoor activity on an Assessment Centre if the target job is for the most part practical and hands-on, such as in the armed services or emergency services.

If you're applying for an operational role, then you might be asked to take part in an outdoor exercise where you're required to show your ability to handle potentially dangerous and challenging tasks that test your leadership skills under pressure. For example, for the job of a senior police officer, you may be asked to assume control of a situation where a serious incident has occurred and you need to follow procedures to contain the incident, while ensuring the safety of your officers and the general public. This type of task can have similarities to the multiple role-play exercises we describe in Chapter 6, although an outdoor exercise is likely to be physically challenging as well as mentally challenging.

A lot of the outdoor activities focus on testing leadership, teamwork and communication skills. These activities often have a strong physical element, such as tackling a task on an assault course or making effective use of survival skills to test your mental and physical fitness for the target job.

For a lot of people in office-based jobs, tasks like these can be seen as having little relevance to their real-life job. If by chance you're asked to take part in an outdoor activity, you need to accept that this is the way the organisation has chosen to assess the skills required for the target job. You may find it difficult to see how this type of outdoor task relates to the skills needed by a department manager in a leading retail store. But if this is what the organisation has chosen as its basis for assessment, you need to try to identify what abilities and skills the activity is trying to highlight, so you can display those skills to good effect within the task.

The military connection

The Assessment Centre method was first employed during the Second World War, by both Allied and Axis forces, because of the need to select people with the leadership potential to perform in a highly pressurised military environment. These centres, which were also used to select people to join the Special Operations Executive (SOE) in the UK, and the Office of Strategic Services (OSS) in the US (the forerunner to the CIA), made much use of practical, outdoor tasks as part of the assessment process.

Don't allow your scepticism about the suitability of the task to cause you to withdraw or disengage from what you're being asked to do, even if you think the activity has little relevance. If you feel strongly about being asked to take part in an activity that you believe isn't appropriate, then you can give the organisation feedback later on, but you must be careful not to give the impression that you're trying to make excuses for your performance.

Reviewing personal performance

A standard feature of many Assessment Centres is that you're asked to complete a simple, formal review of each individual exercise. This review can take different forms. In the following sections we describe two popular review methods.

In Chapter 14 you find out how to review your overall performance on the Assessment Centre. To do this effectively it's important that you review your performance on each of the individual exercises as you go along.

The Participant Report Form

Some Assessment Centres ask you to fill in a Participant Report Form, asking questions such as:

- **What were your aims for this task? What was your plan? What was the outcome?** These questions focus on the reality of what happened while carrying out the task and any attempt to mislead or misrepresent the truth is to be avoided. It's going to be obvious to the assessor who observed and recorded your performance what actually happened, so make sure your answers are frank and honest, as this will show the assessor you have good self-awareness.

Being totally honest is important for a successful outcome to the exercise. You won't do yourself any favours by saying that the outcome was highly successful if you had a bitter argument with the role-player, particularly as the assessor will probably ask the role-player for his views.

✔ **How satisfied are you with what you achieved?** Even though you truly believe the exercise went brilliantly try showing a little modesty and humility by asking yourself, 'how could this have gone better?'. This makes sure that you don't overstate your level of satisfaction with the outcome, but it also helps with your answer to the next question.

✔ **If you had to do this task again what, if anything, would you do differently?** Organisations usually prefer employees who are ready to acknowledge weaknesses and limitations but who are seen as keen to improve, rather than employees, who although they may consistently perform well, can't see any room for improvement.

✔ **Is there anything else you want the assessor to know when evaluating your performance?** Try not to read this question as your chance to make excuses for your performance. This is your opportunity for telling the assessor anything else of importance that wasn't addressed by the previous questions. Often this is going to be something that the assessor is unlikely to have known, such as your report being rushed at the end because your laptop battery ran out during the analysis exercise, causing you to lose a valuable 10 minutes while the administrator was trying to find a spare power lead.

A Participant Report Form is a useful way of letting the assessor see how you approached the exercise and gives you an opportunity of highlighting anything you think is important. Generally the Participant Report Form isn't assessed, because your comments are subjective. However, when you're filling in the form think carefully about what you're saying so as to avoid putting across the wrong impression.

A face-to-face review

Some organisations prefer to carry out a more formal face-to-face review at the end of each exercise to find out what you've learned from the activity. A face-to-face approach is usually taken if the organisation wants to assess your capability to learn quickly and to change your behaviours accordingly. This quality is usually called 'Learning Agility' and sometimes features as one of the competencies on the Assessment Centre. This approach is more commonly used at the graduate level where a person is expected to polish and develop his skills, and is more relevant the younger and less experienced you are.

If a face-to-face review is used on your Assessment Centre you're likely to be interviewed after each exercise by an assessor, who may well ask you the same sorts of questions given on the Participant Report Form (see the previous section).

Taking Part in Information Sessions

A briefing session is an essential part of the Assessment Centre. It's the usual practice to brief all participants at the start of the event to make sure they know exactly what they're going to be doing and when, and what the Assessment Centre expects of them.

When Assessment Centres are used as part of an external recruitment campaign, they usually occur towards the end of the selection process and the participants are effectively on 'the short list'. It is therefore important that the process provides some form of two-way communication, as the organisation must 'sell' itself to the participants, who are choosing the organisation as much as the organisation is choosing them.

Even when Assessment Centres are run for development (Development Centres), a need remains for some form of briefing session. The participants, who will be internal, want to know about the purpose of the centre and what impact it will have on their professional development and their career within the organisation.

Responding to company presentations

As we stated in the previous section, it's important that the Assessment Centre includes a session that explains the purpose of the centre and provides all the information the participants need to know about the organisation. It's therefore common practice for someone from the organisation to make a presentation covering these details.

You may be a graduate applying to an organisation to join their graduate or management trainee programme and it's highly likely that your Assessment Centre will include a presentation from the organisation. The presentation is usually made by someone at line management level or staff from HR. The purpose of the presentation is to tell you what life is like in that organisation, in the event that you're offered a job there.

If you're due to attend a company presentation, here are few tips for getting the most out of the event:

✔ Prepare any questions you want to ask in advance of the presentation. Don't be afraid of asking the same questions that you've already asked in an interview, as you may benefit from getting a slightly different answer, particularly if you put a different slant on the question.

For example, maybe you asked the line manager in your interview: 'I'm keen to develop my technical skills, so what sort of training and support can I expect to get in my first year or two?' Then at the presentation you can ask the HR representative: 'What support does the company provide in the first year or two in the area of Continuing Professional Development?'

✔ While listening to the presentation try to think of any relevant questions that you can ask that show your interest in the company and/or the job, or the working environment.

✔ Make brief notes on points about the organisation that you think may be important so that you can refer to the points later if needed. But don't be tempted to start doodling because you may lose track of what is being said.

✔ If the presenter attempts some humour, then be sure to respond politely with a smile and appropriate laughter,

> but don't overdo it because you may come across as
> insincere or, worse still, mark yourself out as a creep!

Try to make the company presentation a positive experience.
Although on an Assessment Centre you aren't actually competing with the other candidates, it doesn't hurt to make yourself known and stand out from the crowd.

Tackling Q&A sessions with recent recruits

Choosing the right job in order to follow your career path is
hugely important. And recruiters recognise the need to provide as much insight as possible into what life is like in their
organisation so that you can make an informed choice. On an
Assessment Centre you're very often given an opportunity of
talking to experienced staff working in the business area you're
thinking of joining. This is particularly the case in graduate
recruitment, where your first job in your chosen career is
likely to be a major event in your life.

As part of a graduate recruitment campaign the organisation
involved usually gives you the opportunity for meeting and
talking informally with some recently employed graduates on
their view of the organisation; perhaps over lunch, or dinner if
an overnight stay is required.

Bring some prepared questions with you to your meeting;
they can be the same or similar to those you anticipate asking
at the interview or when you're at the company presentation.
This is your opportunity for getting an inside look at the
organisation because you're going to be talking to graduates
who've recently joined the organisation and whose perspective is going to be very similar to your own.

Information sessions are very much for your benefit and
although you're not being assessed on these events, be careful not to do anything that can undermine your prospects of
working for the organisation. You're not likely to be selected
by the organisation simply because you know how to behave
appropriately but you can certainly blow your chances if you
display unsuitable, negative behaviours.

In order to get the most out of the information sessions and to avoid any chance of putting yourself at a disadvantage, bear in mind the following:

✔ Make sure you mix with as many people as possible. Don't just talk to one or two people and don't limit your conversation to the current internal staff of the organisation and ignore your fellow candidates, or worse still do the opposite.

✔ Try to be as natural as possible and don't talk solely about the company and/or job. Be prepared to talk about anything that is topical or in the news.

✔ Be polite and courteous at all times and be careful what you say, as you never know who might be listening!

✔ If alcohol is on offer, be careful about how much you drink. You certainly don't want to get tipsy and suffer the consequences later, or say things you know you shouldn't.

Providing Feedback on the Assessment Centre

Assessment Centres are highly sophisticated processes, requiring a significant amount of time, money and effort to organise, so organisations are generally keen to make sure that an Assessment Centre is as effective as possible. As a participant you're more than likely to be invited to give some feedback on how you found your experience of attending the Assessment Centre. This feedback can be in the form of a Feedback Questionnaire or a brief discussion at the end of the event. Sometimes organisations do both.

Filling in a questionnaire is the most likely choice for the organisation and it usually includes questions such as:

✔ **Before the Assessment Centre:** Was the information timely, clear, complete?

✔ **Facilities:** How good was the food, and how satisfactory were the rooms used for the interviews and other activities?

✔ **Exercises:** Were they realistic? Were the instructions clear, with enough time to carry out the exercises?

✔ **Staff (centre manager, centre administrator, role-players):** How well did they fulfil their roles? Were the staff helpful and approachable?

Try to be frank and honest with your feedback, as the organisation is likely to appreciate constructive criticism. Do avoid being defensive or making it look as if you're making excuses for your performance. If you felt an exercise was difficult to relate to, given that it didn't seem to bear any resemblance to the nature of the job, then now is your chance for saying so, giving the organisation the opportunity of improving or making any necessary changes to the Assessment Centre.

Be careful not to overdo praising the Assessment Centre because you may come across as insincere and sycophantic and you're more likely to lose rather than gain support.

You need to be aware that experienced assessors are very good at spotting attempts by candidates to manipulate situations, both within the exercises and during the event as a whole. Make it your guiding principle on the Assessment Centre of 'Being true to yourself'. Let the assessors see the real you, otherwise the final decision on your performance may be based on a false supposition leading to regrets on both sides.

Site visits

As well as having the opportunity of talking with some recently hired staff you may also be given a tour around the company site, especially if the Assessment Centre is being run on their premises. A site visit gives you an on-the-ground picture of what it's like to be part of the company. This is particularly useful if you're planning to be working in a specialist area and you've no experience of what it's going to be like. For example, most office set-ups are much the same, but factories can be very different from one another according to the nature of the business. Similarly, a dealing room of a City trader, a control centre for one of the emergency services, and a courtroom all have very different working environments and it 's very difficult to appreciate what working in such environments is like until you actually visit one and see them in action.

Chapter 14

Learning from Attending an Assessment Centre

. . . .

In This Chapter

▶ Doing your own thing – reviewing your performance

▶ Seeking feedback

▶ Applying what you've learned

. . . .

*A*ttending an Assessment Centre can be quite an intimidating experience – but it can be fruitful and enriching too. Turn your assessment experience into your big opportunity for discovering more about yourself. In this chapter we explain how you can apply a practical approach to reviewing your own performance on the Assessment Centre and making the most of what you've learned.

Many Assessment Centres make a point of offering feedback as part of your assessment – and if this is the case we strongly advise you to take up the offer. If feedback doesn't appear on the menu – then ask for it! Regardless of whether you're given feedback at the Assessment Centre or some time after the event, make sure you grab it with both hands.

Having received your feedback, now's the time for action. We show you how to make positive use of your feedback for helping you in preparing for the next time you attend an Assessment Centre, or an event very much like it.

Reviewing Your Own Performance

When looking over your performance on the Assessment Centre you need to look at what you did and in what ways you can do better. This involves both reviewing your performance on each activity and reviewing your performance as a whole.

Reviewing each activity

In Chapter 13 we explain that the Assessment Centre may ask you to complete a written review of your performance after each exercise, using a Participant Report Form. However, not all Assessment Centres do this, in which case you have to decide whether you want to keep a record of your performance for each exercise. To help you make up your mind, think about the following:

- ✔ **Is there enough time between activities to review my performance?** Usually you have very little time in between the various activities, so making a record of how you performed is going to be difficult.

- ✔ **How should I spend my time between the activities to best prepare for the next one?** You may prefer to just sit and relax and not distract yourself from the forthcoming task by dwelling on what you have just done, especially if you feel the last task didn't go so well.

 If you have 15 minutes or more before the next activity, you may want to conduct a quick review of the activity. For example, if you've just come out of a group discussion and you know that one of the forthcoming tasks is a one-to-one role-play, you can think about your interpersonal skills and what you can learn from the group discussion that can be applied in the role-play.

When you're reviewing your performance in the activity, ask yourself:

- ✔ What went well?
- ✔ What could have gone better?
- ✔ What can I do differently next time?

Keep your answers to these questions close by you, so you can go into the remaining activities armed with a plan for raising your game in areas you think need improving.

Reviewing your performance as a whole

You may decide there simply isn't time on the Assessment Centre to review your performance as you go along and instead you're going to do your review once the Assessment Centre is over. The following section shows you a useful and practical approach to take.

Completing a learning log

Invitations to attend an Assessment or Development Centre don't occur that often – perhaps only once or twice in your career. However, it's generally agreed that attending an Assessment Centre is a great experience and can have a significant impact on how you carry out your job in the future. Try looking at your attendance at an Assessment Centre as a great opportunity for finding out what makes you tick and use the experience to help prepare you for the next time you get to attend a centre or for applying what you've learned to your present job and future career.

A good way of carrying out your own review is by completing a learning log, following a simple three-step process:

1. Review what happened by describing the key events.

2. Draw your conclusions and identify what you've learned.

3. Plan what you're going to do next time.

A learning log is a tool developed by psychologist Dr Peter Honey, aimed at encouraging people to learn from their experiences. It's linked to the long-established idea of the Learning Cycle, which you can see in Figure 14-1.

Experiences come in all shapes and sizes: giving a presentation, being appointed as a project leader, chairing a meeting, taking your driving test, going out on that first date, getting married, becoming a parent . . .

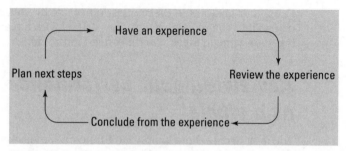

Figure 14-1: The Learning Cycle.

The idea of learning from experience is called *experiential learning* and is based on the theory that learning is ongoing and isn't just something you do as part of your education. It's very important to recognise the value of learning from experience, otherwise you run the risk of repeating the same old mistakes over and over again.

In this case the Assessment Centre is your experience and what you've learned from it can be recorded in your learning log by following the three steps we outlined in the previous section. Here's an example of what a learning log looks like.

1. Review the Experience

The 1st exercise was a group discussion with 5 other candidates. We each had to present a case for our nominee to receive a college grant. We had 15 minutes to prepare and 45 for the discussion. I analysed the details about my nominee and identified the reasons he needed financial support and the arguments that could be used against him, such as his parents having a good income. When we started I offered to take notes on the flip chart and the group agreed. We each had 3 minutes to present and that left about 20 minutes to discuss who should get the £4,000 grant. We got bogged down with each person trying to persuade the rest to go with their nominee. I was making notes on the flip chart, so I spent less time arguing in favour of my guy. I realised we were going round in circles, so I suggested a few criteria, such as financial circumstances, commitment to the college and their course, to help us decide between the nominees. The group agreed and we identified 5 criteria to discuss each candidate against. My guy fell behind because of his better financial circumstances and we ended up with two nominees who we split the £4,000 between as we were about to run out of time.

The 2nd exercise was a written analysis exercise with an oral presentation about a marketing campaign to launch a new product. We had 90 minutes for the written task and I spent 30 minutes reading the brief, analysing the data and planning the structure of my report. I started to write the report but realised that I needed to spend more time analysing the sales figures for the competitive products, so I could determine the market potential of our product. This took me another 10-15 minutes before I resumed writing the report which I finished just in time, although I didn't have enough time to write an Executive Summary as I had intended. We then had 25 minutes to produce a 10-minute Powerpoint presentation, explaining our recommendations. I produced 5 slides, which covered my analysis and recommendations and I had about 5 minutes to run through them quickly and think about what I wanted to say. I then went to make my presentation to one of the assessors and this appeared to go well, although I did struggle to answer a couple of the questions she asked me. One question was 'What would I recommend the company should do if the projected sales figures weren't achieved in the first 3 months?' and I hadn't thought of this, so I fudged my answer. The other question was 'What did I think were the main threats to my recommended launch plan, particularly from competitors?' and I could only think of them cutting their prices, even when she asked me if I could see any other threats, so she was obviously expecting more.

The 3rd activity was a verbal reasoning test and this seemed to go well, as I got all the example questions right and I managed to complete all of the questions in the allotted time and didn't find it too hard.

The 4th activity was a 45-minute Interview and I seemed to get on pretty well with the assessor. He asked me about my time at University and why I wanted to go into marketing. I managed to answer his questions OK and was able to provide some examples of my teamwork on projects and how I planned my final year dissertation to ensure it was submitted on time.

The day finished with them telling us when we would hear from them and that we could get feedback if we wanted by telephoning HR next week. I collected my expenses, thanked the Administrator for an interesting day and left.

2. **Draw conclusions**

In group discussions I must be careful not to get distracted from achieving my brief by taking on a role such as being the scribe or the timekeeper, although these roles do show that I am trying to be a helpful team member. I guess the important thing is to get the balance right. Also in this type of task it is no good just trying to 'out-argue' one another. We needed to have some criteria to help us choose between the nominees, so my suggestion here was a good one and it helped the group to move on. I guess the reason I spotted this requirement was because I wasn't as engaged in arguing about my nominee, due to my scribing role, so I could see more clearly what was happening but it would have been more helpful if I had spotted this earlier.

With the analysis exercise/oral presentation I should have planned my time allocation more carefully as I underestimated the time needed to analyse the data and this meant I didn't have enough time to include an Executive Summary. The structure and content of my presentation was pretty good but the questioning showed that I hadn't given enough thought to contingency planning about what might go wrong with regard to my recommendations.

My verbal reasoning test went well, so I don't think I need to worry about this.

The interview was also pretty good and unless the feedback suggests otherwise, I think my answers to the questions were appropriate.

3. **Plan next steps**

The next time I do a group discussion on an assessment centre I will try to get a balance between helping the group achieve the task and focusing on my own goals, showing I can be an effective team member who can contribute to both. So I will offer to take on a role, fulfil that role and will observe how the group is operating, but will focus on my own brief as well.

I will plan my time better with written tasks and allocate enough time to analysis and not rush into writing the report. I must also give more thought to risks and contingencies, rather than just analysing what is presented. If there is an oral presentation exercise I should recognise that the Question and Answer session will probably raise questions that go beyond what is presented and in future I should anticipate such questions and have some form of answer prepared.

Discovering what you've learned

After you've attended an Assessment Centre you'll have some information about your performance from a couple of different sources:

✔ **Feedback,** either on an individual exercise basis or in relation to your performance as a whole. (We cover this in more detail later in this chapter.)

✔ One or more **learning logs**, from which you can draw your own overall conclusions. Decide what you want to do with this information.

Playing to your strengths

The Chinese have dominated the gold medal position at table tennis ever since the sport first entered the Olympic scene. On one occasion the Chinese team were asked about their domination of the sport and their training routine, and their coach responded: 'We practise eight hours a day perfecting our strengths. Our philosophy is that if you develop your strengths to the maximum, the strength becomes so great it overwhelms the weaknesses. Our top player only plays his forehand. Even though he cannot play his backhand and his opponents know this, his forehand is so invincible that it cannot be beaten.'

Ignoring what you've learned from your feedback is definitely not your best course of action. If you do, you run the risk of squandering a great opportunity for improving your performance. Take heed of the solemn warning from Winston Churchill:

> 'All men make mistakes, but only wise men learn from their mistakes.'

Assuming that you decide to act on the findings of your review, you're now facing an interesting question: 'What is more important, overcoming my weaknesses or playing to my strengths?' The answer of course, is a bit of both. The natural reaction to a disappointing performance is to look at what didn't go well, and wipe out ineffective behaviours by doing things differently or better next time. However, it's just as appropriate for you to look at what worked well and to build on it. Concentrating on building up your strengths may well mask or compensate for your weaknesses to such an extent that they're no longer obvious.

Why not take the two-way approach? Work on removing your weaknesses, while at the same time building on your strengths:

✔ Look at your most serious weaknesses and work out how you can get rid of them.

✔ Be aware of any other weaknesses you have and keep them out of sight as far as possible.

✔ Identify your strengths and think about how you can use them to your advantage. Try to engineer situations where you can bring your strengths into play so that they form an important part in allowing you to perform at your peak.

Getting Feedback on Your Performance

Most organisations have a policy of providing feedback after an Assessment Centre as a matter of course. However, in those few cases where they don't, it's in your interests to ask. Although an organisation has no legal obligation to give feedback after an Assessment Centre, most see it as a moral obligation. Indeed the British Psychological Society (BPS) recommends giving feedback as part of their Best Practice Guidelines for Assessment Centres and Development Centres.

Asking for feedback

If feedback isn't offered either during or after the Centre, ask for it! Your opportunity to do so may come at the end of the event when the Administrator may ask you all for any comments about your experience of the Centre. Don't be embarrassed or reluctant to ask about the arrangements for feedback.

BPS Assessment and Development Centre Best Practice Guidelines

Feedback to candidate/participant

A number of issues link to best practice in the provision of feedback:

✔ If the results have been stored there is a legal requirement through the Data Protection Act, to give candidates/participants meaningful feedback, should they request it.

✔ All candidates/participants should be offered feedback on their performance at an assessment/ development centre and be informed of any recommendations made.

✔ In development centres feedback would automatically be given as part of the process.

✔ Ideally feedback should be provided 'face-to-face', particularly for internal candidates; for

external candidates, it is likely to be both practical and more convenient to offer telephone feedback and/or a written feedback summary. The involvement of line manager input may be valuable to offer support in the workplace to address identified developmental needs.

✔ It is recommended that feedback should be provided promptly after an assessment process (ideally within 4 weeks).

✔ Feedback should at a minimum cover key themes emerging from the assessment/development centre (ideally structured by competencies), the outcome of the process and reasons why the candidate/participant was not selected (if applicable).

If feedback is intended but hasn't been scheduled during the event, then most likely it'll to take place later, once the assessors have finished discussing your performance and reaching their decision. When this happens, feedback is usually only made available to you after you've been told whether you've been successful or otherwise.

Some organisations tell you that feedback is only going to be available after reaching their decision on the successful candidate. When this happens the organisation writes to you about their decision, inviting you to phone the HR department to get your feedback. If feedback is offered in this way it's important that you take advantage of the offer.

We're always amazed that some individuals fail to ask about feedback if none is on offer or, worse, fail to take advantage of the feedback when it is. It's as if the person is simply too busy getting on with her life to recognise what she's missing. This was well expressed by John Lennon, who said:

> *'Life is what happens to you while you're busy making other plans.'*

So don't let this happen to you and always try to get some feedback if you can.

Getting your feedback

When you get your feedback take a close look at what the feedback is saying about different aspects of your performance, for example:

✔ **How well you performed on the Assessment Centre event as a whole.** What your feedback shows is going to fit in with the outcome of the assessment. If you're told that you're successful and have been offered the job or the promotion, then you're going to have every reason to be proud of your achievement.

However, don't assume that your performance was perfect and that you can learn nothing from the experience; if you do, you may come across as arrogant or conceited. There's always room for improvement and if you see your feedback as an opportunity for performing even better, you're going to be seen as a person with a great career ahead of you.

If on the other hand you've been told that you were unsuccessful, then you have to recognise that this doesn't make you a failure. It just means that some aspects of your performance failed to meet the standards the assessors were looking for, or your performance wasn't as strong as some of the other candidates. Either way you're going to get some useful insight on your performance by listening carefully to what you're being told.

✓ **How well you performed against the competencies.** Feedback is often broken down into the specific competencies linked to the activity and your feedback tells you how you performed on each competency. This can be very helpful, as it lets you view your performance in more detail and gives you a clearer picture of your strengths and weaknesses.

✓ **How well you performed on the different exercises.** Your feedback also tells you how you performed on the various exercises and you may find that you're generally better at some tasks than others.

✓ **How well you performed on any psychometric tests or questionnaires.** If your centre included the use of any psychometric tests or questionnaires (refer to Chapter 12), then your feedback explains what was being measured and how you performed. They may also be able to supply you with a candidate's narrative report, which goes into greater detail, based solely on your performance on each of these psychometric instruments. So ask if this is possible, if one isn't volunteered.

While waiting to receive your feedback think about the sort of things you'd really like to know about your performance and make a list of the questions you want to ask. This makes sure that you're not just hearing what the assessor wants to tell you, but lets you dig deeper into how your performance went. Don't forget, you've taken part in the whole assessment process so it isn't unreasonable for you to ask some searching questions. Although, you do need to accept that there may be some practical and ethical restrictions as to how much detail the assessor is allowed to go into.

Receiving feedback in style

Your feedback is going to have added value if you take it in a good spirit and you're receptive to the comments of the assessor. Here are a few tips for getting the most out of your feedback:

✔ **Listening carefully to everything that is said.** It's very tempting to just hear what you want to hear and to employ 'selective listening' and tune out when something you don't like is being said. Also don't miss out on the positive comments and just focus on the negatives. Neither of these behaviours is helpful, because they can give you the wrong impression about your performance. You have to train yourself to pay attention throughout the feedback session.

✔ **Taking some brief notes.** It can be very difficult to remember everything that is being said, particularly if you're a bit anxious and you're hearing things said about you for the first time, or things that touch a raw nerve. So it's helpful to take some brief notes to help you remember for later what was said.

Don't get so engrossed in note taking that you lose eye contact with the person giving you feedback, as this is going to undermine the relationship with the assessor and devalue the feedback.

✔ **Not becoming defensive.** Try to avoid at all costs arguing with the person giving you the feedback. If you get argumentative it can be interpreted as a lack of open-mindedness on your part and may be read as justification for their decision. If you're absolutely sure that what's being said is blatantly wrong, there can be a case for saying so. However, it's highly unlikely that any decision by the assessors is going to be overturned unless an established appeals procedure exists.

✔ **Asking for points to be made clear.** If you're given some feedback that you think is vague or ambiguous, then you may find it helpful to rephrase what was said in your own words, to check the meaning. For example: 'So are you saying that I didn't manage to get her to tell me how she was really feeling about her new role?' By getting things clear in your mind you can then decide if you need to ask any more questions to fully understand what you failed to do, or didn't do well enough.

✔ **Summarising what you've heard.** As the feedback session draws to a close try to summarise the key points you've heard. This can be done for you by the person giving you the feedback, but it's better if it comes from you, because it shows the assessor that you've taken everything on board and gives the assessor the chance of putting right any misunderstanding.

✔ **Closing the feedback session positively.** It's polite to thank the assessor for her time and effort. You never know if you're going to be attending another Assessment Centre with that organisation and it always pays to end on a warm and friendly note.

Optimising different forms of feedback

The purpose of an Assessment Centre is for job selection and feedback is usually given after the centre is over and can take more than one form: face to face, written or by telephone. In contrast a Development Centre (refer to Chapter 1) is for development and the feedback is an integral part of the event and usually takes place face to face to maximise the impact of the feedback.

Finessing face-to-face feedback

Face-to-face feedback is definitely the most satisfactory option because a face-to-face meeting gives you the opportunity of going into more detail, helped by being able to build up a relationship with the person giving the feedback. A typical face-to-face feedback session lasts between 30 and 90 minutes, depending on the purpose of the assessment, whether it's for selection or development, and the level of the job in question. For example, if you're being assessed for a more senior role the feedback session is likely to last longer.

Try treating the feedback session like any other one-to-one session you've experienced. For example, the behaviours you displayed during an interview (refer to Chapter 11) and in a role-play (refer to Chapter 6) can be transferred to your face-to-face session, helping you to get the best value from the session. If you can establish a good relationship with the person giving you the feedback, she may go beyond telling you what you didn't do so well and offer you some advice about what you can do differently next time. Offering advice isn't likely to be part of that person's brief, but if you have the right relationship, then the person giving the feedback may be willing to help you in this way.

Tackling telephone feedback

Some Assessment Centres, such as those being run for graduate recruitment, usually offer feedback by telephone. The main reason for giving feedback in this way is because of the sheer number of candidates who are going through the process, coupled with the fact that candidates usually come from a wide geographical area and it's desirable to cut the costs and time spent travelling. However, feedback over the telephone is generally more impersonal and less detailed because little time is spent on building the relationship.

Here are a few tips for helping you handle telephone feedback effectively:

- ✔ Make sure you make or receive your phone call in a quiet location where you won't be disturbed.

- ✔ You won't be making eye contact, so you can prepare and take notes, for which you need to have a pen and paper handy. You can use a hands-free phone making it easier to take notes, but mention this to the person giving the feedback before you start so that she can judge how much detail she can go into. You may even want to record the session, although if you do, you need to ask permission, as some people may be a bit uncomfortable about being recorded.

- ✔ Building a relationship over the phone is tricky but using a friendly but businesslike tone can help get the call off to a good start and prompts the person giving the feedback to respond in the same way. Be sure to thank the person for calling you or for taking your call, as well as thanking her at the end for her time and effort. It's also a good idea to say how helpful the feedback has been, because people generally like helping and this may lead them to provide you with further help at a later date.

Working with written feedback

Some Assessment Centres back up face–to-face or telephone feedback with a written report listing the main observations made by the assessors and the conclusions they've reached about your performance. However, occasionally feedback is only delivered in writing. Feedback in this form is inevitably distant and impersonal and the comments made about your performance may not be entirely clear to you, so you have to look at ways of making the best use of this type of feedback.

Make sure you read what the assessors are saying very carefully and you fully understand what's being said. More than likely your written feedback won't go into a lot of detail and you may find that some of the remarks made about your performance need explaining. If this is the case, try contacting the organisation and ask if you can discuss some of the comments in the feedback report with the appropriate person. Don't be afraid of asking for comments in the feedback to be made absolutely clear, as the organisation is likely to recognise that this is a perfectly reasonable request. If the organisation seems reluctant to respond, you may well decide that this isn't an organisation you'd want to work for in any case!

More than anything try to avoid giving the impression that you're questioning the organisation's final decision, as this may lead them to see you as someone who is going to cause trouble, rather than someone who just wants to have things made clear and easily understood.

Bringing Together What You've Learned

> *The illiterate of the 21st century will not be those who cannot read and write, but those who cannot learn, unlearn, and relearn.*
>
> Alvin Toffler

Attending an Assessment Centre is likely to be an important event in your career and a powerful learning experience. So after putting yourself through the 'pain' now is the time for realising the 'gain'.

Peeking through the Johari Window

Evaluating your performance (see the earlier sections in this chapter 'Reviewing Your Own Performance' and 'Getting Feedback on Your Performance') may not give you the complete picture. Take a look at the model in Figure 14-2 of the Johari Window. The model shows four windowpanes (areas) illustrating how you can develop your self-awareness.

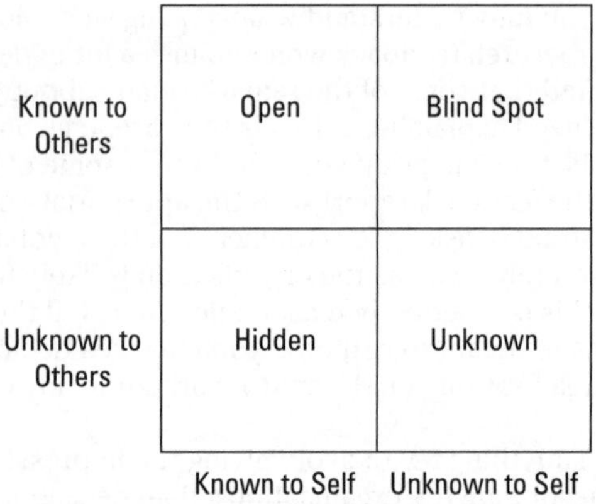

	Known to Self	Unknown to Self
Known to Others	Open	Blind Spot
Unknown to Others	Hidden	Unknown

Figure 14-2: The Johari Window

What everyone knows (Open)

The Open pane refers to those things that everyone can see. For example, you know that you're a naturally chatty and gregarious person who likes to be the centre of attention, so it's going to be no surprise to you, and obvious to everyone else, that you're going to be one of the participants taking a dominant part in a group discussion exercise.

Known to others, but not you (Blind Spot)

Your Blind Spot refers to things that others see in you but are totally oblivious to yourself. You're only going to discover your blind spots through feedback. For example, you may not be aware that you have an irritating way of swaying from side to side when giving a presentation, or that you overuse words like 'basically' in one-to-one and group discussions.

The Johari Window

The Johari Window, so called in the 1950s after the first names of its inventors, American psychologists Joseph Luft and Harry Ingham, is one of the most useful models describing the process of human interaction. A four-paned 'window' divides self-awareness into four different areas, represented by the four panes of the window: *Open, Hidden, Blind Spot* and *Unknown*. The lines dividing the four panes are like window shades, which can move as an interaction progresses, indicating the amount of disclosure (openness) emerging from that area.

What you know but others don't (Hidden)

The Hidden pane represents those things that aren't apparent to others but are only known to you and that you may want to keep close to your chest. However, during the course of your feedback session after discovering that one of your blind spots is a tendency to talk more to the men in the group than the women, it may come up that the reason for your behaviour is because you're nervous and uncomfortable in the company of women, having spent most of your life in a male-dominated environment. This type of self-disclosure can sometimes lead to a more fruitful feedback discussion and the person giving the feedback may be able to offer some helpful advice about how to get along with women in your place of work.

What no one knows (Unknown)

The Unknown pane is the most intriguing of all. No one knows what's going on, but during the feedback session what you didn't know about yourself may come to light through a combination of disclosures from your Hidden pane and what you learn about your Blind Spot. For example, you may come to realise that not only are you nervous in the company of women, but your normally gregarious and forceful behaviour in a group discussion evaporates if the group contains female participants who are equally forceful. Looking back at a group discussion you realise that you find it difficult to oppose the views of strong-minded women for fear of being seen as confrontational and bullying.

An Assessment Centre is an ideal vehicle for helping you to find out things about yourself that you never knew before. Assessors are usually looking to assess your potential, so you're placed in situations that you've never met before. How you respond to these situations inevitably reveals new behaviours and skills not previously known to you, or others.

Putting all the information together

In order to make sure that you make full use of everything you've learned from attending your Assessment Centre you need to go through the following steps:

1. Review your learning logs (see the earlier section 'Completing a learning log') noting what you learned about yourself and any action you need to take.

2. Review the feedback you received at the end or after the Assessment Centre, again looking at what you've learned about yourself and actions you need to take.

3. Bring together your findings from the review you carried out on your own performance and the feedback you received, and pinpoint common statements about yourself or any interesting differences in the way you see yourself and the way others see you.

4. Review the newly merged data to find out if anything new about yourself comes to light and add the new information to the existing information.

5. Use all the information you now have for identifying your strengths – the things you do well; and your weaknesses – the things that you fail in, or don't do well.

After finishing your self-analysis, you're now in a great position to make a plan of action that helps you do even better the next time you attend an Assessment Centre.

Preparing for the Next Time

While it may be some time before you attend another Assessment Centre and have the opportunity of applying what you've learned from this assessment, there are nevertheless some general things you can start thinking about in order to prepare yourself for next time.

Your path to improvement: Using the Ability-Awareness model

To raise your game for the next Assessment Centre you attend, it can help if you understand the stages that you naturally go through in developing your skills and improving your perform-ance. The process entails raising your level of consciousness so that you become fully aware of what you're doing right and what you're doing wrong, enabling you to give the right amount of attention to improving your skill level. This process is referred to as the Conscious Competence model or the Ability-Awareness model, as shown in Figure 14-3.

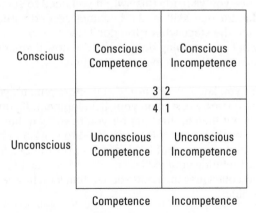

	Competence	Incompetence
Conscious	Conscious Competence 3	2 Conscious Incompetence
Unconscious	4 Unconscious Competence	1 Unconscious Incompetence

Figure 14-3: The Ability-Awareness model.

Your journey to self-improvement usually starts in the Unconscious Incompetence quadrant, as this is where you're blissfully unaware of your lack of skill or ability in relation to a particular competency, for example Persuasive Oral Communication when giving an oral presentation.

The natural transition is for you to move up to Conscious Incompetence (quadrant 2) after becoming aware that you're lacking a particular skill, usually after finding this out through feedback or through carrying out your own review.

Once you're fully aware of your Conscious Incompetence you can move to Unconscious Incompetence. For example, you may now be aware that your presentation skills need to be improved, but you may not fully understand which aspects of them need to be addressed. Only when you're fully aware of what aspects of the skill are lacking can you hope to put it right and the journey from Conscious Incompetence to Conscious Competence (quadrant 3) begins.

Moving from quadrant 2 to quadrant 3 is all about improving your level of skill and this means introducing new behaviours or replacing failing, unsuitable behaviours with more suitable ones. Once you've made this switch you need to spend time practising the new skill until it becomes second nature. You then reach the stage where you don't need to even think about what you're doing because you're now in quadrant 4 and displaying Unconscious Competence!

Now that you know your path to self-improvement, you're in a position to start working on your development. If you follow the steps outlined in this chapter you're going to have no diffi-culty in identifying the things you need to work on and you're likely to find a number of work-based opportunities for prac-tising and refining your skills. Try also to get the help of your boss and colleagues in giving you feedback on how well you're doing.

Once you've developed your new level of competence, be careful not to become complacent, because when you're in a state of Unconscious Competence you may not be aware that you're slipping back into Unconscious Incompetence. Make it a habit of regularly reviewing your performance by asking for feedback from colleagues and friends. This way you're going to be able to maintain your level of performance and not allow bad habits to creep in.

Applying your learning

If you happen to get invited to another Assessment Centre, then once you've done your homework and prepared yourself well for the event as we describe in Chapters 3, 15 and 17, you can turn your attention to sharpening your skills, based on what you've learned from your previous experience.

Go through the list of things you've decided you need to work on, identifying the specific actions you need to take for building on your strengths and tackling your areas of weakness. Draw up an action plan that includes practising suitable skills, taking note of any feedback you get, and polishing up those skills for your performance on the day. By taking action you're sure of avoiding repeating earlier mistakes and more than likely increasing your chances of success.

Part IV
The Part of Tens

'I realise you used to be a Shakespearian actor but can't you give an oral presentation in a more normal and less theatrical way?'

In this part . . .

Welcome to The Part of Tens – the short and snappy
For Dummies chapters. In Chapter 15 we suggest
ten ways of impressing the assessors, whose opinion
determines whether or not you're successful on the
Assessment Centre. In Chapter 16 we focus in some of the
key behaviours you can adopt to maximise your chances
of success. Finally, we provide some general advice in
achieving peak performance at an Assessment Centre.

Chapter 15

Ten Ways to Impress the Assessors

In This Chapter

▶ Preparing to look and be your best

▶ Showing willing

▶ Getting the results

*T*he assessors are undoubtedly the second most important people at an Assessment Centre, after the participants! The assessors have a key role to play (refer to Chapter 2) as they have the responsibility for selecting the right person for the job. You're going to be seeing and feeling their presence throughout your Assessment Centre, as they busy themselves with observing and recording your performance on the exercises. Therefore it's essential that you seek to impress and convince them that you're the ideal person for the job. In this chapter we give you ten tips for enhancing your chances of success.

Dress to Impress

Looking your best as well as looking the part shows the assessors that you really mean business. What you wear for the big day is all-important for making you look and feel confident and catching the assessor's eye.

Dressing appropriately is the name of the game. Well in advance of the Assessment Centre try to find out if the organisation has a dress code. Try matching your outfit to the target job – for example, if you're applying for a job in the City or a professional services company then it's more than likely that they expect you to wear a suit. If however, you're applying for a job in an advertising or design agency then you can probably be a bit more adventurous, signalling your creative flair but still wearing an outfit suitable for an important meeting. But whatever you do, make sure you get it right.

Try looking on the organisation's website to see if you can get any ideas about their dress code, or alternatively ask the Assessment Centre point of contact. If the Assessment Centre is going to last longer than a day, you may like to take a range of clothes so that you can change as appropriate.

Align Yourself with the Organisation's Values

Every organisation has a set of values and beliefs that are core to the organisation's business and govern the way it operates. The organisation fully expects its employees to embrace and promote those values both inside and outside the organisation.

Before applying for any job, try to find out what the organisation believes in. You can do this by going on their website or even speaking to someone in the organisation. At your interview (refer to Chapter 11) show the interviewer that you've done your homework. Try getting across in the interview how you would promote these values in the job. For example, if a core value is 'Flexibility in Response', think how you might be able to operate flexibly and still perform to the highest standards. Showing the interviewer that you've given some serious thought to what makes the organisation tick is likely to mark you out as a suitable person for the job, as well as winning you brownie points.

You need to be absolutely sure before applying for any job that you feel comfortable with the values and beliefs of the organisation. It's possible that you may relate to some of their values more strongly than others or alternatively feel there are some key values missing. You may need to think twice about whether this is the best organisation for you and choose another organisation with a better 'fit'.

Play to Your Strengths

Take time out to sit back and work out what your strengths are and how you can best use them to secure that all-important job. Knowing what you're good at and demonstrating those strengths helps to boost your confidence, so you can give a good performance that is likely to impress the assessors. Being strong in a particular area can also help compensate for those areas where your behaviour is less effective. This is equally true in your current job and your Assessment Centre.

Try to find out in advance of the Assessment Centre what competencies (refer to Chapter 11) are going to be assessed and think how your strengths align to the core job skills. Knowing this gives you the opportunity to work out how you can play to your strengths.

Read through the other chapters in this book to find out about the different exercises you do on an Assessment Centre and how you can apply your strengths to each of the exercises.

Be Prepared

Showing the assessors that you're well prepared for the event and ready for action is going to win you marks. If you followed the advice we give in Chapter 3 then you've made all the right preparations for your Assessment Centre and you should be well equipped to tackle the challenge before you.

Assessment Centres are well organised and keep to a strict timetable because there are a lot of people involved and the centre manager is working to a very tight timescale. You can play your part in the smooth running of the process by always being in the right place and on time. For example, if you know that each exercise is going to last for a set amount of time, you can impress the assessors by being ready and fully prepared to move onto the next activity when required.

Exhibit Your Enthusiasm and Commitment

It goes without saying that throughout the Assessment Centre you need to show the assessors how keen you are to get the job. Although it seems obvious, in the past we've known candidates turn up to an event and boldly state that they're not sure they want the job! Although this may score full marks for honesty, it certainly isn't going to impress the assessors!

You can communicate your enthusiasm and commitment for the job by the way you speak, your behaviour and your body language. Make sure you speak in a confident voice, set at the right tone and pitch, use the appropriate behaviours in each activity you take part in, and move around purposefully and with assurance. You'll also get credit for enjoying the Assessment Centre experience.

Nobody is going to be impressed by someone who speaks in a monotonous voice, slouches around and generally comes over as laid-back – least of all the assessors, so don't do it.

Signal a Willingness to Learn

As we mention in Chapter 14, feedback plays an important part because it not only highlights your strengths and weaknesses, but also shows you where your development needs lie.

Be positive when receiving your feedback and this will impress the assessors and is likely to be noted in your profile. What you learn from your feedback can help to guide you as to where you can apply your skills in your career now and in the future.

Even if you don't get the job you've set your heart on, the assessors are going to be impressed by candidates who show a willingness to have a go and learn from the Assessment Centre experience. And remember, if you attend another Assessment Centre, you have the opportunity of applying all that you've learned to a similar target job.

Retain Your Composure

During the exercises, the assessors are busy observing and recording your behaviour and it's therefore important that you always act in a professional manner.

Don't allow yourself to get upset or angry when performing in an exercise, especially in a role-play. Bear in mind that some exercises are designed to show how you handle highly charged situations and will therefore test your stress tolerance. The assessors are going to be impressed if you keep your cool, and are likely to give you top marks.

Show Respect Towards Others

The assessors are going to be impressed by the way you show consideration and respect for your fellow candidates and other people at the Assessment Centre. Being respectful shows a maturity and generosity of spirit, which are valuable assets in any job. You can demonstrate your respect and concern for others by taking into account the different backgrounds and attitudes shown by fellow candidates and adjusting your behaviour towards them accordingly.

Even if you dislike another candidate or disagree with an assessor it's important not to let this get the better of you. Other people may see things from a totally different angle and are equally entitled to their own opinion. Your job is to show yourself in the best possible light throughout the assessment process.

Convince the Organisation of Your Worth

In order to convince the organisation that you're the right person for the job, you've got to show them what you can offer that makes you hard to resist.

One of the most obvious opportunities you're going to have of showing your worth is in your interview. The interviewer may even ask the direct question: 'What do you think you can bring to the organisation?' Now is your big opportunity to sell yourself and talk about your skills and capabilities in terms of their worth – how your skills are going to benefit the organisation.

When you're telling the interviewer what a good organiser you are, don't stop at the obvious 'I'm a really good organiser', but give a clear account of yourself in action: the occasion, what you did, and the outcome. The interviewer is going to be looking at what impact your organisational skills had on the event and how your skills can be transferred to his organisation.

Convincing the interviewer of your worth and what an asset you're going to be to the organisation is your most important job right now. As the saying goes: 'If you don't blow your own trumpet, someone else will use it as a spittoon.' Say what you've achieved and what you want to achieve in relation to the job and the organisation confidently, but not arrogantly.

Get It Right for the Assessors

Before your assessment begins make sure you know what you're supposed to be doing and what's expected of you. Carefully read and digest all the information that you've received prior to the Assessment Centre and decide what skills and behaviours you're going to need to display during the event.

Once you have a clear understanding of what is expected of you, be ready to show off those behaviours from the moment you walk through the door. For example, if one of the skills you're being asked to demonstrate relates to organising, you can show the assessors how well organised *you are* by being on time for the activities, at the right location, and with all the necessary materials so that you're not wasting anybody's time.

Avoid taking 'being organised' to an extreme. If you come across as always having everything prepared, you can give the impression that although you're good at organising your-self and others, you may lack the flexibility and skills to cope and respond to the unexpected.

Chapter 16

Ten Ways of Behaving Effectively

In This Chapter

▶ Being confident

▶ Interacting with others

▶ Achieving your aim

Selecting the right person for the job is the main task on an Assessment Centre. The assessors are busy comparing your behaviour to the behaviour required to do the job successfully. You have to remember that your behaviour is under close scrutiny during the exercises, and possibly in other activities throughout the event. In this chapter we offer you ten tips for making sure that your behaviour will be noted so you can achieve your aim.

Behave Assertively

On an Assessment Centre you're constantly interacting with other people, such as in a role-play exercise or in a group discussion. You're likely to be in a position where you have to express your point of view. Some people are going to agree with you, while others might take an opposing point of view. In this situation you need to know how to behave assertively.

Acting assertively is about being willing to express your point of view without showing disregard for the views and opinions of others. It is about standing up for your rights, whilst at the same time recognising that other people also have rights.

Acting assertively portrays you as an individual who is willing to speak her mind but also knows when to keep quiet and listen, and this should appeal to most employers. So if you're offering an opinion, don't be shy about telling the other person why you hold this belief and the strength of your conviction. Providing your reasoning may help to win others round to your point of view or at least allow them to understand why you're taking that point of view.

Acting assertively needs a degree of self-awareness. You have to get the right balance between being too aggressive or too submissive in your behaviour. So pause and think about what you're going to say before saying it, and how what you're saying is going to come across. Ask yourself: 'Is the person going to think I'm being too critical or challenging, or am I going to be seen as soft or over-accommodating?'

Show Confidence

Acting confidently inspires confidence in others and makes you get noticed. You look and sound like a person who knows exactly what you're doing or talking about and other people put their trust in you, believing that you know best.

Showing confidence is as much about non-verbal communication as it is about what you're saying. A confident person will interact with you positively, taking charge while still asking for your opinions and acknowledging your viewpoint.

Before attending the Assessment Centre, assess your level of confidence by making a video of yourself in action. You can get friends or colleagues to help by taking part in a simulated group meeting. Afterwards you can analyse your behaviour with your friends or colleagues and work out how you can appear more confident if need be.

Although it's important that you appear confident, especially on the Assessment Centre, it's easy to start acting over-confident and appearing arrogant. Displaying this sort of behaviour is extremely unlikely to go down well with the assessors, because they're not behaviours that are sought after for successful job performance!

Earn the Respect of Others

On an Assessment Centre you're going to be meeting a lot of new people and how you interact with them will be observed and recorded by the assessors. Your guiding principle in establishing rapport with your fellow candidates and earning their respect is to:

> *'Do unto others as you would have them do unto you.'*

You won't have much spare time on your assessment for socialising but whenever you can, make an effort to get to know your fellow candidates. Be ready to listen to what they have to say while being ready to reciprocate. In this way you can quickly create a bond of mutual respect. Although you aim to stand out, it's good to show consideration for others by helping to make sure everyone else is equally involved and has their share of the limelight. This is as true during the exercises as it is during the breaks. Listening attentively to the other candidates' ideas and suggestions shows respect even if you don't necessarily agree with them.

Gain the Support of Others

Gaining support is about convincing others to believe in you and your opinions and winning them over to your side. Having good communication skills is essential in most jobs and this is one of the most important skills that the assessors are going to be watching out for. Being able to get your ideas and opinions across clearly and persuasively is going to stand you in good stead when making a presentation or taking part in a group discussion. Gaining support for your ideas is about being able to see the other person's point of view and her values. To find out what others think and believe in, you need to engage with them and ask questions. The more questions you ask, the more you're going to find out about their views on the matter under discussion.

Don't fall into the trap of getting into an argument with someone in a vain attempt to convince her that you're right. In the end you may just have to accept that everyone is entitled to her opinion, no matter how different that opinion is from your own.

Be Genuine and Sincere

Being genuine and sincere builds trust. In your place of work, being able to trust your colleagues is important for maintaining a harmonious and effective working relationship. When you first meet someone on an Assessment Centre you have no way of knowing if you can trust that person and that person has no way of knowing if she can trust you. However, you can quickly build up trust by acting in a way that shows you're genuine and sincere in all you do, as trust will grow or lessen depending on how genuine and sincere you are. So, it's always important to be honest and truthful. If you lie or exaggerate, even slightly, you run the risk of others picking up on this and beginning to distrust you.

Being genuine means speaking with sincerity. For example, when you're in a group discussion you can acknowledge another person's ideas by saying, 'that's a good idea'. If you say this at a few appropriate points during the meeting, it's likely to be noted, and you're going to be credited with displaying sincere and genuine behaviour.

However, be careful not to overdo it or use superlatives, like 'what a fantastic idea, that's the best idea ever'. If you do, you're going to appear insincere and people may think that you're simply going through the motions, and worse still your behaviour will be regarded as irritating and annoying.

Be Friendly and Approachable

Appearing friendly and approachable seems like a lot to ask when you're feeling nervous and apprehensive on your arrival at the Assessment Centre. To get rid of the butterflies in your stomach you need to start interacting with other participants as early on as possible. The more you interact with your fellow candidates, the more comfortable you're likely to feel, and the more you will see your assessment experience as positive.

You don't need to overdo the friendliness as you aren't looking to make lifelong friends; you don't even need to pull out your best jokes, although you can if you feel they're okay for

the occasion and they're going to help you relax. Instead, try
using simple conversation starters, like:

- ✔ Always saying who you are and if appropriate shaking
  hands.

- ✔ Asking for the other person's name and when she tells
  you, repeating it to help you remember it.

- ✔ Asking the person a question, for example what her job is
  or where she's from.

- ✔ Throughout the day remaining positive and enthusiastic,
  and smiling.

- ✔ During breaks continuing to make an effort, asking 'How's
  it going?' or 'How are you finding it?'

You don't have to fill all the silences, but when you're seen to
be making an effort you're likely to find that your friendliness is
reciprocated helping to make you much more approachable – a
desirable quality in most jobs.

Act with Assurance

When you're on your assessment you're more than likely
going to be taken out of your comfort zone. You're presented
with new challenges where you feel uncomfortable and self-
conscious. You may also start having doubts about yourself
and make self-effacing remarks, such as: 'I've no idea how to
do that', or 'I'm probably going to make a complete mess of it'.

While you might be careful to make sure these remarks aren't
overheard by the assessors, such comments can undermine
your self-confidence, leading you to expect to fail. Once you
fall into a downward spiral of self-doubt, it can be very difficult to pull yourself out of it, especially during a challenging
event like an Assessment Centre, so don't go there!

During the Assessment Centre, say to yourself; 'Right. I'm
going to have a go', and think carefully about what sort of
behaviours you're going to display before starting, and trying
to act with assurance. This shows the assessors that you have
confidence in yourself and your abilities, and you truly believe
what you're saying.

Stay Focused

An Assessment Centre is a tiring and sometimes draining experience and it can be difficult to stay focused when you're taking part in a lot of different activities. But staying focused is all-important. You have to keep in mind that you're continually being assessed. You need to focus on displaying the appropriate skills that go with the exercise.

It's very easy to become distracted by the presence of the assessors while you're performing the exercises. You can help yourself by trying to ignore them unless they address you, as they too need to keep focused on their part of the job. Admittedly ignoring the assessors is easier said than done, but it's important that you at least try!

Use Appropriate Body Language

We're all familiar with the saying, 'Actions speak louder than words', which is as true on an Assessment Centre as it is for any other situation. *How* you say something can be as important as *what* you say. This is because body language betrays your emotions and can support or contradict what you're saying.

The assessors are there busy recording what they're seeing and hearing so make sure that your body language confirms your words. Be conscious of your body language, making sure you come across as positive and that your actions convey the message you want to send:

✔ Stand up straight when shaking hands.

✔ Smile or nod to acknowledge the other person.

✔ Make eye contact and lean towards people to keep them engaged.

✔ Avoid 'closed' gestures such as sitting with your arms and legs crossed.

Make Sure You Get Noticed

This is your time to shine! You want the job as much as the other candidates and if you're going to nail it and secure the job you need to make sure that you're getting noticed. In order to get noticed you have to get involved in the day right from the start. You can do this simply by chatting to everyone you meet, rather than just saying a brief hello.

Give a little thought about what you can say to the other candidates or HR staff when you meet them. Try opening gambits like:

- ✔ Where are you from/working at the moment?
- ✔ Have you been to anything like this before?
- ✔ Do you run lots of these events?

It isn't that important what you say. It's more important that you start talking, as this is going to get you noticed as someone who is comfortable and at ease in an unknown situation and eager to get involved. Being noticed is a great boost to your confidence.

There are likely to be any number of sessions throughout the day when you're going to have the opportunity for getting noticed: the exercises, the Q&A session, or during lunch when you're mixing freely with the other participants.

Make sure you ask at least one question in a Q&A session, demonstrating your interest in the target job. Don't keep on asking questions though, as you may be seen as pushy as well as stopping other people having their turn.

Chapter 17

Ten Tips for Achieving Peak Performance

*N*o matter how much preparation you do before the Assessment Centre, your performance on the day is what counts. In this chapter we give you ten tips for making sure that you go into the event with the right mindset and you're performing at your peak to achieve maximum success.

Arrive in Good Time, Relaxed and Ready to Perform

Anxiety stops you from performing at your best, so minimising feeling tense and anxious is vital. Help yourself by making sure that you've got everything ready that you're going to need for the day. This may mean getting time off work, checking out the location of the Assessment Centre, and how long it's going to take you to get there.

Here's a checklist of some of the key things to think about and do, so that you arrive at the Assessment Centre feeling relaxed and ready to tackle your first challenge:

✔ Get up early – a bit earlier than you do normally so that you have time to get ready without feeling rushed.

✔ Eat and drink something to fuel your brain and to keep you hydrated and alert.

✔ Know where you're going – make sure you have a map and directions to get to your location. If you're driving, find out beforehand where you can park. If you're travelling by train, find out if you have to book your ticket or if the organisation is doing it for you.

✔ Sort out all the necessary documents – letter of introduction, ID, a copy of your CV – and get them ready the night before.

✔ Make sure you know who to ask for when you arrive. It may also help to take any contact details with you, such as the phone number of the administrator, the name of the event and the address.

✔ Leave in plenty of time to get to the location. If for any reason you get delayed and are going to be late, make sure that you phone the organisation to let them know. This allows the organisers to adjust their schedule and they'll be thankful for this.

Pay Careful Attention to All Instructions (Oral or Written)

Pay close attention to any instructions you're given before starting a task. This ensures you know what the activity is, what you can (and can't do) during the task, and what output or response is expected from you. Your instructions may be given verbally or in writing, but if they're verbal, have a pen and notebook ready to write down things that you need to remember.

Every instruction is given for a reason, so if something is unclear, do ask. Once the task begins you're unlikely to be given another chance to ask questions. Don't feel shy about asking for something to be made clear; this shows the administrator that you're paying attention and want to do well.

If you don't pay attention to what's being said you can end up doing the wrong thing, which you then get penalised for. You don't want to lose marks just because you didn't read or listen to the instructions properly!

Focus Clearly on the Aim of the Task

Keeping focused on what you're trying to achieve is important if you wish to arrive at a successful outcome. What you want to achieve will vary according to the type of task you're carrying out. It's important before starting that you're sure you fully understand the task and what you're meant to be doing.

Making a note of what you're trying to achieve and keeping it handy for reference while you're involved in the task can help keep you focused on what you're doing, and still need to do, to reach the task's objective.

Use Preparation Time Effectively

In some exercises you're allowed preparation time before the 'real task' begins. The 'real task' will often be the interactive part of the task, such as the actual group discussion or the role-play. Make sure you're clear about exactly how much time you have to prepare and if not, then ask. The chances are that you're not going to have as much preparation time as you'd like and it's important to know how to make best use of the time you're given.

Spend at least the first five minutes reading the info and deciding what you can realistically get done in the time. It may help to draw up a rough plan of how you can best use your preparation time and the time you're given for the 'real task'. If you're unsure about what's more important to focus on, go back and check out the aims of the task to see if you can afford to spend a bit more time preparing than completing the 'real task', or vice versa.

Manage Your Time

'Time flies' – especially on an Assessment Centre and so you need to keep an eye on the clock when you're busy performing the tasks. Try to work out before you start how much time you can afford to spend on each part of the task. Be prepared to speed up if needed, or reprioritise if you find yourself running short of time. Keep in mind that reaching your goal is all-important.

Make sure you're wearing your watch if you've got one, or else sit near or not far from the clock in the room. Checking the time at regular intervals is going to keep you focused and on track.

Focus on One Task at a Time

In the first session of the day, you can expect to be given an overview of how the day is going to run. You're told what's happening when and where, as well as the number of tasks you're going to be carrying out, which may include specific information about the tasks themselves.

Don't allow yourself to be overwhelmed by the enormity of the challenge and the number of tasks before you, just concentrate on one task at a time and give your full attention to the task at hand. If you're busy thinking about a later task while trying to finish the one you're doing you're unlikely to keep focused on exactly what needs to be achieved, and you may not complete the task to a high standard.

Don't Dwell on Disappointments

Give each task your 'best shot' and don't worry if you feel that you've had a bad task or exercise. Assessment Centres are all about selecting the best candidate for the job. For this reason the tasks are designed to stretch and push you, so that the assessors can see where your strengths and development needs lie. Having this information helps the assessors decide which candidate best fits the requirements of the job.

Be positive, as you don't know exactly what the assessors are looking for or how you performed against the job criteria. Keep your head held high; you may well have done better than you think – most candidates usually do!

Don't let what you may think of as a poor performance, spoil your day. You need to banish any negative thoughts and press on, performing to the best of your ability.

Relax During Breaks

Some participants on the Assessment Centre genuinely believe their behaviour is being assessed during breaks – not so! It doesn't matter a jot if you're eating your peas with a knife, or slurping your soup – the assessors aren't there observing and recording your behaviour. Knowing which piece of cutlery to start with isn't in any way relevant to the target job.

Your breaks are for relaxing and recharging your batteries, ready for your next task. So if you have a 10- or 15-minute break, you're free to do whatever you like with it. However, make sure that you don't go too far away and that you're back promptly – you don't want to delay starting the next task.

What you certainly don't want to be caught doing is letting off steam and swearing or arguing with other participants during your break. Although your behaviour isn't being observed and recorded by the assessors during breaks, they may get to hear about your negative behaviour, which might raise a question mark in their minds about your suitability for the target job.

Be Yourself

Assessment Centres are designed to give you the opportunity to show your suitability for the target job. The tasks you're asked to do on an Assessment Centre are in place to give you a realistic overview of what doing that job is like. If you find that you're doing tasks that you really don't like and couldn't face doing on a daily basis, then you have to seriously consider if this is the right job for you. For this reason, always be yourself and use your assessment experience for checking out whether the job and the organisation suit you.

If you're in a job that doesn't match your skill set, the chances are that you won't enjoy it and before long you'll want to leave. Finding this out before you start the job is much better for you and for the organisation.

Enjoy the Experience!

You may find it hard to imagine, but being on an Assessment Centre can be an enjoyable experience. Think about the positive aspects of your time on the Assessment Centre: you've learned a lot about yourself, the job and the organisation. This is very important when considering your future career and what job or organisational setting you're likely to enjoy.

Whatever the outcome of the Assessment Centre, the feedback you receive (don't forget to ask for it if it isn't offered) is one of the best parts of the experience (refer to Chapter 14). Your feedback highlights what you did well and what you may want to focus on and develop.

Most likely you'll find some aspects of the Assessment Centre challenging – don't worry, the challenges are there to help you find out where your strengths and development needs lie and this will be detailed in your feedback, so treasure it and consider it as a gift!

Index

• *A* •

ability/aptitude test. *See also*
    specific types
    briefing pack materials, 53–54
    purpose of, 200
    research about, 17
    types of, 202–208
Ability-Awareness model, 251–252
abstract ability test, 205, 207, 208
accounting job, 205
acting, 100
active listening
    company presentations, 228
    exercise briefings, 274–275
    fact-finding exercises, 124, 125
    group exercises, 75
    interview tips, 191
    oral presentations, 87, 93
    panel interviews, 180
    receipt of feedback, 244
    role-play exercises, 111, 114
    show of respect, 267
activity-based group exercise,
    65–66
adjustment, for disability, 58
advert, for job
    described, 50–51
    interview preparation, 195–196
    organisation research, 51
aggression
    inbox exercises, 164
    role-play exercises, 112–113,
        115–116
agreeableness, 210
aim, in written report, 134
airtime, 64–65
alcoholic drink, 230

analysis exercise
    described, 38–39, 131–132
    effective behaviour, 138–142
    example of, 35
    formats, 132–137
    job-related competencies,
        137–138
    link to oral presentation, 83–84
    preparation tips, 139, 142–143
anecdote, 92
anger
    role-plays, 115–116
    tips for success, 261, 267, 277
*Answering Tough Interview
    Questions For Dummies*
    (Yeung), 196
anxiety
    arrival at Assessment Centre, 220
    described, 218
    oral presentations, 94, 95
    planning and scheduling
        exercises, 155
    role-play exercises, 112
    tips for controlling, 218–219
appearance
    behaviour during interviews,
        193–194
    dress for interviews, 190–191
    icebreakers, 221
    tips for success, 274
appendix, of written report, 134
The Apprentice (TV series), 10
argument, 267
arrogance, 266
assertive behaviour, 265–266
Assessment Centre
    advantages of, 16–19
    arrival at, 218–221, 273–274

Assessment Centre (*continued*)
  common questions about, 12–13
  common uses of, 19–25
  defined, 8–10
  described, 1, 7–12
  versus Development Centre, 23
  feedback on, 230–231
  history of, 9, 225
  key features, 13–16
  learning from, 234–239, 278
  purpose of, 27–28
  tour of, 231
assessor
  Assessment versus Development
    Centre, 23
  bias, 13, 43, 44
  decision-making approach, 44–46
  described, 43
  features of Assessment Centres,
    14–15
  feedback on, 231
  group exercises, 77
  oral presentation types, 88–90
  organisation research, 48
  positive impression on, 190–191,
    257–263
  role-play observations, 102
  tasks of, 44
assigned role group discussion,
    68–70
attendance
  described, 31–32
  exercise preparation, 35
  preparatory information, 32
attention, audience, 93
Attention to Detail competency
  analysis exercises, 137, 138
  planning and scheduling
    exercises, 150, 151
attitude, during assessment
  competency based interviews, 190
  oral presentations, 94
  organisation research, 47
  tips for impressing assessors,
    260–261

audience, for in-basket/inbox
  exercise, 168–169
audience, for presentation
  common presentation
    mistakes, 98
  effective presentation behaviour,
    92–93, 95–96
  stages of presentation, 86, 87
  types of presentations, 88–90

• *B* •

banking job, 205
*Basic Math & Pre-Algebra For
  Dummies* (Zegarelli), 205
behaviour. *See also specific
    behaviours*
  analysis exercises, 138–142
  briefing sessions, 229, 230
  business games, 223
  classifications, 44
  company presentations, 228
  competency based interviews,
    190–195
  competency components, 30
  defined, 28
  fact-finding exercises, 125–129
  group exercises, 72–77
  in-basket/inbox exercises, 166–173
  interviews, 180
  levels, 31
  oral presentations, 92–97
  performance review, 225–227
  planning and scheduling
    exercises, 151–153
  preparation tips, 55–56, 59
  purpose of Assessment Centres, 28
  receipt of feedback, 244–247
  role-plays, 107, 108, 110–117
  tips for success, 261, 265–271
behaviour evaluation
  assessor's role, 44
  learning from experience, 234–240
  procedure, 225–227
  tips for improvement, 251–253
  tools for, 248–250

behavioural description interview, 181, 183

benchmark, 31

bias
advantages of Assessment Centres, 17
assessor training, 43
assessor's objective, 44
common questions about, 13
fact-finding exercises, 127–128

Biodata method, 17

body language
one-to-one interviews, 178
oral presentations, 94, 95
tips for success, 270

Body Language For Dummies (Kuhnke), 95

boredom, 112

boss
in-basket/inbox exercises, 169
role-play scenarios, 105

break, relaxation, 277

brief, exercise
analysis exercise, 132, 133–136
attention to details, 274–275
fact-finding exercises, 120
in-basket/inbox exercises, 158–160
planning and scheduling exercises, 146–149, 151
role-play exercises, 100–105, 111, 118

briefing pack, Assessment Centre
described, 51–54
group exercises, 79

briefing session, 227–230

British Psychological Society, 24, 240–241

business analyst job, 132

business game, 222–224

business meeting
dress code, 257–258
in-basket/inbox exercises, 169
role-play exercises, 105–106, 110–111

• C •

calm behaviour
fact-finding exercises, 127, 130
group exercises, 76
panel interviews, 180
planning and scheduling exercises, 155
role-play exercises, 114, 115–117
tips for impressing assessors, 261

candidate, fellow
Assessment Centre features, 15–16
described, 42
group exercises, 72–77, 78
group introductions, 219–220
icebreakers, 221
presentation types, 88–90
respectful behaviour, 261, 267

case-study
described, 38–39, 131–132
effective behaviour, 138–142
example of, 35
formats, 132–137
job-related competencies, 137–138
link to oral presentation, 83–84
preparation tips, 139, 142–143

CBI. *See* competency based interview

centre manager/administrator, 42

chairperson, panel, 180

chart, organisational, 169

cheating, 79, 201

clarity, of presentation, 85

classification, behaviour, 44

clock, 276

closed question, 128

clothing
dress for interview, 190–191, 193
positive impression on assessors, 257–258

coaching, 25

coffee, 216

Cold War scenario, 223

Commercial Awareness
competency
analysis exercises, 137–138
competency based interview, 188, 190
commitment, 260
communication
briefing sessions, 230
competency based interviews, 184–187
group exercises, 73, 74–77
in-basket/inbox exercises, 164, 171–173
interview tips, 191–195
introductions at arrival, 219–220
one-to-one interviews, 178–179
oral presentations, 84–88
outdoor activities, 224
panel interviews, 180
performance review, 248–249
receipt of feedback, 244, 246
role-play exercises, 102, 107–109, 111–117
tips for success, 260, 266, 269, 270, 271
two-to-one interviews, 179
verbal ability tests, 203–204
company presentation, 228–229
competency, job-related
competency
advantages of Assessment Centres, 16
assessor's decision making, 44–45
briefing pack description, 52
versus competences, 29–30
competency based interviews, 188–190, 195–196
defined, 28
described, 30
exercise matrix, 34–35
fact-finding exercises, 123–124
features of Assessment Centres, 14
feedback formats, 243
group exercises, 70–72

in-basket/inbox exercises, 165–166
oral presentations, 90–91
planning and scheduling exercises, 150–151
preparation tips, 55–57
role-play exercises, 108–109
competency based interview (CBI)
assessed competencies, 188–190, 195–196
described, 40–41, 183
detailed and relevant examples in, 184–187, 196
effective/ineffective behaviours, 190–195
key principle of, 184
origin of, 184
preparation tips, 195–197
process of, 184–187
Competitive Tender scenario, 223
competition among participants, 10, 12–13
competitive group discussion, 36
comprehension test, 203, 204
compromise, 75
computer skill, 174
confidence
competency based interviews, 186
group exercises, 79
interviews, 191, 193, 197
oral presentations, 85
panel interviews, 180
role-play exercises, 112
tips for success, 260, 266, 269
confrontational participant, 76, 77
confusion, 152
conscientiousness, 210
content, exercise
discussions, 73
oral presentations, 92
conversation starter, 269
co-operative group discussion, 36
Corporate Announcement scenario, 222–223
critical thinking test, 203

criticism, 76, 77
crystallised intelligence, 202
culture, organisational, 48
current event, 66
Customer Service competency
  competency based interview, 188,
    190
  role-play exercise, 109
customer service role-play, 106, 109

• *D* •

data collection
  assessor's role, 43, 45
  features of Assessment
    Centres, 15
DDA (Disability Discrimination
  Act), 58
decision making
  analysis exercises, 140–142
  common approaches to, 44–46
  discussion leaders, 67
  fact-finding exercises, 122,
    126–127, 130
  features of Assessment Centres, 15
  matrix tool, 45, 46
  situational judgement tests,
    212–214
Decisiveness competency
  analysis exercises, 137, 138
  fact-finding exercises, 123, 124
  in-basket/inbox exercises,
    165–166
defensive behaviour, 244
Delegation competency, 165, 166
delegation task
  discussion leaders, 67
  in-basket/inbox exercises, 162, 172
delivery, oral presentation, 85,
    86–87, 91
dependent event, 152–153
detailed response, 171–173
determination, 193, 194, 260
Development Centre, 22–25
diary, 169, 235–239

diplomatic job, 223
Disability Discrimination Act
  (DDA), 58
discussion exercise
  analysis exercises, 136–137
  assigned roles, 68–70
  described, 36, 66
  example of, 35
  group dynamic, 64–65
  leader role, 66–67
  link to oral presentation, 83–84
  non-assigned roles, 67–68
  timing, 64–65
  typical topics, 64, 66
distraction, 98, 270, 274
Diversity Awareness
  competency, 109
drawing conclusions, 238
dress code, 190–191, 257–258
dyslexia, 58

• *E* •

electronic inbox exercise. *See*
  inbox exercise
email, 163–164, 174
emotional stability, 210
empathy, 114, 115
enthusiasm, 260
essential competency, 45
ethics, 48
evaluation, behaviour
  assessor's role, 44
  learning from experience,
    234–240
  procedure, 225–227
  tips for improvement, 251–253
  tools for, 248–250
executive summary, 134
exercise simulation. *See also*
    specific types
  assessor's tasks, 44–45
  briefing pack information, 52–53
  described, 34–35
  features of Assessment Centres, 14

exercise simulation *(continued)*
  feedback on, 231
  matrix, 34–35
  misunderstandings about
    Assessment Centres, 11
  personal review, 234–240
  preparation tips, 54–57
experiential learning
  evaluation tools, 248–250
  feedback session, 235–239
  self-improvement, 253
  tips for success, 260–261, 278
external recruitment, 19, 20–21
external role-play, 106–107
eye contact
  interview tips, 191
  introductions at arrival, 220
  oral presentations, 89, 95
  panel interviews, 180
  receipt of feedback, 244
  role-play exercises, 111, 112
  tips for success, 270

• *F* •

face-to-face review, 227, 245–246
facial expression, 95
fact-finding exercise
  described, 38, 119–120
  effective/ineffective
    behaviours, 125–129
  job-related
    competencies, 123–124
  preparation tips, 129–130
  structure of, 120–123
failure, past, 192–193, 277
fast-track programme, 24
feedback
  on Assessment Centre, 230–231
  Assessment Centre structure, 32
  described, 23, 240–241
  evaluation tools, 248–250
  forms of, 245–247
  group exercise practice, 78
  ignoring of, 240

learning from, 235–239, 247–250
  preparation tips, 59
  receipt of, 244–247
  request for, 241–242
  review of, 242–245
  360º feedback questionnaire,
    214–215
first impression, 190–191, 257–258
Flexibility competency
  competency based interview, 189,
    190
  group exercise, 71, 72
  oral presentations, 90, 91
  role-play exercise, 109
flip chart, 82
fluid intelligence, 202
fly-in email, 163
focus on task, 270, 275, 276
formal presentation, 88
friendliness, 268–269
frustration
  role-play exercises, 112, 116
  tips for impressing assessors, 261

• *G* •

Gantt chart, 148
GCSE maths paper, 205
genuine behaviour, 268
grammar test, 203, 204
group discussion exercise
  analysis exercises, 136–137
  assigned roles, 68–70
  described, 36, 66
  example of, 35
  group dynamic, 64–65
  leader role, 66–67
  link to oral presentation, 83–84
  non-assigned roles, 67–68
  timing, 64–65
  typical topics, 64, 66
group exercise. *See also specific*
    exercises
  described, 63–64
  effective behaviour, 72–77

group size, 64
icebreakers, 221
job-related competencies, 70–72
oral presentations, 89–90
preparation tips, 77–79
response to, 11–12, 13
timing, 64–65, 67, 68, 69
types of, 65–69, 66
typical topics, 64

• *H* •

hand gesture, 94, 95, 112, 270
Healy, Liam (*Psychometric Tests For Dummies*), 200
highlighting text, 151, 164
honesty
feedback questionnaire, 215
interviews, 194–195
role-play exercises, 112
Honey, Peter (psychologist), 235
humour
company presentations, 228–229
oral presentations, 96
hypothetical situation, 194

• *I* •

icebreaker, 221
Impact competency
competency based interview, 189, 190
oral presentations, 91
improving performance, 251–253
in-basket exercise
described, 38
effective/ineffective behaviours, 166–173
example brief, 158–160
versus inbox exercise, 158, 162
job-related competencies, 165–166

preparation tips, 173–174
prioritisation, 160, 161–162
purpose of, 157
sorting tips, 162–163
inbox exercise
computer functions, 164
described, 163
effective/ineffective behaviours, 166–173
emails, 163, 164
example brief, 158–160
versus in-basket exercise, 158, 162
job-related competencies, 165–166
preparation tips, 173–174
prioritisation, 160, 161–162
writing tips, 164
incompetence, 251–253
independent exercise, 39–40
individual exercise, 38–39
informal presentation, 88
information session, 227–230
Ingham, Harry (psychologist), 249
Initiative competency
competency based interviews, 189, 190
group exercises, 71, 72
in-basket/inbox exercises, 165, 166
oral presentations, 91
introducing yourself, 219–220
Integrity competency, 189, 190
intelligence, 202
interlinked exercise, 40
internal promotion, 19, 22
internal role-play, 105–106
Internet resources
oral presentation preparation, 84
organisation research, 48
practice tests, 53
psychometric tests, 201, 205, 207, 216
verbal ability tests, 203

Interpersonal Sensitivity
   competency
   competency based interview, 189,
      190
   oral presentations, 91
   role-play exercises, 109
interview. *See also specific types*
   job analysis, 29
   misunderstandings about
      Assessment Centres, 11
   most commonly used, 40–41, 183
   popularity of, 177
   preparation tips, 182, 195–197
   role-play scenarios, 107
   structure of, 181–183
   styles of, 178–181
Interview Simulation. *See* role-play
   exercise
investigation exercise. *See* fact-
   finding exercise
IQ test, 202
irrelevant question, 128–129, 181

• *J* •

jargon, 97
job. *See also specific jobs*
   accountability, 54–55
   analysis, 28, 29
job advert
   described, 50–51
   interview preparation, 195–196
   organisation research, 51
job description
   described, 49–50
   interview preparation, 195–196
   organisation research, 51
job-related competency
   advantages of Assessment
      Centres, 16
   assessor's decision making, 44–45
   briefing pack description, 52
   versus competences, 29–30
   competency based interviews,
      188–190, 195–196

defined, 28
described, 30
exercise matrix, 34–35
fact-finding exercises, 123–124
features of Assessment Centres, 14
feedback formats, 243
group exercises, 70–72
in-basket/inbox exercises,
   165–166
oral presentations, 90–91
planning and scheduling
   exercises, 150–151
preparation tips, 55–57
role-play exercises, 108–109
Johari Window (performance
   evaluation tool), 248–250
joke, 96
Judgement competency
   analysis exercises, 137, 138
   fact-finding exercises, 123, 124
   group exercises, 71, 72
   in-basket/inbox exercises,
      165–166
   oral presentations, 90, 91
   planning and scheduling
      exercises, 150, 151

• *K* •

Kuhnke, Elizabeth (*Body Language
   For Dummies*), 95

• *L* •

laid-back attitude, 193, 194
layout, room, 86
leader role, in group discussions,
   66–67
leadership allocation, 36, 224
Leadership competency
   competency based interview,
      188, 190
   group exercise, 71, 72
   role-play exercise, 109
   skills linked to, 55

leading question, 128
learning from experience
  evaluation tools, 248–250
  feedback session, 235–239
  self-improvement, 253
  tips for success, 260–261, 278
listening
  company presentations, 228
  exercise briefings, 274–275
  fact-finding exercises, 124, 125
  group exercises, 75
  interview tips, 191
  oral presentations, 87, 93
  panel interviews, 180
  receipt of feedback, 244
  role-play exercises, 111, 114
  show of respect, 267
Listening competency
  competency based interviews,
      189, 190
  fact-finding exercises, 124
  oral presentations, 90, 91
  role-play exercises, 109
log, learning, 235–239, 250
logic
  analysis exercise, 132
  planning and scheduling
      exercises, 152–154, 155
logistics manager job, 145
Luft, Joseph (psychologist), 249

• M •

main body, of written report, 134
making decisions
  analysis exercises, 140–142
  common approaches to, 44–46
  discussion leaders, 67
  fact-finding exercises, 122,
      126–127, 130
  features of Assessment
      Centres, 15
  matrix tool, 45, 46
  situational judgement tests,
      212–214

managerial job, 170
maths, 205, 206
matrix, priority-setting, 161, 167
mechanical and spatial ability test,
      207–209
meeting
  dress code, 257–258
  in-basket/inbox exercises, 169
  role-play exercises,
      105–106, 110–111
message, of oral presentation, 87
military, 225
mobile phone, 197
modesty, 186
motivation assessment, 200, 212
multiple questions, 128
multiple role-play exercises,
      102–105
multitasking, 167, 174, 276

• N •

needs, personal, 114–115
negotiating skill
  business games, 223
  role-play scenarios, 106, 107
nervousness
  arrival at Assessment Centre, 220
  described, 218
  oral presentations, 94, 95
  planning and scheduling
      exercises, 155
  role-play exercises, 112
  tips for controlling, 218–219
newspaper, 66, 129, 143
non-assigned role group discussion,
      67–68
non-verbal behaviour, 112, 266. *See
      also specific behaviours*
norm group, 201
note taking, 125, 228, 244, 274
numerical ability test, 205, 206

• O •

OAR (Overall Assessment
  Rating), 45
objectivity
  advantages of Assessment
    Centres, 17–18
  fact-finding exercises, 127–128
observation, assessor's, 44
office manager job, 49–50
office-based job, 224
one-to-one exercise
  role-plays, 100–102
  types of, 36–38
one-to-one interview, 178–179
online test, 201
open personality, 210
opening, of presentation, 87
Openness to Change competency,
    189, 190
operational role, 102, 224
oral presentation
  analysis exercises, 135–136
  common mistakes, 97–98
  described, 37
  effective behaviour, 92–97
  formats, 81–84, 87
  job-related competencies, 90–91
  stages of, 84–88
  tips for success, 271
  types of, 88–90
organisation, researching an
  general questions, 47–48
  job advert, 50–51
  job description, 49–50, 51–52
  tips for impressing assessors, 258
organisational chart, 169
organisational need, 114–115
Organisational Sensitivity
    competency, 165, 166
outdoor activity, 224–225
Overall Assessment Rating
    (OAR), 45
overhead projector, 82, 93

• P •

panel interview, 180–181
panicking, 117, 127, 180
paper shuffling, 173
paper-based in-basket exercise
  described, 38
  effective/ineffective behaviours,
    166–173
  example brief, 158–160
  versus inbox exercise, 158, 162
  job-related competencies,
    165–166
  preparation tips, 173–174
  prioritisation, 160, 161–162
  purpose of, 157
  sorting tips, 162–163
participant, other
  Assessment Centre features,
    15–16
  described, 42
  group exercises, 72–77, 78
  group introductions, 219–220
  icebreakers, 221
  presentation types, 88–90
  respectful behaviour, 261, 267
Participant Report Form, 225–226
patronising participants, 98
pattern finding, 207
People Development competency,
    188, 190
percentile, 201
performance review
  learning from experience,
    234–240
  procedure, 225–227
  tips for improvement, 251–253
  tools for, 248–250
personal need, 114–115
personality questionnaire
  described, 210–211
  purpose of, 41, 200
  types of, 211–212

Persuasive Oral Communication
  competency
  competency based interview, 188,
    190
  fact-finding exercises, 123, 124
  group exercise, 71, 72
  oral presentations, 91
  role-play exercise, 109
persuasive technique
  fact-finding exercises, 122–123
  role-play exercises, 113
phone call
  feedback, 246
  interviews, 197
  research methods, 48
pictorial question, 205, 208
Planning and Organising
  competency
  analysis exercises, 137, 138
  competency based interviews,
    188, 190
  fact-finding exercises, 123, 124
  group exercises, 71, 72
  in-basket/inbox exercises,
    165, 166
  oral presentations, 90, 91
  planning and scheduling
    exercises, 150
  role-play exercises, 109
planning and scheduling exercise
  described, 39, 145–146
  effective/ineffective behaviours,
    151–153
  example brief, 146–149
  job-related competencies,
    150–151
  planning and implementation
    steps, 149–150
  preparation tips, 153–155
positive thinking, 94, 277
posture, 95, 112, 193
power test, 202, 205
PowerPoint presentation, 82, 93

practice test
  abstract ability tests, 207
  briefing pack materials, 53–54
  group exercises, 78
  mechanical and spatial ability
    tests, 209
  numerical ability tests, 205, 216
  oral presentations, 94
  verbal ability tests, 216
praise, 268
prejudice
  advantages of Assessment
    Centres, 17
  assessor training, 43
  assessor's objective, 44
  common questions about, 13
  fact-finding exercises, 127–128
preparing for assessment
  accountabilities-skills match,
    54–55
  analysis exercises, 139, 142–143
  briefing pack, 51–54
  disability notification, 58
  fact-finding exercises, 129–130
  group exercises, 77–79
  in-basket/inbox exercises,
    173–174
  interviews, 182, 195–197
  job research, 48–51
  newspaper articles, 66
  oral presentations, 84–86, 87, 91
  organisation research, 47–48
  planning and scheduling
    exercises, 153–155
  prior feedback, 59
  psychometric tests, 216
  response plans, 55–57
  role-play exercises, 110, 117–118
  second visit to centre, 251–253
  situational judgement tests,
    213–214
  tips for success, 259, 275–276
presentation. See analysis exercise;
    oral presentation
press interview, 107

prioritising tasks
  in-basket exercise,
    160–162, 167–168
  inbox exercises, 163, 167–168
Problem Analysis competency
  analysis exercises, 137, 138
  competency based interviews,
    188, 190
  fact-finding exercises, 123, 124
  group exercises, 71, 72
  in-basket/inbox exercises, 165, 166
  planning and scheduling
    exercises, 150, 151
problem-solving exercise, 67–68
process, discussion, 73
productivity, 16
project manager job, 145
project plan, 154, 155
promotion, 19, 22, 215
promptness, 197, 274
proofreading, 97
prospect role-play, 106
psychometric test. *See also specific*
    types
  administration guidelines, 200–201
  briefing pack materials, 53–54
  described, 41, 199
  interpretation and scoring, 201
  misunderstandings about
    Assessment Centres, 11
  preparation tips, 216
  purpose of, 200
Psychometric Tests For Dummies
    (Healy), 200
public relations, 107
punctuality, 197, 273–274

• *Q* •

Quality Standards competency,
    189, 190
questioning
  abstract ability tests,
    205, 207–208
  briefing session, 229–230

company presentations, 228
fact-finding exercises, 120–122,
    125, 127–130
interview tips, 191, 192, 194, 196
mechanical and spatial ability
    tests, 208–209
numerical ability test, 206
oral presentations,
    84, 85, 87–88, 91, 271
panel interviews, 180, 181
personality tests, 210, 211, 212
receipt of feedback, 244
situational interviews, 182
situational judgement tests, 213
360º feedback questionnaire,
    214–215
verbal ability tests, 204
questionnaire. *See specific types*
quiet participant, 75

• *R* •

rapport building, 111
reading test, 203
record, assessor's, 44
relaxation time, 277
relaxed appearance,
    193–194, 221, 274
research exercise
  described, 38, 119–120
  effective/ineffective behaviours,
    125–129
  job-related competencies,
    123–124
  preparation tips, 129–130
  structure of, 120–123
researching organisations
  general questions, 47–48
  job advert, 50–51
  job description, 49–50, 51–52
  tips for impressing assessors, 258
resistance, 113
resource scheduler job, 145
respect, 261, 267

review, performance
  learning from experience,
    234–240
  procedure, 225–227
  tips for improvement, 251–253
  tools for, 248–250
role-play exercise
  assigned role group discussions,
    68–69
  described, 37, 43, 99–100
  effective/ineffective behaviours,
    110–117
  example of, 35
  job-related competencies,
    108–109
  popular scenarios, 105–107
  preparation tips, 117–118
  role-player's behaviour, 108
  types of, 100–105
room layout, 86
round-table discussion
  analysis exercises, 136–137
  assigned roles, 68–70
  described, 36, 66
  example of, 35
  group dynamic, 64–65
  leader role, 66–67
  link to oral presentation, 83–84
  non-assigned roles, 67–68
  timing, 64–65
  typical topics, 64, 66

● **S** ●

sales-focused exercise
  business games, 223
  oral presentations, 89–90
  role-plays, 106, 113–114
scheduling exercise
  described, 39, 145–146
  effective/ineffective behaviours,
    151–153
  example brief, 146–149

job-related competencies,
  150–151
planning and implementation
  steps, 149–150
preparation tips, 153–155
script, 97, 108
self-awareness, 248–252
self-confidence
  competency based
    interviews, 186
  group exercises, 79
  interviews, 191, 193, 197
  oral presentations, 85
  panel interviews, 180
  role-play exercises, 112
  tips for success, 260, 266, 269
self-disclosure, 249
self-improvement, 251–253
self-worth, 262
silence, 193–194, 220
simulation. See also specific types
  assessor's tasks, 44–45
  briefing pack information, 52–53
  described, 34–35
  features of Assessment Centres, 14
  feedback on, 231
  matrix, 34–35
  misunderstandings about
    Assessment Centres, 11
  personal review, 234–240
  preparation tips, 54–57
sincerity, 268
situational interview, 181, 182
situational judgement test,
  212–214
skimming text, 139–140
smiling, 191, 197, 270
sorting items, 162–163, 164
spatial ability test, 207–209
speed test, 202, 205
spelling test, 203, 204
stand-alone oral presentation, 82–83
standard, Assessment Centre, 24

Strategic Perspective competency
analysis exercises, 138
competency based interview,
188–189, 190
in-basket/inbox exercises,
165–166
strength, personal
discussion leaders, 67
playing to, 239, 240, 259
preparation tips, 56
Stress Tolerance competency
competency based interviews,
189, 190
fact-finding exercises, 123, 124
oral presentations, 90, 91
role-play exercises, 109
structured interview, 181–183
subordinate role, 105
suit, 257–258
summary
analysis exercises, 134
oral presentations, 87
receipt of feedback, 245
role-plays, 115
superficial behaviour, 171
supplier role-play, 107
support, from others, 267
surprise event, 114, 222
survival skill, 224

• *T* •

task objective, 67
task simulation. *See also specific
exercises*
assessor's tasks, 44–45
briefing pack information, 52–53
described, 34–35
features of Assessment Centres, 14
feedback on, 231
matrix, 34–35
misunderstandings about
Assessment Centres, 11

personal review, 234–240
preparation tips, 54–57
team exercise
described, 63–64
effective behaviour, 72–77
group size, 64
icebreakers, 221
job-related competencies, 70–72
oral presentations, 89–90
preparation tips, 77–79
response to, 11–12, 13
timing, 64–65, 67, 68, 69
types of, 65–69, 66
typical topics, 64
Teamwork competency
competency based interview,
188, 190
group exercise, 71, 72
technology
inbox exercises, 163–164
oral presentations, 86
telephone call
feedback, 246
interviews, 197
research methods, 48
themed exercise, 39–40
theoretical answer, 194
360º feedback questionnaire,
214–215
timetable
example of, 33
in-basket/inbox exercises, 170
management tips, 276
planning and scheduling
exercises, 148
preparatory information, 32
psychometric tests, 202
title, competency, 30
trainable competency, 45
trait questionnaire, 211
trust building, 268
two-to-one interview, 179
type questionnaire, 211

• U •

unstructured interview, 181

• V •

values, organisational, 258
verbal ability test, 203–204
visual aid, for presentations
  common mistakes, 97
  preparation, 82, 85, 86
  presentation behaviour, 92–93
visual impairment, 58
volume, speaking, 73, 98

• W •

War and Peace scenario, 223
wash-up. *See* decision making
water intake, 216
ways of working, 35–39
weakness, personal, 57, 240
work experience
  abstract ability tests, 207
  competency based interviews,
    184–187

interview tips, 192–193
versus performance at
  Assessment Centres, 12
Work Sample method, 17
Written Communication
  competency, 137, 138
written feedback, 247
written work
  analysis exercise reports,
    132–135, 139, 143
  email tasks, 164

• Y •

Yeung, Rob (*Answering Tough
  Interview Questions For
  Dummies*), 196

• Z •

Zegarelli, Mark (*Basic Math & Pre-
  Algebra For Dummies*), 205

Notes

....

_____

_____

_____

_____

_____

_____

_____

_____

_____

_____

_____

_____

_____

_____

_____

_____

_____

_____

_____

Notes

Notes

FOR DUMMIES®

LF HELP

UK editions

978-0-470-01838-5

978-07645-7028-5

978-0-470-51501-3

NANCE

978-0-470-99280-7

978-0-470-99811-3

978-0-470-69515-9

JSINESS

978-0-470-51806-9

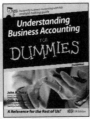

978-0-470-99245-6

978-0-470-05768-1

British Sign Language
For Dummies
978-0-470-69477-0

Buying & Selling a Home
For Dummies, 2nd Edition
978-0-470-99448-1

Diabetes Cookbook For Dummies
978-0-470-51219-7

DIY and Home Maintenance
All-in-One For Dummies
978-0-7645-7054-4

Emotional Freedom Technique
For Dummies
978-0-470-75876-2

English Grammar For Dummies
978-0-470-05752-0

Green Living For Dummies
978-0-470-06038-4

IBS For Dummies
978-0-470-51737-6

Inventing For Dummies
978-0-470-51996-7

Job Hunting and Career Change
All-in-One For Dummies
978-0-470-51611-9

PRINCE2 For Dummies
978-0-470-51919-6

Psychometric Tests For Dummies
978-0-470-75366-8

Raising Happy Children
For Dummies
978-0-470-05978-4

Stop Smoking For Dummies
978-0-470-99456-6

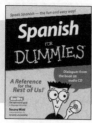  
 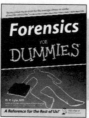 
  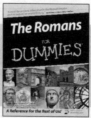

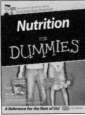